Seated by the Sea

New Perspectives on Maritime History and Nautical Archaeology Working in the Americas

UNIVERSITY PRESS OF FLORIDA

Florida A&M University, Tallahassee
Florida Atlantic University, Boca Raton
Florida Gulf Coast University, Ft. Myers
Florida International University, Miami
Florida State University, Tallahassee
New College of Florida, Sarasota
University of Central Florida, Orlando
University of Florida, Gainesville
University of North Florida, Jacksonville
University of South Florida, Tampa
University of West Florida, Pensacola

Seated by the Sea

The Maritime History of Portland, Maine,
and Its Irish Longshoremen

Michael C. Connolly

Foreword by Governor Joseph E. Brennan, Federal Maritime Commission

University Press of Florida
Gainesville/Tallahassee/Tampa/Boca Raton
Pensacola/Orlando/Miami/Jacksonville/Ft. Myers/Sarasota

Copyright 2010 by Michael C. Connolly
Printed in the United States of America. This book is printed on Glatfelter Natures Book, a paper certified under the standards of the Forestry Stewardship Council (FSC). It is a recycled stock that contains 30 percent post-consumer waste and is acid-free.
All rights reserved
All images are from "Collections of Maine Historical Society" unless otherwise indicated.

16 15 14 13 12 11   6 5 4 3 2 1

First cloth printing, 2010
First paperback printing, 2011

Library of Congress Cataloging-in-Publication Data
Connolly, Michael C.
Seated by the sea : the maritime history of Portland, Maine, and its Irish longshoremen / Michael C. Connolly; foreword by Joseph E. Brennan.
p. cm.—(New perspectives on maritime history and nautical archaeology. Working in the Americas)
Includes bibliographical references and index.
ISBN 978-0-8130-3469-0 (cloth)
ISBN 978-0-8130-3722-6 (paperback)
1. Stevedores—Maine—Portland—History. 2. Irish—Maine—Portland—History. 3. Irish Americans—Maine—Portland—History. 4. Working class—Maine—Portland—History. 5. Labor unions—Maine—Portland—History. 6. Social change—Maine—Portland—History. 7. Portland (Me.)—Economic conditions. 8. Portland (Me.)—Social conditions. 9. Portland (Me.)—Ethnic relations. 10. Port cities—Maine—Case studies. I. Title.
HD8039.L82U65125 2010
331.6'2415074191—dc22   2009044785

The University Press of Florida is the scholarly publishing agency for the State University System of Florida, comprising Florida A&M University, Florida Atlantic University, Florida Gulf Coast University, Florida International University, Florida State University, New College of Florida, University of Central Florida, University of Florida, University of North Florida, University of South Florida, and University of West Florida.

University Press of Florida
15 Northwest 15th Street
Gainesville, FL 32611-2079
http://www.upf.com

This book is dedicated to all Portland longshoremen
such as Coleman Connolly and Larry Welch, and to their families who
were the beneficiaries of their work and who shared their dreams.

Often I think of the beautiful town
That is seated by the sea;
Often in thought go up and down
The pleasant streets of that dear old town,
And my youth comes back to me.

Henry Wadsworth Longfellow, "My Lost Youth"

Contents

List of Illustrations xi

Foreword xiii

Acknowledgments xv

Chronology xix

Introduction 1

1. "Delightfully Situated on a Healthy Hill": The Port of Portland before the Civil War 6

2. Black Fades to Green on the Waterfront: Nineteenth-Century Social, Racial, and Ethnic Change 36

3. A Mixed Blessing: Portland at the Turn of the Twentieth-Century 65

4. Lost Strikes and Union Affiliation: Early Twentieth-Century Labor Militancy Alongshore 84

5. Apex of the Union and Catholic Hierarchical Influence 113

6. Longshore Culture and the Decline of the Port of Portland in the Mid- to Late Twentieth Century 141

Conclusion: The Port of Portland in the Twenty-First Century and Its Maritime Future 181

Appendix A. *Portland Town* 195

Appendix B. *Day of the Clipper* 197

Appendix C. PLSBS Retirement List as of January 1983 199

Appendix D. Oral Histories 201

Appendix E. Longshore Nicknames 203

Appendix F. Membership Levels of the Portland Longshoremen's Benevolent Society   215

Notes   219

Bibliography   243

Index   269

Illustrations

Figures

1. Fort Loyall, 1678–1690 8
2. Portland Head Light 14
3. Mariner's House (1931) 15
4. Portland Observatory 19
5. Map of Portland (1823) 21
6. Clay Cove (1840) 24
7. Munjoy Hill and Observatory (1845) 26
8. John Alfred Poor 28
9. Old Grand Trunk Depot (1854) and grain elevator 30
10. View from Ferry Village boatyard (1854) 32
11. SS *Oregon* January 21, 1884 33
12. Eastern Steamboat House 34
13. J. B. Brown's Portland Sugar Company 42
14. *Jeanie Johnston* (August 9, 2003) 58
15. Grand Trunk railroad yard and Portland Company 71
16. Grand Trunk Railroad Station, c. 1904 72
17. Commercial Street with railroad beltline 73
18. Schooner *Viking* with longshoremen 75
19. Deering Wharf hauling lumber 77
20. PLSBS banner (July 4, 1894) 79
21. ILA Charter Local 861 (1914) 106
22. KKK parade in Portland, c. 1923 138
23. KKK headquarters (Klavern), Witham Estate 139
24. Composite of former longshoremen Larry Welch, Phil O'Donnell, Tom Mulkern, and Roy Caleb 143

25. Composite of retired longshoremen Pat Malone, Steve Concannon, Jack Humeniuk (active), and Pat O'Malley   144
26. Composite of longshoreman Larry Welch   146
27. Loading flour   147
28. Unloading whisky at Grand Trunk Wharf (1920)   148
29. Maine State Pier, opened 1923   150
30. Joseph Ryan, president of ILA (1927–53)   156
31. Harry Bridges, president of ILWU (1937–77)   159
32. Exporting potatoes   166
33. Entering Portland harbor   171
34. *Prince of Fundy* at International Marine Terminal   176
35. Pat Malone (December 29, 1969)   179

Tables

1. Black Population Concentration in Portland and Boston (1840–60)   44
2. Total Population of Portland (1800–1900)   66
3. Major Commodities Shipped to and from Portland (1895 and 1900)   70
4. Origin of First- and Second-Generation Immigrants in Portland (1900)   78

Charts

1. Total Membership Levels of the PLSBS (1882–1978)   216
2. New Membership Levels of the PLSBS (1888–1977)   217

Foreword

Portland, Maine's Longshore Legacy

When my father, John J. Brennan, arrived on the shores of America from Ireland in the late nineteenth century, he was able to secure a job loading and unloading ships on the Portland waterfront. He was among friends. Many of his fellow longshoremen were, like both my father and mother, Irish (Gaelic) speakers from the same region of County Galway, Ireland, that they had only reluctantly abandoned. They were all in search of work, security, religious and political freedom, and ultimately the chance for a new life and a place to realize their dream of raising a family. My mother, Catherine Mulkerrin, was from Callowfeenish (*Calibhfuinse*) in the heart of its *Gaeltacht* or Irish-speaking region and quite near my father's birthplace. Although they arrived in America separately, they married in Portland and eventually raised a family of eight children, of which I was the fifth child born.

Life in Portland in the late nineteenth century was not easy. My parents, however, had been well prepared for hardships by the nature of their childhood and early life in Ireland. Portland, Maine, must have seemed like a dream to them because it gave my parents the opportunities that were lacking in their ancestral homeland, and they were eager to take advantage of these new opportunities. They embraced their new lives and they worked hard, as did nearly all of their fellow immigrant families in this new home. Here they found institutions that understood their needs and supported them in their search for security and fulfillment in work, religion, and eventually even in politics. This city provided a sound educational and cultural base for their children.

I attended local schools on and around our Munjoy Hill home on Kellogg Street, and I eventually graduated from Cheverus High School in 1952. In 1958, after two years in the Army, I graduated from Boston College and then proceeded on to the University of Maine Law School from which I graduated in 1963. My career since then has included many honors and public service, including Cumberland County District Attorney; Maine House of Representatives (1965–1971); Maine Senate (1973–1975); Maine Attorney General (1975–1978); Governor of Maine (1979–1987); U.S. House of Representatives (1987–1991); and two terms as Commissioner of the Federal Maritime Commission (1999–present).

My story, although perhaps unusual in some of its details and highlights, is really the story of the immigrant families in Maine and in America. It is the story of almost unbelievable mobility and opportunity for those who came and are still coming to these shores. The details of my individual life's accomplishments are perhaps being lived out at this very moment by some other son or daughter of an immigrant family in Portland, or Maine, or beyond in this great country of possibilities for those who dream and work hard to fulfill those dreams.

I am happy to support Mike Connolly in promoting his book, *Seated by the Sea: The Maritime History of Portland, Maine, and Its Irish Longshoremen*. I do this because I can see my own family experience in the lives of these predominantly first- and second-generation Irish dock laborers. This is not only the story of dreamers but also of hard workers and realists who labored to find a way to put food on the table for their growing families. It is the story of sacrifice by those who had recently come to America for the benefit of those who would be born here. Their children would identify themselves as Americans, even if they might add a prefix to proudly proclaim their ethnic background as Irish Americans.

My work these last eight years on the Federal Maritime Commission has only increased my appreciation for my parents' efforts on my behalf. I am proud of their hard work. I am also proud to lend my name to the effort of this book to analyze and remember the labor of Portland's Irish longshoremen over one and one-half centuries. I hope that this book may help to preserve this aspect of the maritime history of Maine as a strong and vibrant legacy, and to memorialize the labor of these longshoremen who helped to keep the commerce of this country flowing rapidly, smoothly, and predictably. I hope all who read *Seated by the Sea* will share a sense of appreciation even if they have no direct connection with these laborers because, in the final analysis, we are all working in our own ways to promote our individual, family, and national growth and security. As is often said in Ireland, "God bless the work!"

Governor Joseph E. Brennan, Federal Maritime Commission

Acknowledgments

Of the many people who have had a hand in the evolution of this book over the past twenty years, I would especially like to mention a few who stand out. Foremost among these would be my father, Michael F. Connolly, and his best friend, Larry Welch, who over the years filled my head with stories about these longshoremen and their earthy but seemingly "heroic" daily endeavors.

I must acknowledge the Portland Longshoremen's Benevolent Society (PLSBS) for granting me permission to review their records, even though I was not a member of the union. Bill and Jack Humeniuk, together with Vinny O'Malley, willingly made these private records available to me at the Labor Temple on Exchange Street. Years later, in collaboration with Prof. Robert Babcock of the University of Maine at Orono, these invaluable records were stored safely at the Maine Historical Society (MHS) in Portland. Now, future generations of historians, both professional and amateur, and the children and grandchildren of these longshoremen may learn from them. They were the first set of union records in the MHS collection. Professor Babcock must also be recognized for his seminal research comparing the development of the port of Portland with that of Saint John, New Brunswick, in journal articles published in 1979 and 1982. The staff at MHS, especially Bill Barry, Matt Barker, Nick Noyes, Alissa Lane, Jamie Kingman Rice, and Steve Bromage have been especially helpful. Bill Barry must be thanked above all, not only for his scholarship but also for his enthusiasm, insight, and good Irish humor.

Thanks go to the several retired longshoremen who allowed me to interview them in the early 1980s. The PLSBS remains ready to resume its position as a labor force on Portland's waterfront, and its public face is represented especially by Matty Connolly and Jack Humeniuk. At Boston College Andy Buni and Kevin O'Neill were especially encouraging. My colleagues at Saint Joseph's College (SJC) in Standish, Maine, in my twenty-five years there have always supported my efforts at publishing. Faculty scholarships and faculty development grants have provided incentives for completing these efforts. At SJC Renée LeBrun of the marketing department was very generous in her help with my image collection, and my student intern, Joshua Bell, now a graduate student in political science at Suffolk University, helped with typing and computer tasks. Other colleagues, such as Bill Jordan, formerly of Westbrook College, and Ed McCarron of Stonehill College in North Easton, Massachusetts, have often sent me off on productive avenues of research. Charles P. M. Outwin, an expert on eighteenth-century Falmouth in Casco Bay, and labor historian Charlie Scontras were generous in their advice in areas of their expertise. Scontras, especially through his work at the Bureau of Labor Education at the University of Maine at Orono, has published many very rich and thorough studies of the Maine labor movement especially in the last two centuries. The Scontras texts will assist those working in this field for years to come. Joe Conforti of the American studies program of the University of Southern Maine conceived and edited *Creating Portland: History and Place in Northern New England* and kindly took the time to review my manuscript.

Ken Nilsen of Saint Francis Xavier University in Antigonish, Nova Scotia, has been supportive of my research since I first met him as an Irish-language professor at Harvard University in 1980. Ken deserves special acknowledgment here because since 1984 he has undertaken an extensive study of Irish speakers in Portland, including several of the longshoremen in this book. Of the nine male Irish speakers interviewed for his most recent study of Portland (2004) fully six, or two-thirds, had been longshoremen—and, by the way, all seven of the females in this same study had served as domestic workers. Ken Nilsen has placed Portland forever on the map of Irish-speaking enclaves in North America, and for this we are in his debt.

Joan Hansen, Phil "The Harbormaster" O'Donnell, Larry Welch, and many others helped to preserve longshore nicknames, an always amusing staple of Portland's cultural life, especially when locals would ask a probing question like, "Which Foley are you?" One's nickname was always a good starting point for a conversation. Claire Foley, Tom Wilsbach, and many members of the Irish American Club of Maine and the Maine Irish Heritage Center were constantly supportive of this research.

Lincoln Paine of Munjoy Hill in Portland is a neighbor and a maritime historian who is currently undertaking the ambitious task of writing the maritime history of the world. Lincoln was one of the first to urge me to contact the University Press of Florida because of its acclaimed Maritime Series, and for this I am most grateful.

The staff at University Press of Florida has been very supportive, especially director Meredith Babb, with whom I have worked closely since the beginning. I thank the reviewers of my manuscript for their valuable suggestions for improvements, particularly the extensive editorial work of Patricia Bower. I thank the series editors of *New Perspectives on Maritime History and Nautical Archaeology* for deciding to broaden the scope of maritime history by including the study of "the people, communities, and industries that support maritime endeavors."

Locally, I am honored to include the words to two of the best-known maritime songs, not only in Portland but internationally: *Portland Town*, and *The Day of the Clipper*, by Chuck and Steve Romanoff of Schooner Fare. Their music taps into the essence of what it means to live in a maritime city such as Portland and region such as New England.

Former Maine governor Joe Brennan, now Federal Maritime commissioner and the son of a Portland (Munjoy Hill) longshoreman, was generous in his willingness to provide the foreword for this book. He is a prime example of the upward mobility of the second-generation Irish in Portland and in Maine. His support and his long public service are much appreciated by this author and by many others in his hometown and state.

My partner, Becky Hitchcock, has been with me for most of the twenty-seven years during which this book has been evolving, as has our *anam cara* relationship. I thank her, again, for making such a pleasant environment for me to do the research and writing that I so enjoy doing, all the more because of her support.

To my brother and sister, Peter Lawrence and Mary Frances Connolly, and in memory of our parents Michael Francis and Norma Scribner Connolly, I say thank you for our shared inheritance and interest in all things Irish.

To the courage and hope of my paternal grandparents, and even one great-grandmother, who emigrated from County Galway to this country with its strange language, weather, and customs—they made any difficult tasks before me seem simple by comparison.

Finally, all honor must go to the back-breaking effort of the many thousands of Portland longshoremen whose labor on this city's waterfront over more than 150 years allowed several generations of their numerous offspring to succeed and prosper in their chosen land of opportunity.

Chronology

1623	Christopher Leavitt (Levett) provisioned House Island
1633	George Cleeve and Richard Tucker settled peninsula
1658	Falmouth in Casco Bay settlement began to emerge
1676	Falmouth destroyed by the Abenaki (Wabanaki)
1690	Falmouth again overrun by Native Americans
1690–1715	Settlement virtually abandoned
1718	Incorporation of town of Falmouth in Casco Bay
1718	Arrival of *McCallum* from Ireland with twenty families
1727	First masts shipped to British Navy from Stroudwater
1774	Intolerable Acts
1775 (June 3)	O'Briens seized HMS *Margaretta*
1775 (October 18)	Falmouth destroyed by Lt. Henry Mowatt
1786	Portland (Neck) incorporates, separated from Falmouth
1796	Launching of the *Portland*
1807–08	Embargo Act crippled Maine shipping
1807	Portland Observatory built by Lemuel Moody
1808	St. Patrick's Catholic Church (Damariscotta Mills) built
1813 (September 5)	*Enterprise* defeated the British *Boxer*
1820 (March 15)	Maine statehood
1820–32	Portland served as Maine's capital
1823 (August)	Kennebec Steam Navigation Company founded
1828	Abyssinian Church (Sumner, now Newbury Street) built
1830 (November 1)	First Mass at St. Dominic's Church (Portland)

1830–70	Cumberland and Oxford Canal completed
1832	Portland incorporated as a city
1832–66	Portland's cultural and economic "Golden Years"
1843	Portland Steam Packet Co. (Portland to Boston) founded
1845–49	Irish potato famine and large-scale emigration
1853 (July 18)	Portland linked to Montreal by Atlantic and St. Lawrence Railroad (A&StLRR)
1853	A&StLRR leased to Grand Trunk Railroad
1853	Arrival of the SS *Sarah Sands* (service to Liverpool)
1855	Portland Sugar Company chartered (John Bundy Brown)
1850s	Know-Nothing (Nativist) agitation in Maine
1860	International Steamship Co. (to Boston and Maritimes)
1861–65	Civil War
1863 (June 26)	*Caleb Cushing* seized by Confederate raiders
1864 (February 22)	RMS *Bohemian* sank off Cape Elizabeth
1864 (May and July)	Portland Longshoremen's Benevolent Association strikes
1866 (June)	Fenian Brotherhood invasion of Canada from Eastport
1866 (July 4)	Great Portland Fire (1,800 buildings lost)
1866	Cathedral of the Immaculate Conception (Portland) built
1869	Transcontinental railroad completed
1871 (September 5)	Death of John A. Poor (born 1808 in Andover)
1875–1900	Bishop James Augustine Healy serves the Diocese of Portland as the first black Catholic Bishop in America
1880 (November 15)	Portland Longshoremen's Benevolent Society (PLSBS) incorporated
1885	Meeting of Bishop J. A. Healy and Terence Powderly, president of the Knights of Labor (KOL)
1886 (December 24)	Wreck of *Annie Maguire* off Portland Head
1892	International Longshoremen's Association (ILA) founded

1892–1909	Daniel J. Keefe is ILA's first president
1898 (November 26)	Sinking of the *Portland* off Cape Cod
1900	Portland serviced by seven transatlantic shipping companies
1901–06	Bishop William Henry O'Connell
1904	Workingmen's Club opened (21 Commercial Street)
1906–24	Bishop Louis S. Walsh
1909–21	T. V. O'Connor is ILA president
1911 (November 1–January 9)	Longshore strike in Portland
1913 (November 11–22)	Longshore strike in Portland
1914 (February 10)	PLSBS affiliated with ILA (Local 861)
1917–18	United States in World War I
1919	Highest membership level for PLSBS (1,366)
1920s	KKK active in Maine and Portland; Red Scare
1921	Dillingham Act restricted immigration
1921 (May 20)	James Walker beaten to death on waterfront
1921 (December 21–28)	Longshore strike in Portland
1923 (January 20)	Grand Trunk (GTR) nationalized under Canadian National (CNRR), steady loss of Canadian grain exports begins
1923	Maine State Pier (MSP) completed
1923	(November 1–2) "Port's busiest 48-hour period" with four steamships discharging 4,363 passengers through immigration
1924	Johnson-Reed Act further restricted immigration
1927–53	Joseph P. Ryan is ILA president
1934 (May 9–July 31)	"The Big Strike" on Pacific Coast
1934 (July 5)	"Bloody Thursday"—two killed, forty-three injured in San Francisco longshore strike
1936	Harry Bridges takes International Longshoremen's and Warehousemen's Union (ILWU) into the Congress of Industrial Organizations (CIO)
1941 (October 31)	USS *Reuben James* DD 245 (home base in Portland) sunk by German U-Boat off Iceland

1941 (November)	Portland Pipeline to Montreal opened
1941–45	United States in World War II
1941–45	Casco Bay (Hussey Sound) as home staging area (inner base) for the North Atlantic Fleet (COMDESLANT)
1942–45	South Portland Shipbuilding Corporation launched 274 Liberty ships
1947	Taft-Hartley Act passed over Truman's veto
1950s	McCarthyism/Red Scare
1953–63	William Bradley is ILA president
1955	Jarka Corporation ends stevedore service to Portland
1955–99	Jarka replaced by International Terminal Operating Company (ITO)
1956	Launch of *Ideal X* by Malcolm McLean (first container ship)
1956	Sea-Land Container Company founded
1963–87	Thomas W. "Teddy" Gleason is ILA president
1979	$10 million Bond passed for Maine State Pier (MSP)
1981 (December)	Last vessel handled by PLSBS at MSP
1981–86	No cargo handling work for PLSBS
1980s	Merrill Marine bulk cargo pier enhanced
1984	$5 million bond for container facility in Portland
1985	International Marine Terminal (IMT) rebuilt (east)
1987–2007	John Bowers is ILA president
1987	Working Waterfront Referendum passed
1991 (March 21)	*Yankee Clipper*, first container ship to visit Portland
1991–2008	Hapag-Lloyd stevedoring services in Portland
1994	$4 million jobs bond to rebuild IMT (west)
1998	Sea-Land merged with Maersk container line
2000–2008	P&O Ports/Dubai Ports/AIG (now Ports America)
2004	*Shamrock* container vessel repossessed
2005	Gulf of Maine Ocean Research facility opened
2007–present	Richard P. Hughes Jr. is ILA president

2007 (July–December)	Eimskip (Icelandic) container ship with service to Halifax, Nova Scotia
2007 (August 19)	Columbia Coastal Transport (Boston & NY/NJ)
2007	Olympia Company (Kevin Mahaney) chosen to develop Maine State Pier (MSP)
2008 (May 30)	*The Cat* to Nova Scotia from Ocean Gateway
2008	Maine Port Authority a division of the Maine Department of Transportation (MDOT) considers control of IMT from Portland
2008 (June)	Columbia Coastal suspends service to Portland
2008 (November)	Red Shield (Old Town) seeks bankruptcy
2008 (December)	Olympia withdraws its offer to develop MSP
2008 (December)	Ocean Properties (Tom Walsh) chosen for MSP
2008–9	Major worldwide recession begins
2009 (January)	Ocean Properties withdraws from MSP project
2009 (March 29)	Old Town Fuel and Fiber (former Red Shield) reestablishes paper shipments by container from IMT
2009 (June 1)	Maine Port Authority takes control of IMT
2009 (Summer)	Negotiations for Portland as cruise line home port; also for new container feeder service to Halifax at IMT

Introduction

Why is this book needed? It seems a logical question to ask at the start of a project such as this. At the very least one should determine what this book could add to the existing body of work. Scholarly and creative treatments of the maritime world abound. This is true on the national, regional, and even state levels, and many of these works have impressive historical relevance. Some of these studies and novels concentrate on ships and shipbuilding. Some concentrate on the sailors who, often while being portrayed romantically, took these ships to the four corners of the globe and, in the age of sail, put Maine close to the center of the maritime world. Other studies have concentrated on issues of commerce, trade, and facilitating the ocean-borne transportation of raw materials and manufactured goods.

What has largely been neglected in most of these studies, however, has been a thorough treatment of the workers who stayed at home and who loaded and unloaded these ships—the longshoremen, otherwise known as dockworkers or, imprecisely, as stevedores. Lacking the romance of "those who go down to the sea in ships," these hardy souls only went as far as the wharves. Their labor, though, was every bit as crucial as that of the more thoroughly documented related areas of manufacturing; agriculture; mineral and natural resource extraction, including fishing; and shipping. The dearth of documentation on these longshore laborers in New England is particularly stark given the pivotal role of the shipping industry, sailing, whaling, and all other maritime-related functions on the regional economy and the historical development of New England, generally, and the state of Maine, in particular.

Ironically, other maritime regions in the United States do not suffer from this apparent oversight. Documentation of the Pacific Coast longshoremen—specifically the International Longshoremen's and Warehousemen's Union (ILWU), led by the radical firebrand Harry Bridges—is quite extensive and growing. Scholarly treatments of Gulf Coast dockworkers, particularly in the racially diverse and pivotal port of New Orleans, are readily available. Even Great Lakes shipping and longshore labor has been better documented than that of New England or Maine.

This book represents a social history of a relatively large group of predominantly ethnic and unskilled laborers. It is essentially a study of this seemingly powerless group and its efforts to adapt and survive in the potentially hostile environment along Maine's rugged coast. It documents, therefore, a history of survival and an attempt to live "the American Dream." It records the creative thinking and actions that allowed these largely Irish and Irish-American workers to make a home for their growing families and neighborhoods. They eventually were able to fulfill their own dreams through the gains and mobility of their children and grandchildren. It is a narrative of struggle and failures but also, at its very core, one of hope and ultimate success. "The dreams of the first generation were lived by the second."

Fortunately, abundant primary records exist to document the labors of many thousands of the longshoremen of Portland over their more than 125 years of labor along the docks of Maine's largest city. In 1985, at the urging of Dr. Robert H. Babcock (University of Maine at Orono, Emeritus Professor of History) and myself, the Portland Longshoremen's Benevolent Society (PLSBS), International Longshoremen's Association (ILA) Local 861 agreed to archive and store its records at the Maine Historical Society (MHS) in Portland. This forward-looking decision by the union instantly resulted in the presence of the first labor-related manuscript collection at the historical society. This collection, numbering nearly one hundred individual components, contains the minutes of regular union meetings starting in 1880; financial, dues, and sick reports; and even a few volumes of the predominantly Italian Freight Handler's Union, ILA Local 912. These manuscripts [MA 85-15] in collections 359 and 360 will preserve these vital records for future analysis by the union itself, local and regional historians, Maine and ethnic and labor scholars, and many others well into the foreseeable future.

This book has employed a multifaceted and thematic approach. The abundance of resources, including the union records, allows one to analyze these maritime laborers in several ways. Any study over such a lengthy period must be selective by its very nature, thus consciously choosing to leave out far more than it includes. My choice has been to concentrate on the critical years of 1880–1923 and to analyze these important issues not by any one paradigm alone, but rather treating labor, ethnic, racial, business, and maritime issues collectively. Emphasis in each chapter is given to the issues or themes that appear to be most crucial to the understanding of that corresponding period. By chapter, therefore, the major emphases of this book will be as follows:

Chapter 1—historical development of the port over 250 years
Chapter 2—ethnic, social, and racial trends in the late nineteenth century
Chapter 3—a snapshot in time at the turn of the twentieth century
Chapter 4—labor unionization and affiliation in the early twentieth century
Chapter 5—religion and Catholic hierarchical influence on the workers
Chapter 6—decline of the port in the late twentieth century
Conclusion—status quo and hopes for the future

Ultimately, if this book stands for anything it is that these longshoremen were real people, not just records or statistics, and that they had real families who entirely depended upon their job security and income. Dating before the year 1880 and down to the present, many thousands of longshore laborers in Portland have attempted to realize their dreams—not alone by dreaming but by backbreaking and sustained effort as well.

Over the decades of this study their labor would change with technological innovations and, therefore, changing working conditions. Sometimes these dockworkers and their union would resist these innovations, especially when they believed that these changes would harm their safety, wages, or job security. Symptomatic of this issue was the sling load, the weight of each individual unit of product to be moved by a longshore gang at any one time, and the related issue of the size and composition of these work gangs themselves.

Sometimes these longshoremen must have felt like a dying breed—almost like cowboys, but this time on the eastern frontier. As the "skull-dragging," that is to say the physically demanding, nature of strictly manual labor evolved technologically to include the use of the steam-powered winch, and as the sling load itself eventually gave way to the large and ponderous container, the workers were caught in a dilemma. They were forced to choose between short-term job security by sticking to traditional methods and long-term survival of the industry in what was becoming a relatively small-volume North Atlantic port via mechanization and innovation. There was a constant and predictable struggle between this longshore union and the forces of innovation and efficiency represented by the cost-conscious shipping companies and their local stevedore agents who ultimately hired these dock workers on mutually agreed terms and conditions.

Was there any reality to local entrepreneur John Alfred Poor's well-publicized dream of Portland, Maine, as the hub in a major international shipping nexus between Europe and the North American continent? Or, on the other extreme, was Portland ultimately destined to devolve into a relatively minor feeder port to the larger and more modern maritime facilities located near population centers to the south, Boston and New York, or to the east, Saint John, New Brunswick, and Halifax, Nova Scotia? Could the Portland longshoremen and their union, together with city political and business elites, have made a series of drastically different developmental decisions that realistically might have prevented the downward spiral of the port of Portland?

Finally, this book attempts to put the past into perspective and to document the struggles, successes, and failures of thousands of workers in Maine's largest city over a century and a quarter. In a small way this may serve to partially fill the gap that has existed in American historiography with its lack of any substantial treatment of this important labor force and of this significant North Atlantic port. The maritime labor of northern New England should be recognized along with that of the other important regional ports of this country.

No clear picture of the future is ever possible without a thorough understanding of the past. In this regard, the leaders and citizens of Maine may wish to consider the issues that have been raised in this book as they ponder the future development of this port that is so crucial to the entire state and region. Today, Portland is a leading Atlantic Coast oil port, supplying eastern Canada with huge quantities of petroleum through the Portland Pipeline that commences in Portland harbor. Portland continues to receive and ship large quantities of bulk cargo in and out of the Merrill Marine facilities at the western end of the harbor. A small number of unionized Portland longshoremen have attempted to continue the long tradition as they handle container cargo and function primarily as a feeder port from the International Marine facility just east of the Casco Bay Bridge.

The history of the port of Portland and this largely unseen and unrecorded labor force is now before you. Perhaps this book may chronicle in some small way their mighty and crucial efforts over the past several decades. It is my hope that this book may help to answer the probable and innocent question of some future young citizen of this city, state, or region when pondering the past, present, and future of Maine's maritime tradition: "Daddy, what's a longshoreman?"

1

"Delightfully Situated on a Healthy Hill"

The Port of Portland before the Civil War

Europeans first settled the area now known as Portland more than 375 years ago, in 1633, with the arrival of George Cleeve and Richard Tucker. Although originally a squatter, Cleeve by 1637 had obtained a grant for the peninsula, surrounding lands, and islands from the English proprietor Sir Ferdinando Gorges. The earliest enterprises of European settlers were fishing, lumbering, and fur trading.

Capt. Christopher Leavitt (Levett), while sailing the Maine coast in 1623–24, found no settlements between the mouth of the Piscataqua River (present-day Kittery, Maine, and Portsmouth, New Hampshire) and Newagen (below present-day Boothbay Harbor at the southern tip of Southport Island). Earlier British fishing expeditions had been attacked by Native Americans along the coast, and Leavitt thought it advisable to provide for the safety of these fishing crews and their valued catches. He may well have provisioned House Island in Casco Bay around 1623.

Before his death at sea in 1630 Leavitt's plan gained the support of King Charles I, who "ordered all churches in the realm to take up a contribution to aid this enterprise on the Maine coast." Perhaps today's House Island, the innermost island at the mouth of a well-protected natural harbor, might suit their needs. Captain Leavitt eventually fashioned a plan in England: "One harbor to which all the boats along the coast could be brought for storage and protection must be fortified. For this he had in mind what is now Portland Harbor."[1]

George Cleeve, one of Portland's two original European settlers, first settled on Richmond Island off Cape Elizabeth. The island was named for its first settler in the early 1620s, John Richmond, of Bandon Bridge, Ireland. His region of Ireland had been planted by English Protestants in the time of Queen Elizabeth, and many of its Puritans had been unhappy in Ireland. "The names of several of them are found on the *Mayflower's* passenger list and in John Winter's accounts."[2]

Both nineteenth- and twentieth-century historians have focused on the importance of the ocean. In the words of Robert D. Foulke, the sea was "largely unchanged since the first separation of earth and water." Foulke continues, "Throughout all centuries, unlike the land, the sea has been a constant for those who sailed on it, variable in mood but immutable in essence."[3]

A local historian, Edward Elwell, wrote in 1876, "The impenetrable forest was behind them, the open ocean before them, and this was their highway and the chief source of their sustenance."[4] One hundred years later a nearly identical view was expressed by a more contemporary American historian who wrote that "the ocean was the highway connecting the Old World and the New and the seaport towns were the vital link between the two."[5] Today, this view is still widely supported. Maritime historian Felipe Fernández-Armesto writes that "global history became a reality. It grew out of maritime history." In the same maritime resource, the Newfoundland-based maritime historian Olaf Janzen subscribes to Elwell's much earlier conceptualization by titling his essay "A World-Embracing Sea: The Oceans as Highways."[6]

This settlement became known by its Native American name, Aucocisco, or Casco, from Wabanaki words for a muddy bay or, alternatively, a great blue heron. An earlier aboriginal name for the peninsula had been Machigonne (Machegonne) meaning elbow or knee or, according to John Neal, bad clay from the words "*matchi*" (bad) and "*gon*" (clay).[7] By 1658, Massachusetts had taken control of this entire area and in the process changed the town name to Falmouth, along with countless other English place names along the Maine coast and inland. The growth of the area was slow. By 1675, more than forty years after its first settlement, there were only forty families living on the peninsula, which was then referred to as the Neck.

In 1675, a series of wars began in response to the white traders' ill-treatment of the Native American population along the New England coast.[8] In 1676 Falmouth was destroyed and would lay dormant for two years. However, resettlement between 1678 and 1688 caused Falmouth to double in population, reaching between six hundred and seven hundred persons living within approximately eighty families.[9] By 1688, a second phase of these

1. Fort Loyall, 1678–1690, at Clay Cove near Fore and India (Broad) streets.

wars had started, and in 1690 Native Americans again overran Falmouth. This phase of the fighting continued intermittently for ten years and was followed in 1703 by yet another major outbreak.

Thus, during the years 1690 to 1715, Falmouth was virtually abandoned. Even as early as 1669, however, British political economist Sir Josiah Child worried that a reawakening of American commercial and entrepreneurial interests, such as ship building specifically, might promote an "animating spirit" among the citizenry that could become antithetical to colonial domination by the "Mother Kingdom."[10]

The year 1715 marked the beginning of the second major period of Portland's growth. In that year there was but one family living on the peninsula, often called the Neck. Still known as Falmouth, or more specifically Falmouth in Casco Bay, the town incorporated in 1718, by which time twenty families lived on the Neck. Although the presence of Native Americans in the area continued to periodically alarm the white population, the town itself was never again placed in jeopardy by the Abenaki (Wabanaki). Gradually the frontiers were expanded toward the north and west, and Falmouth's security was enhanced as it became the major supply post for an ever-expanding hinterland. Colonial Falmouth would have included much of the land of the modern cities and towns of Portland, Falmouth, Westbrook, Cape Elizabeth, and South Portland.[11]

Also in 1718 the ship *McCallum* arrived bearing twenty immigrant families from Ireland. These were Scots-Irish Presbyterians mainly from the city of Londonderry whose first winter in Falmouth was so desperate that the local inhabitants had to petition the General Court in Massachusetts: "That there are now in this town about three hundred souls, most of whom are arrived from Ireland, of which not one-half have provisions enough to live upon over the winter, and so poor that they are not able to buy any, and none of the first inhabitants so well furnished as that they are able to supply them."[12] As a result, some one hundred bushels of Indian meal were sent to Falmouth, paid for by the public treasury of Massachusetts.

Many of these early Irish immigrants and their families proceeded to Londonderry, New Hampshire (then known as Nutfield), while others settled in Maine in the Brunswick-Topsham area then known as Pejepscot. Some, however, decided to stay in Falmouth. Commerce, shipbuilding, fishing, and other ocean-related industries became the core of Falmouth's growth in the years prior to the American Revolution. The spirit of this period was reportedly optimistic. "The forest as well as the sea was made a source of profit." Commerce was on the increase, with exports consisting largely of lumber, fur, and fish, all natural resources locally in abundance. To transport these exports, vessels were needed; Edward Elwell as early as 1727 reported that thirty ships were anchored in Falmouth harbor. "Population gradually increased; in 1753 it numbered 720 souls on the Neck, and in the whole town, 2,712, including 21 slaves, Parson Smith owning one. In 1774 the population of the Neck had increased to 2,000."[13]

Early in the eighteenth century, Falmouth merchants supplied large amounts of cordwood, fish, and lumber to Boston as well as to southern ports. "The merchants of Falmouth were canny, having been trained by the best not only at home but also in Boston, New York, and Britain itself."[14] It soon became clear that there was money to be made in the transport as well as in the sale of these Maine resources.

Shipbuilding eventually became a crucial component of the local economy, and "the ancestors of many of our present men of property laid the foundation of their fortunes in this profitable pursuit." The cove located east of India Street became the site of the first shipyard in the city and remained so engaged well into the mid-nineteenth century.[15]

In March 1727 Parson Smith recorded in his diary, "About this time Mr. Reddin came down with a considerable quantity of goods to build a sloop." Thomas Smith lived at the foot of King Street, now India Street, in the area then known as Clay Cove. After five months had passed, Parson Smith reported that the "sloop built before my door was launched to-day." Maritime historian William Hutchinson Rowe wrote that the site of this shipyard is now lost, "a circumstance which illustrates the difficulty in reconstructing the maritime past of a water front." Ironically, one form of bulk transport would by the mid-nineteenth century be partially replaced by another, when maritime shipping was forced to compete with rail transport. Clay Cove together with much of the town's waterfront was filled in. "In 1850, in order to give railroad connection between the eastern and western parts of the city, a granite retaining wall was constructed and the space within it was filled in. The right of way created was given the name of Commercial Street."[16]

Another closely related shipbuilding trade came into being in 1727 when Falmouth became the American center for the procurement of tall, straight trees to be used for masts in the British Royal Navy. An agent for the trade was sent to Falmouth and the first shipment of masts was made in May of 1727.[17] This trade in masts was representative of much of the town's early commerce. Many of the early merchants were of Ulster, Scottish, or English backgrounds, and it was not uncommon to load a newly built ship with merchandise, sail to England or another European destination, and then sell the whole cargo, ship included. Falmouth, as the most important port for masts in the pre-Revolutionary period, failed to create many fortunes, however. This was because the mast business was a Royal monopoly and profits were retained by the British. The few exceptions to this rule would be the officially sanctioned mast agents, and their names are still locally significant: Col. Thomas Westbrook, Brig. Samuel Waldo, and Capt. George Tate Sr.[18]

The colonial relationship between Great Britain and America was clearly demonstrated in the ever-expanding system of taxation and tariffs imposed on the colonies. After 1700, regulations were established by the Royal Navy and fee schedules implemented for duty collection in the various American ports. Commodities liable for taxation were limited at first to wines and spirits, but eventually the list grew to include most dry goods, except for a few necessities. Falmouth was the only collection point in Maine prior to the Revolution, and in 1758 Francis Waldo was appointed the first collector.

According to William Willis, Portland's preeminent nineteenth-century local historian, these various acts of trade only served to highlight to an increasing number of American merchants and businessmen the disadvantage of remaining a colony. "By these narrow laws, the whole industry of the colonies was hampered and made subservient to the manufacturing industry and wealth of England."[19]

After Britain's victory in the French and Indian War, and the proclamation of several legislative initiatives such as the Boston Port Act (1774), England attempted to recoup some of its financial outlay in the colonies by a stricter enforcement of these taxes and tariffs, and surer prosecution of colonists convicted of smuggling rum, sugar, molasses, and the like. Falmouth's citizens resisted these British regulations, which would have adversely affected the local economy. "On the day the Boston Port Bill took effect, the bell of the Falmouth first parish was muffled and tolled from sunrise until nine o'clock in the evening."[20]

In July of 1770, John Adams traveled to the eastern district of Maine and deplored the conditions he found there including, "many sharp, steep Hills, many Rocks, many deep Rutts, and not a Footstep of Man, except in the Road. It was vastly Disagreeable." Later in his autobiography, Adams gave even more graphic details regarding his memory of the lands north and east of the city of Portland:

> From Falmouth now Portland in Casco Bay, to Pounalborough There was an entire Wilderness, except North Yarmouth, New Brunswick, and Long reach. The Roads, where a Wheel had never rolled from the Creation, were miry and founderous, incumbered with long Sloughs of Water. The Stumps of the Trees which had been cutt to make the road all remaining fresh and the Roots crossing the path some above ground and some beneath so that my Horses would frequently get between the Roots and he would flounce and blunder, in danger of breaking his own Limbs as well as mine.[21]

The Intolerable Acts (1774) ran headlong into an emerging spirit of political and economic independence held by many Americans. At the outbreak of the Revolution, of the five customs officers in Falmouth, all but one, a Mr. Child, joined the royal party (Tory) and left the country. Because these customs posts were British appointments, at least before the Revolution, it would seem logical that these officers would largely favor a continuation of British rule. Not surprisingly, Mr. Child was rewarded for his patriotism by his fellow citizens after the Revolution by being given the senior customs post. Toryism, it seems, was also the position of some of Falmouth's leading merchants, many of whom after the outbreak of hostilities fled to Canada's Maritime Provinces where they were able to reestablish successful commercial careers.

The War of Independence had early and disastrous consequences for Falmouth. On October 18, 1775, the British lieutenant Henry Mowatt (Mowat) ordered the destruction of the town, which had refused to surrender its weapons to him. Mowatt apparently also had a score to settle with Falmouth. Gen. Samuel Thompson and members of the Brunswick militia had held him captive there for several hours in April of 1775, after news of Lexington and Concord had reached Maine.

Less than two months later, on June 3, 1775, Jeremiah O'Brien, along with several sons and other American nationalists, seized the British vessel HMS *Margaretta* and two other ships near the mouth of the Machias River in far down east Maine.[22] O'Brien would later be referred to as "the Machias Admiral" and given financial support from Massachusetts to defend the eastern coastline. His son John would make an illustrious career of harassing British shipping and boldly and cleverly escaping imprisonment from Mill Prison in England. John O'Brien eventually returned to Maine to command the schooner *Hibernia*, which continued to plague and capture British vessels.[23]

When British vice admiral Samuel Graves in Boston ordered Mowatt to "pacify" the coast north of Boston in the fall of 1775, retribution was perhaps one factor that led Mowatt to bypass such ports as Cape Ann, Marblehead, Salem, and Portsmouth before anchoring off Falmouth on the morning of October 16, 1775. Falmouth's citizens refused to surrender their arms, as Lieutenant Mowatt ordered. The bombardment by four British naval vessels began the next morning and lasted twelve hours followed by a landing party of some one hundred British marines. Together with the bombardment the British incendiary torches were devastating:

> Approximately three-fourths of Falmouth's buildings were destroyed in the conflagration. The British completely devastated the lower

and compact end of town; almost every store or warehouse was consumed. St. Paul's Episcopal Church, a new courthouse, the old meetinghouse, the public library, a distillery and nearly all the wharves were destroyed. The town lost about 130 dwellings which had housed 160 families. Few structurally sound buildings remained. Many were so damaged that they could not be occupied by their owners.[24]

The list of grievances against King George III in the Declaration of Independence included the accusation leveled at "the tyrant," as the king was called—"He has plundered our seas, ravaged our Coasts, burnt our towns, and destroyed the lives of our people."

No other incident more clearly illustrated this complaint in the Declaration than did the attack on the town of Falmouth. "The Falmouth affair therefore contributed to the desire for independence from Britain."[25] Thus, this town would be forever linked with this integral violent event in the struggle of the American colonists for independence from Britain. Symbolically at least, Jeremiah O'Brien, an Irishman, had played a central role in tweaking the nose of the British Admiralty.

"The Americans were shocked. They were outraged. They were moved to anger and revenge. As propaganda, the raid backfired on the British with as much force as the sinking of the *Lusitania* in later years hurt the German cause." Mowatt was referred to as an "execrable Monster," and George Washington, a man usually not prone to hyperbole, declared that the British action was "effected with every circumstance of Cruelty and Barbarity, which Revenge and Malice could suggest."[26] Washington further claimed that the Falmouth affair demonstrated the "diabolical designs of [the British] Administration to prosecute with unrelenting Fury, the most cruel, and savage war that ever a Civilized Nation engaged in."[27] Once again, however, Falmouth lay in ruin, and its recovery would be delayed until the restoration of peace by the Treaty of Paris in 1783.

It took more than one decade to begin the task of rebuilding, but on July 4, 1786, the Neck, or peninsula, took the name of Portland, thus separating from the rest of Falmouth. Portland's city motto, eventually and appropriately, became *Resurgam* ("I will rise again"). This renaming also served to differentiate Portland from the other Falmouth on Cape Cod that some locals distained as "a poor little miserable sand heap."[28] The name Portland had been used prior to this to describe Cushing's Island, and the mainland

2. Portland Head Light—one of the oldest lighthouses in America, commissioned by George Washington, 1791. Courtesy of the Marketing Department of Saint Joseph's College of Maine.

opposite this island had long been called Portland Head, the present site of one of America's oldest and most recognizable lighthouses.[29]

This local separation was, at least in part, a logical result of geographical divisions, the diverging commercial and agricultural interests of the residents of these two areas, and the secession from the old parish by many of the citizens who had moved away from the peninsula: "a feeling of jealousy no doubt existed, which aided by the inconvenience to the out inhabitants of attending town meetings at so great a distance from the center, prepared the minds of the people for a change."[30] A more contemporary historian added that, "Falmouth's elite, whose members also generally belonged to its commercial community, dominated the town's culture."[31]

Portland's next maritime-related period of rapid growth fell roughly between the end of the Revolutionary War in 1783 and the beginning of the War of 1812.[32] Launched in the spring of 1796 at a cost exceeding sixty thousand dollars, the *Portland* was a joint venture of local shipbuilders Ebenezer Preble, brother of the future commodore Edward Preble, and Joseph Jewett, a Portland merchant, along with Salem's William Gray Jr., who had a large ropewalk in this town. Its initial voyage in that same year took it to Bombay, India.[33]

In 1797, near the middle of these three decades of growth, Dr. Timothy Dwight, the president of Yale University, visited Portland. Dwight's impression, recorded in his travel journal, reported that "no American town is more entirely commercial and of course none is more sprightly. Lumber, fish and ships are the principal materials of their commerce."[34]

Perhaps the most notable of Portland's maritime merchants in this period were the McLellans. Originally having emigrated from Ulster in 1720, Bryce McLellan moved from Wells to Casco Bay. It was there that Joseph McLellan Sr. became the business patriarch, eventually passing on the merchant trade to two of his three sons. By 1800 the family fortune was at its apex, and sons Hugh and Stephen built two of Portland's finest residences. "The family probably owned the largest fleet of vessels in Maine, and headed the first bank and insurance company." What had taken years to accumulate, however, was largely lost in a matter of months owing to the European conflict then under way between Great Britain and France. The McLellans and other Maine merchants and sailors would be caught in the crosswinds of this torrent.[35]

Local historian William Willis writing in 1865 spoke also of this remarkable period of growth that was interrupted by the damaging effects of the

3. Mariner's House (1931) in the Old Port, built by Samuel Butts in 1797.

Embargo Act of 1807: "Probably no period of our history was more prosperous than the three years preceding the first embargo; the navigation had increased twelve thousand tons, and the amount received for duties was higher than it has been until 1862. But the melancholy events of that period had a most disastrous effect upon all the springs of our prosperity."[36]

Available statistics on tonnage of shipping owned in Portland (133,162 tons in 1866) as well as duties collected at the Custom House served to document the port's growth.[37] A comparison with similar statistics from other Atlantic ports revealed that in 1855 the gross tonnage of permanently registered shipping was greater in Portland than in Baltimore (77,107 tons) or Philadelphia (47,739 tons), but it was significantly less than that of Boston (393,577 tons).[38]

A great amount of Portland's commerce had historically been with the West Indies, but British shipping policy resulting from the Treaty of Paris (1783) operated to the detriment of American commercial interests, especially those of New England. The British policy was to prohibit trade between America and British colonies in the West Indies in all but British-owned vessels. Simultaneously, British ships were allowed free trade with all American ports. These events occurred concurrently with Napoleon Bonaparte's rise to power in France and the subsequent increased use of British naval power against the Napoleonic French navy. Portland-owned ships and other American-owned "neutrals" profited greatly from trade with European belligerents in the early 1800s. The lucrative maritime trade in this period, often referred to as the "Neutral Profits Era," was not without its risks, however.[39]

Napoleon controlled most of the coast of Europe from the Baltic to the Adriatic. After the Berlin and Milan decrees of 1806, the French effectively blockaded British trade with mainland Europe. England had likewise opted to use its naval supremacy to also blockade the continent, and all cargoes to Napoleonic Europe were considered contraband. "Neutral" commerce had ceased to exist. In his *History of the English Speaking Peoples*, Winston Churchill colorfully evaluated the thoroughness of this embargo: "The British blockage wrapped the French Empire and Napoleonic Europe in a clammy shroud. No trade, no coffee, no sugar, no contact with the East, or with the Americans! And no means of ending the deadlock!"[40]

Maine merchants profited handsomely from trade with the West Indies and Europe, albeit at the substantial risk of capture by French or British privateers. In 1798, near the start of the Napoleonic wars, Portland handled five thousand tons of shipping. By 1807 that volume increased by nearly a factor of eight, to thirty-nine thousand tons, but at an increased risk of seizure or the impressment of American sailors. The British were also concerned with the tactic of the "broken voyage." A neutral American vessel could, by using this tactic, load sugar in the French West Indies and, instead of proceeding directly to Amsterdam, they might land at Portland. In Portland they would pay duty on the cargo, reload the cargo, receive a full rebate on any duty paid, and then proceed across the Atlantic with an "American cargo." The *Essex* decision of 1805 made such a tactic unlawful, however, and after that a vessel on such a mission could be seized by the British as a fair prize.[41]

The impressing or kidnapping of American seamen, especially by the British navy to relieve its chronic manpower shortage, was the most contentious issue between Britain and the United States. In 1805 the American government decided upon a nonintercourse policy with France and Great Britain. President Thomas Jefferson formalized this concern in 1807 with the passage of the Embargo Act. The suspension of marine commerce by the Embargo Act led to a disastrous decline in American shipping. The Embargo and British impressment were most harmful to New England with its heavy dependence upon maritime trade:

> To no portion of the Union, was the preservation of "Sailors' Rights," viewed with more intense interest, than by our eastern inhabitants. For we had a numerous body of seamen;—the amount of our tonnage was altogether disproportionate to our wealth, or even population; and a large number of our seafaring men were believed to be then holden as impresses, or rather as slaves, on board the British ships of war.[42]

The damage extended to all auxiliary trades, especially to ship chandlers, supply companies, lumber interests, and the many commercial banks that had extended risk capital in these promising areas. Edward Elwell graphically detailed its local consequences: "Great distress prevailed throughout the community, and the grass literally grew upon the wharves."[43] Public soup kitchens relieved the suffering of the unemployed dockworkers. A note sent in late 1807 from the Reverend Edward Payson to his father suggested that the merchants were also in distress. "Such a scene of wretchedness as I have never witnessed. A large number of the most wealthy merchants have already failed, and numbers more are daily following, so that we are all threatened with universal bankruptcy."[44]

Although the Embargo Act lasted only fourteen months, its repercussions for Portland were far more extensive. The previously cited statistics on Portland-owned ship tonnage reveal that the rapid increase experienced since the post-Revolutionary period was not only halted but even reversed for a time following the passage of the Embargo Act. Rev. Edward Payson went on to say that "at least three hundred persons, besides sailors, [are] out of employ." The poorhouse was reported to be full, confidence in short supply, and neighbor distrusting neighbor. Payson concluded, "I can not describe [the] distress we are in."[45]

Local shipping and merchant families were not the only Portlanders affected by European hostilities in this era. An obituary from 1872 tells the tale of Jack Groves, a "colored man," whose life was impacted by events in the earlier years of that century: "He was one of the crew of a vessel belonging to Capt. Arthur McLellan, which was seized by a French man-of-war in 1809, under 'Bonaparte's Berlin and Milan decree,' and assisted the captain, Sam'l. McLellan son of the owner, in retaking the vessel from the prize crew."[46]

By 1812 tonnage figures still had not rebounded to their pre-embargo levels. Likewise the duties collected at Portland's Custom House fell by more than three hundred thousand dollars in the two years between 1806–8. Most of Portland's Federal Period merchants, along with its economy, were ruined. Rev. Edward Payson apocalyptically proclaimed this as God's punishment on an "iniquitous population."[47]

Amazingly, despite these heavy losses, Capt. Lemuel Moody optimistically constructed the Portland Observatory in 1807, at the very start of the embargo. This was a dramatic demonstration of faith in Portland's commercial future and its continued reliance upon maritime enterprise. Located at the crest of Munjoy Hill in the east end of the city, this magnificent structure was used to locate returning vessels long before they entered the harbor and to signal Portland's citizens and commercial interests of their imminent arrival at the docks. A code was devised whereby flags could easily identify the exact ship on the horizon. On one day alone in 1844 it was reported that two hundred vessels could be sighted from the octagonal tower.[48]

4. Portland Observatory (built in 1807)—top of Munjoy Hill.

The observatory serves today as a symbol of both Munjoy Hill and of Portland, and of the defining connection of both with the sea.[49] The Munjoy Hill area was sparsely settled in this period except at its base where much of Portland's small black population resided. After the Great Fire of 1866, this area would serve as a place of refuge for the victims and later still as an entry-level, affordable home for the overflow of Irish and later Italian, Jewish, and other immigrants into the city.

The embargo was not only disastrous but also futile. Within five years of the passage of the Embargo Act the United States and Great Britain were again at war. Local consequences of the War of 1812 included the success of several Portland-owned vessels in privateering raids against British shipping.

In a major sea battle to the east of Casco Bay, the American ship USS *Enterprise* defeated and captured the British Brig HMS *Boxer*. *Enterprise*, commanded by the young Lt. William Burrows, was cruising eastward and happened to be in Portland harbor when *Boxer*, commanded by Cdr. Samuel Blyth and allegedly blockading the Maine coast, was heard firing its guns near the mouth of the Kennebec River. The ships met off Pemaquid and Monhegan on September 5, 1813, and the Americans secured the victory. Lemuel Moody reported on the battle from the new Portland Observatory. A verse from the poem "My Lost Youth" by Portland native Henry Wadsworth Longfellow immortalized this naval battle and the subsequent burial of both dead captains in a common grave within Portland's Eastern Cemetery at the base of Munjoy Hill. A toast was given at a victory banquet attended by the surviving officers of both ships: "To the crew of the *Boxer*, by law enemies; in gallantry, brothers."[50]

Although in reality Longfellow was only a six-year-old boy in 1813, by poetic license in "My Lost Youth," he allowed himself to appear as an eyewitness to history through his stirring verse commemorating this important Anglo-American naval battle:

> I remember the sea-fight far away,
>   How it thundered o'er the tide!
> And the dead captains as they lay
>   In their graves, o'erlooking the tranquil bay,
>   Where they in battle died.

"My Lost Youth" was most likely the result of a visit to Portland in 1846 that the poet remembered as being "a beautiful afternoon, and the harbor was full of white sails, coming and departing." He penned these words nearly one decade later in his Cambridge, Massachusetts, home during a depressed time in his life. His diary of March 29, 1855, recorded: "At night, as I lie in bed, a poem comes into my mind—a memory of Portland—my native town, the city by the sea. Siede la terra dove nate fui sulla marina." This is Longfellow's well-known poem that famously ends with the memorable refrain, "A boy's will is the wind's will, and the thoughts of youth are long, long thoughts." In an earlier verse, Longfellow mentions Portland's waterfront and its sailors and the romantic impressions they made on the young poet:

> I remember the black wharves and the slips,
>   And the sea-tides tossing free;
> And Spanish sailors with bearded lips,
>   And the beauty and mystery of the ships,
> And the magic of the sea.[51]

Politically, the greatest significance of the War of 1812 for Portland was the boost it gave to the movement for separation from Massachusetts and eventual statehood status for Maine. During that conflict many Mainers,

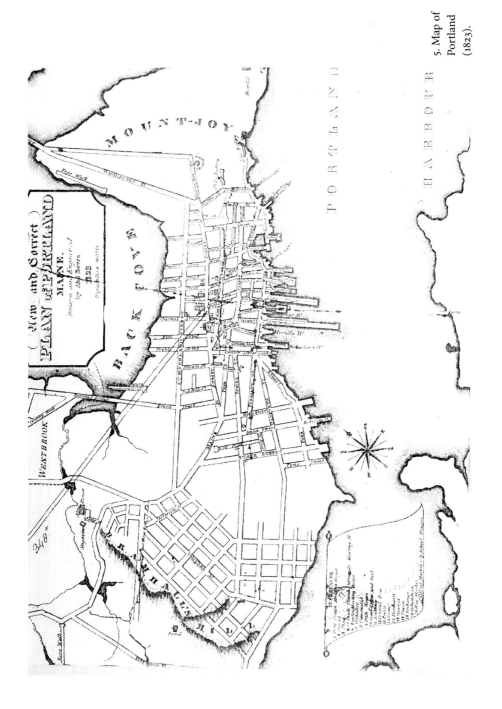

5. Map of Portland (1823).

especially in the eastern coastal regions, may well have thought that they had been abandoned and treated as a mere buffer zone between the Maritime Provinces of British Canada and Massachusetts proper. After several earlier unsuccessful attempts at gaining independence, in 1819 the residents of the district finally voted for statehood status by a margin of seventeen thousand to seven thousand.[52] The Missouri Compromise linked Maine's admission to the Union as a "free" state with Missouri's admission as a "slave" state, and Maine was thus granted statehood on March 15, 1820.

Portland served as the state capital from 1820 to 1832 when the shift was made to Augusta, a more centrally located site. Portland's original designation as Maine's state capital had important economic and political implications. Predictably, Portland struggled to keep its designation as the capital but was only able to delay the move for several years. Augusta, on the Kennebec River, was eventually chosen over several coastal towns because it was "central as to territory, population, and representation." The supporters of Augusta, in an apparent slight toward Portland, also claimed that "it was a place where the business of legislation might be carried on with less embarrassment and more purity than in a larger town."[53]

Despite this political setback, Portland retained the natural advantage of its harbor and, given the condition of roads east of Boston, steamship travel from Boston to Portland and beyond was a desirable transportation option. One example of this would be the service inaugurated in August 1823 between Boston, Portland, and Bath by the Kennebec Steam Navigation Company.[54] One person who availed of maritime transport to Portland from the south was Anne Royall. In her 1828 memoir of travels in the United States, Royall favorably recounted her first impressions of the city:

> Just as the sun was setting we arrived in sight of Portland, fifty-four miles from Portsmouth. Nothing can be handsomer than Portland as you approach it, floating as it were on the bosom of Casco Bay, it being almost surrounded by water—a long handsome bridge over part of Casco Bay. The square brick houses and the observatory seventy feet high, and the great bay of Casco, is beautiful beyond description.[55]

Portland was incorporated as a city in 1832, notwithstanding the opposition of the older and wealthier inhabitants who feared the loss of political control. They were concerned that the new government would be extravagant and spend money much too freely on public works.[56] These "established" families were opposed by Portland's rising merchant class that was anxious to translate statehood and city status into personal and citywide economic independence and prosperity. Two of the most successful maritime merchants in the late Federal period of Portland were Capt. Asa Clapp and Matthew "King" Cobb, who both reportedly "survived handsomely." In addition to diversifying their holdings with banks and other onshore businesses and avoiding the pitfall of overextending in these perilous times, these entrepreneurs acting either individually or as partners "sent ships all over the Atlantic and, in rare instances to India."[57]

Local historian William David Barry colorfully described Asa Clapp as "the last Nabob and the first modern businessman." He also referred to him as "the last full-fledged maritime hero-model [whose] business was regional, diversified and connected to centers of power." By the time of Captain Clapp's death in 1848, the *Merchant Magazine* claimed "There are few persons in New England who have built so many ships, and employed so many mariners, mechanics and laborers or who have erected so many houses and stores and done so much to promote the interest and prosperity of Maine."[58]

The incorporation of Portland was aided by its prior status as a major maritime port, the shire town of Cumberland County, and, from 1820 to 1832, the capital of the newly admitted state of Maine. In anticipation of this municipal change, certain lanes and alleys were appropriately renamed to reflect the greater dignity of Portland's new status. Some of the street name changes included: Hampshire Street (formerly Chub Lane); Franklin Street (Fiddle Lane); Exchange Street (Fish Lane); Lime Street (Lime Alley); and Center Street (Love Lane).[59]

Also of significance was the change from a selectman form of government to a mayor/alderman system that survived from 1832 until 1923 when it was replaced by a city council, largely selected at-large, and a ceremonial mayor elected by the council itself rather than directly by the electorate. In 1832 Andrew L. Emerson was elected as Portland's first mayor.

Around this same time, a Portland-built ship, *Friendship*, was involved in the Dutch East Indies (Sumatra) pepper trade when it was attacked and captured off Quallah Battoo by Malayan pirates. As an act of retaliation, Capt. John Downes aboard the frigate *Potomac*, under direct orders from President Andrew Jackson, "stormed the place in 1832, destroying its forts and killing the Sultan Po Mahomet with 150 of his followers. This is said to have been the first American naval battle in the Pacific."[60]

6. Clay Cove (1840) east of India Street (now Thames Street).

This episode near the present-day Strait of Malacca has corroboratively also been referred to as "the United States' first ever official military intervention in Asia." President Andrew Jackson believed that "the piratical perpetrators belonged to tribes in such a state of society that the usual course of proceedings between civilized nations cannot be pursued." Believing this to be true, the president gave orders to "inflict chastisement."[61]

Portland's Golden Years

The period between 1832 and 1866 has often been referred to as Portland's "Golden Years." Many factors contributed to the city's growth, but they all centered on Portland's geographic placement on a sheltered, ice-free, deep-water port nearer to Europe than any other major American port. This geographical advantage, in addition to the natural resources of the area—chiefly, fish and lumber—and the rapid development of more northern and eastern sections of the state, gave Portland a degree of commercial prominence.

Thomas Mooney, a wandering Irish version of Alexis de Tocqueville, was traveling throughout the United States just before 1850 and recording his impressions for transmission back to Ireland. Mooney's account of

Portland at midcentury, in the very midst of its "Golden Years," was quite favorable:

> A full day's walk still northward [from Portsmouth] is Portland, having twenty thousand inhabitants, the commercial capital of the state of Maine. This city is one hundred and seven miles north-east of Boston, connected with it by railway, and on the other hand Portland is about to be connected by railroad with Montreal, and other business cities of Canada which will make it a most important city, and double its population and wealth. Portland is delightfully situated on a healthy hill, which commands a fine view of the harbour and surrounding country. Mr. Cartan, shoe maker, Mr. Hughes, merchant-tailor, Mr. O'Connor, general merchant, will give the stranger information.[62]

Portland quickly became the major exporting center for the produce of its large and rapidly developing hinterland. This same region required many imported goods and services that were also largely supplied through Portland. Thus, even though the city was strategically located to serve an expanding region, geography alone was not enough to ensure that commercial success would automatically follow. By 1860, just prior to the start of the Civil War, "Boston owned 464,200 tons of shipping with an export-import trade of $54,535,000. Portland, with 131,800 tons, had $3,442,000 worth of trade and was the busiest of Maine's ports. Portland had a large and fairly well protected harbor and early became a distribution center for the back country."[63]

The key ingredient needed to provide a dependable and economical link between Portland and its markets and natural resources was a transportation system. The mid-nineteenth century witnessed a revolution in maritime transportation away from the use of sailing ships, many of which were built along the Maine coast, to the larger and more dependable steamship.[64]

As early as 1822, records show the steamer *Kennebec* made runs between Portland and Yarmouth. By 1824, the steamer *Patent* of the Kennebec Steam Navigation Company connected Bath to Portland and Boston, and in 1826 the steamer *Legislator* was purchased by this same company. Service was marginal and intermittent, at best, and explosions occurred with some frequency in this experimental stage of the development of steam engine technology.

7. Munjoy Hill (1845), Observatory, and Casco Bay islands.

By 1828 this company was liquidated and its assets were sold at auction in Boston. "Profits were marginal because of the then-current economic depression and because wood-burning paddle-wheel steamers required such large quantities of room for fuel that there was little comfortable accommodation for paying passengers and freight."[65] Slightly later, a more dependable steamship connection between New England's two premier maritime centers emerged. The steamer *Portland*, built at Portland and owned by the Cumberland Steam Navigation Company, was a commercial success between 1835 and 1850. The *Portland* usually connected with the steamer *Bangor* at Portland for transshipments further east along the Maine coast, but in the year 1842 the *Bangor* "was sold to a Turkish Company to transport pilgrims on their way to Mecca."[66] Other lines were active on this route as well. The International Steamship Company was founded in 1860 with runs between Boston, Portland, and the most significant ports in the Canadian Maritime provinces of New Brunswick and Nova Scotia.[67]

The need for more modern and dependable forms of transport was enormous. Maine was, and to a large extent still is, a source of raw materials for the more heavily populated and wealthier regions of the United States to its south and west. Lumber and potatoes were exported in great quantity always, but perishable goods, especially seafood, required a more rapid and predictable form of transport.

One such example would be the early shellfish trade. Canneries sprang up along the Maine coast in the 1840s, and these greatly expanded the market for Maine fish and shellfish such as lobster, mackerel, clams, salmon, and chowder. Sweet corn was another very popular Maine export using this new technology for storing and shipping. The lobster market was vastly expanded in the 1840s with the development of canneries. "In 1844 William Underwood was canning lobsters in Harpswell. From 1852 to 1857 George Burnham and Samuel Rumery were canning corn and lobsters in Portland. They parted in 1867, Burnham to join with Charles Morrill, and Rumery to go with the Portland Packing Company." By the year 1880, some twenty-three coastal factories were involved with the canning and shipping of these perishable, yet highly desirable, Maine exports.[68]

The mid-nineteenth century also witnessed a steady and rapid growth in both short- and long-distance railroad links between American cities. Commercial growth in this period was contingent upon transportation links with American and important world maritime trading centers.

John Alfred Poor: Visionary

It was John Alfred Poor who envisioned the opportunity for Portland to become a major commercial entry port (*entrepôt*) along the Atlantic coast of North America. If Maine in general and Portland in particular were to take advantage of their geographic location, in effect to change their situation at the end of the line from a liability into an asset, the railroad would have to become a key resource. John Poor, one of the pioneers who understood this imperative with both energy and clarity, was born in 1808 in Andover, Maine. By the early 1830s Poor was practicing law in Bangor. After witnessing the initial run of New England's first rail link, between Boston and Newton, Massachusetts, Poor moved to Portland and devoted an increasing amount of his energy to the development of Maine's commercial rail transportation.

Poor's concept of this new technology was formed within a comprehensive and indeed forward-looking framework. He perceived Portland to be the central linkage between Europe and North America for the transport of both goods and people.[69] For Portland to achieve this status, it was essential to ensure adequate rail links from every geographic direction to the city: to the east and Canada's Maritime ports, especially Halifax; to the north and

8. John Alfred Poor, entrepreneur (1808–1871).

Canada's two major ice-bound winter ports of Quebec and Montreal; to the west and America's rich midlands with its cattle and grain; and, finally, to the south and the major commercial and population centers of Boston, New York, and beyond.

In 1836, Poor attempted to convince some of Portland's leading landowners and merchants, including John Neal, Judge William Preble, John Mussey, and John B. Brown, of the practicality of this scheme. Their skepticism concerning Poor's plan for a rail link between Portland and Montreal via the White Mountains of New Hampshire was best illustrated by this retrospectively recorded reaction of John Neal: "I was not a little astonished for it seemed to me at first, that he had overlooked—or overtopped—the White-Hills to begin with."[70]

Unmoved by the criticism, John Poor's vision of the future was both vivid and grand, as evidenced in his majestic prose concerning "a vision, in which I saw the whole line pass before me like a grand panorama, and in continuation a vast system of railroads permeating the whole country

... with new cities with a dense population, with every facility for ocean steamships from every country; and the coast of Maine lined with cities rivaling the cities on the coast of the Baltic."[71]

John Poor's greatest achievement was to convince Canadian investors and businessmen of the superiority of a Montreal to Portland sea–rail link with Europe, as opposed to a similar link via Boston. His skill and imagination in outwitting the financial and political leaders of the much larger city to the south are the stuff of legend. They were demonstrated in an episode that included a daring sleigh ride in 1845 through New Hampshire and Vermont in the midst of a February blizzard to demonstrate the viability of the Montreal–Portland route.[72]

Poor envisioned Portland as the winter port for ice-bound Canadian ports on the Saint Lawrence, such as Quebec and Montreal. "He also envisioned an integrated freight system that would connect Europe and America via train and ship, a concept first articulated by British engineer and designer Isambard Kingdom Brunel, who in 1837 built the steamship *Great Western* for just such a service."[73]

Since 1853, Portland and Montreal cultivated their commercial ties with each other out of self-interest and self-protection. Boston and New York were, of course, commercial threats to Montreal as well as to Portland. A narrow-gauge rail link, incompatible with the wider and fairly standard American gauge, was deliberately chosen to connect Montreal on the St. Lawrence River to the Atlantic Ocean at Portland while simultaneously limiting Boston's access. Poor suggested that by using a narrow "gauge different from that of the Boston railways, the Portland line could prevent interchange of traffic and thereby avoid becoming a 'feeder line' to Boston."[74] Such a narrow gauge would prevent monopoly control by more powerful interests and larger concentrations of capital. It could allow Portland to develop as a "trade center in its own right," quite apart from its larger competitors to the south.[75]

What appeared so promising at the start, however, soon ran into multiple financial problems. Between 1846 and 1853 the Atlantic and St. Lawrence Railway, linking Portland with Montreal, was completed. On Monday, July 18, 1853, the *Eastern Argus* reported the expected arrival of the first railroad cars from Montreal due in at about seven o'clock.[76] That evening more than twelve thousand Portland citizens joined their mayor and John A. Poor in a long-anticipated and enthusiastic public welcome: "When, some seven or eight years since, the scheme was broached of building a Railroad nearly

9. Old Grand Trunk Depot (1854) and grain elevator (India and Fore).

three hundred miles long, from Portland to Montreal, it was scouted as utterly impracticable by thousands of sensible men. . . . A hundred other captious objections were raised. They were all triumphantly answered last evening by the arrival of the first train from Montreal. The victory is won, and we congratulate the people of Portland upon the glorious result."[77]

Just three weeks after its opening, however, due to cost overruns and shortages of capital, the new line had to be leased to the Grand Trunk Railway Company of Canada for 999 years. The railroad line built to connect Maine with the Maritime Provinces, the European and North American line, met a similar fate and was also leased forever to the Maine Central Railroad. The link west was to be made by the Portland, Rutland, Oswego, and Chicago Railway Company, the incorporation of which was chartered by the Maine legislature and approved by the boards of trade of Chicago and Buffalo but not by the Portland Board of Trade. Previous financially shaky railroad corporations proposed by John Poor had made Portland financiers nervous about further risks to their capital.

This regional caution occurred even as the first transcontinental railroad was being completed in 1869, later heroically documented in Portlander John Ford's great silent film epic, *The Iron Horse* (1924). It was at the time of several local financial disappointments when, despite these stunning national achievements in transportation, Poor's life ended on September 5, 1871.

Despite the failure of his more grandiose schemes, the legacy of John Alfred Poor was immense to both Portland and Maine. He was the local representative of a common type of nineteenth-century urban entrepreneur. His own commercial interests were well served by such development, but, more importantly, so too were Portland's interests served. The number of short-term and long-term jobs created in Portland by Poor's enterprises was significant. He had given Maine two important railroad links with major Canadian regions; founded the Portland Company near the Grand Trunk Railway station to build locomotives and heavy machinery; presided over the Portland Gas Light Company; and managed a major newspaper called the *State of Maine*. Poor imbued the minds of many with both his spirit and vision for a future based on commerce and transportation—a future in which Portland would play the major role.

10. Ferry Village Yards—J. W. Dyer launching *White-Sea* (1854).

The Early Irish and Building the Canals

John A. Poor's partial success in developing Portland as a major port for Canada's eastern regions also had an impact on Irish immigration into the city and state. In 1853, in order to handle the increased shipping expected into and out of Portland, the Canadian Steam Navigation Company commenced winter service to the city. Soon after, it was taken over by a major British shipping firm, the Allan Line, which was locally known as the Montreal Ocean Steamship Company, incorporated in 1854. It commenced service into Portland from Liverpool via Cobh, then known as Queenstown, County Cork, Ireland. Thus Irish immigrants could gain affordable passage directly to Portland via Queenstown in ships that the Allan Line would lucratively fill with Canadian grain for the return passage to England.

One of the few images from this period showing immigrants, presumably many of them from Ireland, arriving on the Portland waterfront is the pencil sketch (wash drawing) by Portland artist Frederic Goth titled *Arrival of the SS Oregon, Portland ME, January 21, 1884*. Passengers disembarked at Grand Trunk Ocean Sheds No. 6 at the foot of Hancock Street, adjacent to the Grand Trunk Grain Elevator, the commercial raison d'être for the Allan Line's venture into Portland.[78]

Ironically, this exact location has recently been re-created as the Ocean Gateway facility in Portland for handling passenger liners and the regular, albeit seasonal, catamaran service to Yarmouth, Nova Scotia. Hancock Street, which had previously terminated at Middle Street by the Thomas Laughlin Company, a steel foundry that was a Portland landmark for many years, today continues through to the waterfront. This recent development fortuitously also re-created the street corner on which the poet Henry Wadsworth Longfellow was born in 1807. Finally, Hancock Street has now been extended one block closer to the waterfront and now intersects with the newly re-created Thames Street, its original name, going east along the harbor from Commercial Street. Thus, Portland's new Ocean Gateway facility is situated at nearly the exact location of Goth's unique artistic image of immigration directly to Portland in 1884. The entry to the Ocean Gateway building has even attempted to recreate the image of the clock tower of the old Grand Trunk Railway station that, until 1966, sat only one block to its west. History, albeit with significant chronological and technological modifications, has come full circle in many of these significant waterfront developments.

11. M12550 *Arrival of the SS Oregon, Portland ME, January 21, 1884*. Frederic R. Goth. Courtesy of the Peabody Essex Museum.

12. Eastern Steamboat House (Richardson's Wharf). Courtesy of William D. Barry.

An excellent example of the risk-taking, entrepreneurial spirit at the mid-nineteenth century involved Portland with its natural hinterland to the west and north. This was the Cumberland and Oxford (C&O) Canal (1830–70) that created a continuous waterway from the northern tip of Long Lake, near the town of Harrison, to Portland on Casco Bay. The route via the Songo and the Presumpscot rivers required a system of engineered connections and locks, some of which are still in use today.[79]

The C&O Canal, completed in 1830, employed large numbers of Irish laborers, many of whom would have worshipped at the Saint Dominic's Church in Portland, also completed in the same year. Ironically, many of these same laborers would move on to the construction of the rail lines in Maine that would eventually make the C&O obsolete.[80]

One year before John Poor's death, Gov. Joshua L. Chamberlain, the hero of Gettysburg, in a speech in 1870 to the Maine Legislature demonstrated the entrepreneurial vision of Maine's future that he shared with Poor: "She reminds me more of the Western States than of the rest of New England in her conditions and needs—[with] virgin soil, undeveloped powers, vast forests, and vigorous men, but no money. Like them she is trying to build railroads, invite immigration and develop her resources."[81]

Many in Maine today would continue to bemoan, along with Poor and Chamberlain, the state's perennial lack of the capital necessary to sufficiently develop its natural and human resources. One item of commonality between political and commercial leaders, then and now, would be to acknowledge that taking advantage of Portland and Maine's maritime location will be as essential to its future as it has been to its past.

2

Black Fades to Green on the Waterfront

Nineteenth-Century Social, Racial, and Ethnic Change

New England lies at the periphery of the major concentration of population in North America, and within New England over various time periods certain population groups have themselves been seen as peripheral.[1] This chapter will attempt to explore the relationship in the mid-nineteenth century in Portland between two such marginalized groups, African Americans and Irish, within this major New England maritime port city.

A chronological approach will be used while identifying central themes to explore: the growth of the port of Portland; the arrival of a small but notable black population with a maritime-related occupational niche and demographic comparisons with Boston; labor and racial comparisons with other American ports, including New York, Philadelphia, New Orleans, and Portland, Oregon; racial theories of "whiteness" and their impact; the arrival of the Irish and their dockside hegemony by the mid-nineteenth century; and finally the founding of the predominantly Irish Portland Longshoremen's Benevolent Society (PLSBS) in 1880. Local demographic conditions in Portland, especially in terms of race, will be reviewed in comparison with its larger and major New England rival port of Boston. Literature on whiteness and its impact on the American working class will be analyzed in the context of the replacement of one small peripheral group in Portland, African Americans, by another, albeit much larger group, the Irish.

Portland's maritime location on a deep-water, ice-free harbor together with its plentiful supply of labor made this waterfront a natural place in which to do business. Occupations directly connected to maritime endeavors included ship store and chandlers, repair and supply, as well as the necessary marine insurance that blossomed in Portland during this period.

Examples of the latter included the Portland Mutual Fire Insurance Company (1828), the Ocean Insurance Company (1832), and the Dirigo Insurance Company (1856). Of course, banking and financial services also grew in tandem with maritime and railroad expansion. Many other businesses, such as the Portland Glass Company and the Portland Shovel Manufacturing Company, may have had a less direct connection to the waterfront but still relied on affordable transport.[2]

It is clear that these businesses, together with businesses that were not marine related, were equally dependent on capital accumulated by transport and maritime commerce. They all profited by having a readily available means of distributing their manufactured goods to potentially distant markets. To handle the increasing demand for water-borne merchandise and transportation, several local maritime companies expanded their facilities. The Portland Steam Packet Company had been formed in 1843 to provide safe, dependable propeller service between Portland and Boston. In the first twenty years of business, its boats made nearly 11,200 trips and carried nearly 1.5 million passengers and 2.5 million tons of freight without the loss of a single life.[3] The International Steamship Company was incorporated in 1860 to transport freight and passengers between Portland and major southern and eastern ports, especially Saint John, New Brunswick, and Halifax, Nova Scotia. The New England Screwship Company provided twice-weekly round-trip service between Portland and New York City.

Labor was crucial for this impressive growth during the "Golden Years," 1832–66. Workers and their union supporters did not always see things eye to eye with their employers, of course. When a strike for the ten-hour day occurred by the journeymen mechanics at the Portland Company in 1849, the *Portland Pleasure Boat*, "an ardent defender of the working classes," rhetorically and forcefully attacked the owners:

> If the Portland Company can grind an hour's labor per day out of each man, it will aid them materially in paying for their shares; it will also help to keep the workers in ignorance and poverty. . . . I would not say a word to stir up unnecessary strife between the two classes, but I would be glad if all farmers, mechanics and laborers, were aware that they are the only class of people that the world cannot spare—that the other portions of society are chiefly drones and suckers, living on the heart's blood and vitals of honest industry.[4]

Portland, Maine's "Golden Years" ended with the Great Portland Fire of July 4, 1866, probably the nation's worst non-war-related inferno up to that date. From a boatyard on Commercial Street the fire spread to a lumberyard and then on to John B. Brown's huge Portland Sugar House. Before it burned out at the base of Munjoy Hill, the fire had destroyed 6 million dollars worth of property—nearly 1,800 buildings comprising more than one-quarter of Portland's assessed valuation, including the greatest part of the city's business district. It left nearly ten thousand residents homeless. The poet Henry Wadsworth Longfellow, a Portland native, returned to the city of his birth in July of 1866 and wrote, "I have been in Portland since the fire. Desolation! Desolation! Desolation! It reminds me of Pompeii, the 'sepult city.'"[5]

Portland's citizens of enterprise, however, were up to the enormous task of rebuilding the city, and their economic vitality enabled Portland to bounce back from the disaster in a remarkably short time. Within two years Portland was virtually rebuilt, its vitality in no small part the result of the continued efforts of John Alfred Poor, John Bundy Brown, Charles Q. Clapp, John Mussey, James Phinney Baxter, and other Portland businessmen who had made the city a major shipping and transportation center. Capital gained from these commercial and shipping ventures, as well as from having supplied the Union Army during the recently completed Civil War, was confidently reinvested in Portland's rebirth. The writer John Neal commented that "a new spirit took sudden possession of our property holders . . . and straightway they began building for the future so Portland is now . . . at least fifty years ahead of what she would have been otherwise."[6]

Many of Portland's present-day central structures and services were built in the years following the Great Fire. The business district reappeared as did a beautiful new post office, customs house, Roman Catholic cathedral, and Maine General Hospital on Bramhall Hill. Lincoln Park was created to serve the dual purpose of an urban recreational park as well as a firebreak between the city center and the east end. In 1868 Portland began to pipe water from nearby Sebago Lake as the city's major water supply, which it continues to be to this day. The spirit of public concern and the confidence demonstrated in these years were neither romantic nor entirely altruistic. Portland had revealed its potential as a major commercial center, and its chief natural resource, a deep-water, ice-free port closer to Europe than any other major American Atlantic port, was still there to be exploited for private as well as public gain.

Prosperity bred prosperity. In the period between 1866 and 1880, Portland business concerns grew along with the general expansion of the port and the railroads serving it. Some of this growth was directly connected with transportation, such as the Portland Company that manufactured steam engines, the Portland Sugar House that depended on shipping to provide the raw molasses from the West Indies, and the Portland Dry Dock Company.

By the end of the Civil War, Portland had become Canada's winter port. It was visited by such important shipping companies as the Canadian Line, the Glasgow Line, and the Anchor Line, all of which also served generally as transport connections between Great Britain and eastern Canada. Between the months of November through April, many transatlantic steamers of these companies would dock in Portland with their cargoes bound for Quebec, Montreal, or other ice-bound Canadian cities. Portland benefited greatly from being the conduit for these passengers and commodities. Although Boston and New York handled greater volumes of dry goods and more passengers, the Grand Trunk Railway (narrow gauge) connection was especially advantageous to this much smaller city. Portland served as a major eastern terminus for goods and passengers from eastern or midwestern United States and Canada to be transported back to Europe via these great shipping lines.

One of the challenges for American ports in the post–Civil War period was to generate enough export capacity to initiate and maintain regular service by major international steamship lines. Large railroad conglomerates determined many of the conditions of commerce. Railroad rate structures could serve to make larger more distant ports, such as New York, more economically viable than local facilities in Boston or Portland. Boston, for example, was hurt economically for those very reasons when the Cunard Line suspended service from 1868 to 1871.[7] Portland, however, since 1853, had the distinct advantage of the Canadian grain connection, an economic opportunity it would continue to exploit successfully throughout the next seventy years.

Nineteenth-Century African American Dockworkers

Portland's maritime prosperity and continued growth depended on a vital labor force. In the early nineteenth century, some Portland dockworkers were black. Many of Portland's African Americans were the offspring of ex-slaves or those who had come from the West Indies via the molasses trade. Slavery had been present in colonial Falmouth, and even Parson Thomas Smith was reportedly a slave owner as late as 1753 when there were twenty-one slaves in the town. Slavery was abolished in Maine, however, through the manumission clause of the Massachusetts Constitution of 1780. "The end of slavery would see declining numbers of blacks in [the] old settlements and growing black populations in the new boom towns thriving on the maritime trade—Portland, for instance." Randolph Stakeman has contended that "Portland provided many opportunities for the former slaves and soon became the home of Maine's largest black community."[8]

By 1828 an Abyssinian church was incorporated.[9] Its location near the corner of Mountfort and Newbury (then named Sumner) streets marked the center of Portland's black community at the base of Munjoy Hill, one of the city's poorest neighborhoods. It was located adjacent to the docks in the east end of the city. By 1835 this black church was joined by twenty-two "colored members of the Second [Congregational] Church [who] were set off to unite with the Abyssinian Church." That same year, also in that building, a separate school for black students, averaging fifty in number, initiated a period of segregated education in Portland that lasted until the Civil War. Thus, between 1835 and the Civil War it would appear that Portland's educational system was largely segregated. The end of educational segregation was suggested by historian William Willis who recorded in his study of Portland first published in 1865 that, "the day scholars are, under recent arrangements, distributed in the other schools and the separate establishment for colored children is discontinued."[10]

Gary B. Nash studied blacks living in northern seaport cities between 1775 and 1820. He referred to the black church as the tie between the distant African past, the recent experience of slavery, and the future as free citizens. Nash contended that there were two major reasons for the rise of these separatist "African" churches: "discriminatory treatment in white churches and the gradual rise of a community of interest among the Afro-Americans."[11]

Portland seemed to fit into this pattern of northern seaport cities concerning the emergence of a separate black church. Evidence in the historical novel *Pyrrhus Venture* and many more contemporary sources also suggested that in the early nineteenth century an appreciable number of Portland's dockworkers were black.[12] Local historians have located the city's black neighborhood in the area surrounding the Abyssinian Church at the base of Munjoy Hill: "During the Federal Period black stevedores virtually controlled longshore work at Portland, and the area around Hancock, Newbury and the Hill (above Mountfort) became a distinctly black neighborhood. It was not until Irish laborers arrived in the mid-nineteenth century that the situation on the wharves changed."[13] The degree to which blacks controlled local dock work could be seen in the *Portland Transcript* of January 22, 1895, which described a Portland black as "one of the negro stevedores, who prior to the [eighteen] forties used to do all the stevedoring in this port."[14]

The presence of a significant African American population along Portland's waterfront was clear. That a good number of these blacks had found work as longshoremen in the early nineteenth century was not surprising. The molasses trade between Portland and the West Indies was one source of a local black population that had arrived from the Caribbean aboard Portland-bound ships and who subsequently found work along its waterfront. Longshore work was dangerous, unskilled, labor intensive, and sporadic, totally dependent upon the arrival of loaded ships. Thus, before the large-scale arrival of Irish immigrants into Maine in the mid- to late nineteenth century, African Americans often served as a source of the cheap, unskilled labor necessary for profitable maritime commerce.

The West Indies trade involved the importation of molasses and the export of wooden boxes, barrels, and casks, and the shooks or wooden parts with which to make these items. Suspended during the embargo and the War of 1812, this trade recommenced and expanded throughout the early nineteenth century. In its raw form, molasses was cheap, retailing at fifty cents a gallon, and it was particularly desired in the logging camps that proliferated in the Maine woods during the winter months. The following is an early example of clever advertising for this product: "Foresters float down timber that seamen may build ships and go to the saccharine islands of the south for molasses; for without molasses no lumberman could be happy in the unsweetened wilderness. Pork lubricates the joints, molasses gives tenacity to his muscles."[15]

13. J. B. Brown's Portland Sugar Company (c. 1855).

Two lucrative molasses by-products, sugar and rum, sustained the trade. In 1845 an experimental firm in Portland attempted but failed to produce refined sugar from molasses. Ten years later, however, the manager of that firm, John Bundy Brown, together with Dependence H. Furbish, who had discovered a steam method of refining sugar from molasses, chartered the Portland Sugar Company (1855). This company was for a time the largest importer of molasses in New England.

Maritime historian William H. Rowe wrote that John Bundy Brown was joined by "two other sugar houses of good capacity operating in the city and the market in the vast territory to the west and the east by the Grand Trunk and Maine Central Railroads, made Portland a molasses port that was a close rival of New York."[16] Brown became one of Maine's leading venture capitalists and was eventually an investor and director of the Atlantic and Saint Lawrence Railroad, among several other corporate enterprises. Dependable and affordable transport by land and sea was an indispensable element in this and most businesses, then as now.[17] By 1860 6 million gallons of molasses were being imported to Portland, largely from Cuba and the Caribbean: "[Brown] produced some 250 barrels [of some eleven grades of sugar] a day from 25,000 hogsheads of molasses a year. The business, it was estimated, was 'raising one and a half million dollars annually,' and kept a whole fleet of brigs and schooners from Matanzas and Cardenas coming constantly. Near Portland there is still a Blackstrap Hill, so called because it was the first land to be sighted by these vessels with their cargoes of 'blackstrap' molasses."[18]

In addition to sugar, the production of rum had been significant since the late eighteenth century. "At one point Portland had as many as seven distilleries running day and night converting molasses to rum."[19] It was second only to Medford, Massachusetts, just outside of Boston, as New England's primary rum supplier. Several factors converged to end this lucrative trade. These factors included keener competition from other ports; a new centrifugal system of refining sugar; the shipment of molasses by bulk rather than wooden hogsheads and sugar in bags rather than boxes; a prohibitionist Maine Law initiated by Portland's mayor Neal Dow and passed by the Maine Legislature in 1851; and the complete destruction of J. B. Brown's Portland Sugar House in the Portland Fire of 1866.

Portland historian William Goold, writing in a local newspaper about the old custom house, connected the West Indies molasses trade with Portland's African American dockworkers in a fascinating manner:

> Here in good weather . . . were collected the stevedores, sailors, boarding-house keepers, and all who had an interest in the discharging and fitting away of West Indiamen, which was the principal . . . trade of Portland. Conspicuous among the Sunday crowd was the black crew who discharged all the molasses by hoisting it out by hand, keeping time to their amusing songs while at work. They were sure to have a large audience to hear their singing. Many churchgoing people on coming out of meeting . . . then took Fore Street on their way home, no matter where they lived.[20]

This recollection is further supported by a later well-known maritime historian:

> When a cargo of coffee or molasses came alongside a wharf or when lumber was being loaded aboard, the waterfront resounded with the song of the Negro stevedores. They hoisted the hogsheads from the holds by a tackle (pronounced "taykel") and fall, all the time singing:

> Everybody he lub something,
>   Hoojun - John - a hoojun,
> Song he set the heart a-beating,
>   Hoojun - John - a hoojun.[21]

The incorporation of the Abyssinian church in Portland in 1828 itself suggested a sizable black population. John Neal, a notable contemporary, placed the number as high as seven hundred to eight hundred. "I am told that more than three hundred grown persons regularly meet together for worship. If this is true—if it is true in any degree, our missionary people ought to be applied to forthwith, yea and all others who are favorable to education or morality."[22]

Using Boston as the larger port with which to make a comparison, census returns present a statistical record of Portland's black population and isolate the "free colored" community by sex and place of domicile. Actual census returns from the four decades preceding the Civil War would suggest that John Neal's estimates were somewhat inflated.

The census figures revealed a fairly equal number of black males and females in nineteenth-century Portland, but it also showed the city to have a highly racially segregated housing pattern. At a time when there were seven wards in the city, the black population was squeezed into Ward 1 on Munjoy Hill, derisively characterized as "Nigger Hill."[23]

The relatively small percentage of blacks to whites for Portland was quite similar to that of Boston in these antebellum years. African Americans, as a percentage of population, were slightly higher for Boston in 1830 and 1860, but slightly higher for Portland in 1840 and 1850, and almost always less than 3 percent in each city. Residential concentration in Portland, however, gave the appearance of a larger black population than actually existed, perhaps explaining the source of John Neal's inflated estimate.

Table 1. Black Population Concentration in Portland and Boston (1840–60)

Year	Black Pop. (Portland)	Ward 1 (Portland)	Ward 6 (Boston)
1840	402	310 (77%)	1,088 (45%)
1850	395	321 (81%)	1,219 (61%)
1860	318	209 (66%)	1,395 (62%)

Sources: U.S. Census Office, *Fifth Census of the U.S.* (1830), 2–3; *Sixth Census of the U.S.* (1840), 4–5; *Seventh Census of the U.S.* (1850), 4; *Eighth Census of the U.S.* (1860), 201; *Twelfth Census of the U.S.* (1900), Vol. I, Population (Part I), 619. Boston statistics are taken from Horton and Horton, *Black Bostonians*, 2–5.

Both Portland and Boston had their own "Nigger Hill," the lower slopes of Munjoy Hill and the northern slope of Beacon Hill, respectively. Portland's blacks, at least two-thirds of whom lived at the base of Munjoy Hill in the east end of the city, were relatively more residentially concentrated than were blacks in Boston. Both cities were also beginning to experience the influx of large numbers of Irish by the 1850s, with direct consequences for the racial minority. "Often, a dramatic rise in the number of Irish in a neighborhood resulted in a decline in the area's black population. This was the case in ward two [in Boston] between 1850 and 1860, [where] competition for jobs and housing engendered animosity between blacks and Irish."[24] Even by 1900 when the number of city wards in Portland had increased to nine, the number of blacks living in the east end of Portland (wards 1 and 2) was 179 out of a total of 291, or 62 percent.[25] The newly arriving Irish immigrants would replicate this racial–ethnic pattern of establishing tightly knit communities in the later years of the nineteenth century.

White hostility caused segregated African American neighborhoods to form, Gary Nash has argued, and "in the cities the concentration of free blacks provided some security against a hostile world." It was therefore to areas like Munjoy Hill within American towns and cities that free blacks migrated in the post-Revolutionary decades. "The dense network of urban black institutions and a rich community life made it easier to confront racism in the cities than in the countryside."[26] According to the Horton study, Boston's blacks were still confronting racism in the antebellum years, as reflected in their changing residential patterns. "Much of the black flight from ward two was undoubtedly an effort by blacks to shield themselves from hostility and harassment. Since they were still barred from many neighborhoods, these families moved into predominantly black sections."[27]

Just as residential patterns in Portland produced a compact, albeit small, black neighborhood in the east end of the city, so too there was a certain amount of occupational concentration among African Americans. The Reverend Elijah Kellogg (1813–1901) was a Portland-born novelist, collector of history, and noted local historian for much of his adult life around the fishing community of Harpswell, Maine. In his novel *A Strong Arm and a Mother's Blessing* he described black workers unloading ships to a musical cadence quite similar to William Goold's previously mentioned recollection. Kellogg conjectured that "during the continuance of the lumber trade, Portland could boast of the largest number and most athletic body of negroes that were ever seen together."[28]

African Americans played significant roles in the maritime labor force in Portland as in other major seaports such as Boston, New York, and Philadelphia. This black workforce has been referred to as "part of a literally floating proletariat." In particular, they headed for the maritime towns, for black men had long been important on the coasting vessels and overseas ships of colonial commerce, and black women could hope for domestic service in the homes of an increasingly affluent urban upper class.[29]

African American labor occupied a niche in early-nineteenth-century Portland and other coastal seaports remarkably similar to that occupied by Irish men and women later in the century. The antebellum period, 1830–60, in Portland represented the years of transition along the waterfront. The Irish would replace blacks as longshoremen in Portland, especially in the famine and postfamine years from the late 1840s through the 1850s. The casual, unskilled, and underpaid nature of this work helped make it the occupational domain of those at the bottom rung of the socioeconomic ladder. The native Yankee population for the most part eschewed this menial labor.

The timing of this labor transformation along Portland's waterfront was of paramount importance, occurring nearly simultaneously with the opening of the direct rail link between Portland and Montreal in 1853. The Atlantic and Saint Lawrence (later the Grand Trunk) Railway would give a completely new and much greater significance to this workforce in the second half of the nineteenth century. The Irish were also becoming a more demographically significant portion of the city's overall population, a trend that would continue. Economically and socially this immigration was bound to have profound effects.

In Boston, New York, Cincinnati, and elsewhere, violent confrontations between African American and Irish labor took place, particularly during the July 1863 draft riots in New York City. An earlier confirmation that the contact between black and white dockworkers, specifically the Irish, could be violent came from Cincinnati's waterfront during the Civil War. "Hard times also promoted scattered outbreaks of violence among desperate wage earners. Screaming 'Let's clear out the niggers,' Irish dock workers, angered by the attempts of black laborers to underbid them for jobs, initiated a two-day riot in July 1862, which left a trail of destruction that stretched from the city's docks into the black homes along the levee."[30]

In Portland, racial anxiety and animosity was apparently prevalent as it was in other American cities.[31] Although scant published evidence exists to document similar violent episodes in Portland, there is little doubt that blacks had earlier been driven off the waterfront by the Irish, and that likely only their relatively small overall number prevented the type of overtly violent racial incidents as reported elsewhere.

The first recorded strike in Maine by black workers, as documented by labor historian Charles A. Scontras, occurred in 1866 during the construction of the new city hall building.[32] A "party of Negroes" was brought to Portland from Boston to do construction. This led to the charge that "no white need apply" and of preferential hiring practices for blacks by "their admirers" in the city in the immediate aftermath of the Civil War. Printed advertisements appeared locally stating, "Any employer who wants one or more laboring people and is willing to send South for them, has only to address the Freedman's Bureau at Washington to receive its latest information."[33]

Maureen Elgersman Lee, a historian who has written authoritatively about blacks in Bangor and Portland, has noted that along the Portland waterfront,

> black men were refused union membership, a fact that left them out of group-negotiated wages and benefits. This exclusion also pooled them in service-based unskilled and semiskilled labor. . . . West Indian men, in particular, were employed as seamen. . . . Other men worked on steamers as stewards and waiters.[34]

Daniel Rosenberg's study of New Orleans dockworkers analyzed the complex and unique set of work rules, traditions, and racial composition along the levees of this significant Gulf Coast port around the turn of the century. Not surprisingly, the contrasts with Portland were far greater than the similarities. New Orleans was by many accounts the nation's second-busiest port throughout many of these years. Dockworkers numbered around eleven thousand, roughly ten times the number in Portland. The racial composition of the two cities could hardly have been more divergent. New Orleans in 1900 had a total population of three hundred thousand, with blacks accounting for eighty thousand of the total, or roughly 27 percent.[35]

Similarities with Portland, Maine, however, were also noteworthy. Both were major regional ports, and the nature of dock work in both ports was casual and seasonal, entirely dependent on ships to load or unload. The major export crops, cotton in New Orleans and grain in Portland, were primarily available for shipping in the fall and winter months, thus forcing dockworkers in both ports to scramble for other temporary employment during the spring and summer.

White and black longshoremen in New Orleans joined together for their mutual protection in a system that became known as "half-and-half." For a generation at the turn of the century this work pattern defied local and national trends toward segregation and "separate but equal." Prior to this period, and in contrast with this Gulf port's equal racial allocation of work, the mostly Irish longshoremen of Portland had replaced the black and other non-Irish laborers. They cemented the removal of the former by prohibiting the employment of African Americans in the original bylaws of the Portland Longshoremen's Benevolent Society (1881) stating that "no colored person shall at any time be admitted as a member of this Society."[36]

A clear example of this racial prohibition in action could be witnessed in the following revealing PLSBS record just two years later:

> At a meeting of the Portland Longshoremen's Association held Nov. 26th 1883, the following committee was appointed to wait upon Mr. Neill, Stevedore of the Allan Line (namely Messrs. Lowery, D. J. Leonard, & Jeremiah Bassett), the object of such committee being to inquire into the engaging of a colored man named Green, by above named Stevedore.
>
> Mr. Neill was waited on Nov. 27th by Messrs. Leonard & Bassett and on calling upon him explained. He stated that his only object in giving Green employment was that he was an old and faithful employee of the firm in Boston, that he had no intention whatever of introducing this class of labor, and that he knew of no other man of the above description in his employment, nor was he aware that in employing him that he was doing anything contrary to the rules of the association—and your committee so report.
> (signed) D. J. Leonard
> Jeremiah Bassett[37]

A significant maritime labor similarity is that both of these far-distant ports would eventually be represented by the International Longshoremen's Association (ILA), New Orleans by the turn of the century and Portland in 1914. Contrary to the general American and the local Portland experience, in New Orleans, "The International Longshoremen's Association (ILA) was among the few American Federation of Labor (AFL) affiliates freely admitting black workers and electing blacks to leadership."[38] But by the time Portland's longshoremen had affiliated with the ILA in 1914, the small African American workforce had already effectively been removed from the local docks for more than two generations.

Some evidence exists to suggest that a few blacks continued to work along the waterfront in Portland in the late nineteenth century. The *Portland Transcript*, edited by Edward H. Elwell, in 1880 briefly analyzed the emergence of Portland's black population and even listed some twenty-six personalities, many long since deceased, with brief "anecdotes illustrating their peculiarities." Among these were Jack Groves, mentioned earlier, who "lived to a great age;" Steadman Shepard, a stevedore; Peter Pier (sometimes spelled Pierre), "a native of the West Indies [who] worked about the wharves and occasionally went to sea;" and John Siggs, a "laborer." This "John Siggs of Mountjoy" was later described as "one of the Negro stevedores, who prior to the forties used to do all the stevedoring in this port."[39] Siggs may be found in several city directories, and is often listed as a laborer in the separate sections for "People of Colour." He was even racially parodied, or so it appears, for supporting Neal Dow's temperance crusade of the mid-1850s: a "Spurious Celebration" was to be held on July 4, 1851, with "Esq. Siggs" delivering an address upon "Wool and Wooly Heads."[40]

The two major contrasts between New Orleans and Portland concerning race relations on the waterfront appear to be relative size and self-interest. In New Orleans, black labor contributed half of those available and looking for work, whereas in Portland the much smaller group of black laborers was swamped by an incoming tide of desperate Irish workers by the midpoint of the nineteenth century. The volume of longshore work was about to dramatically increase and become systematized at this very moment by the new Grand Trunk Railroad connection between Portland and eastern Canada.

Perceived self-interest led the workers of these two ports in diametrically opposite directions. The New Orleans dockers, black and white, needed each other to resist the organized and unified demands of the shipping agents and their stevedore foremen for more work from fewer workers. Today this is referred to as "efficiency" or "productivity," but workers saw this as "speed up" or erosion of work rules, especially concerning the size and composition of the work gangs. In Portland, however, the Irish longshoremen were numerous and secure enough in their control of the docks to battle the employer/stevedores exclusively on their own terms.

Another useful comparison regarding race relations alongshore would be with Portland's namesake, three thousand miles to the west on the Pacific coast, Portland, Oregon. One strong similarity was the tiny proportion of African Americans to the total population. As cited earlier, the black population of Portland, Maine, actually declined by half between the Civil War and the turn of the century, from 1.2 percent in 1860 to 0.6 percent in 1900. As late as 1941 and the American entry into World War II, the black population of Portland, Oregon, also stood at a miniscule 0.6 percent. The lack of any sizable African American community in each city made it possible for their longshore unions, and for waterfront employers and stevedores as well, to exclude all black workers. This was accomplished in part in Portland, Oregon, through a type of "grandfather clause" that perpetuated racial exclusivity. In both ports nepotism, "the brother-in-law system of recruitment," was used.[41]

Longshoremen of Portland, Maine, were overwhelmingly Irish or Irish American, but those of Portland, Oregon, were more diverse, predominantly consisting of English, Canadian, Scandinavian, or German.[42] The nepotism in hiring practices was nearly universal in all American ports until the International Longshoremen's and Warehousemen's Union (ILWU) on the West Coast attempted to end the practice in the twentieth century. Nepotism in Portland, Maine, was quite similar to that of Boston where "the [ILA] membership was largely Irish and Irish-American of the second generation with openings being filled by the sons of members."[43]

The universality of nepotism was noted in a major study of American labor that made the claim that laborers' organizations were largely based on ethnic ties. David Montgomery cited black hod carriers in Philadelphia in the 1870s and the following two examples of Irish nepotism in the hiring of "Irish freight handlers of the port of New York in the 1880s as it was of the Irish grain shovellers who brought the International Longshoremen's Association to the port of Buffalo by means of a successful strike against a saloon-based hiring system in 1899."[44]

In terms of Philadelphia, this ethnic and racial cohesiveness certainly was also prevalent. Peter Cole describes this pattern graphically in terms of longshoremen:

Many of them shared ethnic and religious ties, especially as most gangs were separated by ethnicity. Moreover, family ties—fathers and sons, uncles and nephews, cousins and brothers—were deeply interwoven on the docks, helping each other find jobs and work partners. These bonds were cemented further by the fact that most longshoremen lived in the same waterfront districts near the Delaware River, drank at the same saloons, and attended the same fraternal societies and churches. All of these factors contributed not just to a shared identity but also encouraged a particularly militant brand of unionism.[45]

The research of David Roediger, Noel Ignatiev, and a growing number of other scholars concentrates on the theory of "whiteness" and its relationship to race, ethnicity, and nationalism as it pertains to labor patterns in late-nineteenth and early-twentieth-century America.[46] A clear indication of the prevalence of animosity between the Irish and African Americans in Portland could be found in an editorial in the *Eastern Argus*, a pro–Democratic Party Portland daily newspaper, of November 15, 1864, under the title "The Blarney of the Press":

> The miscegenation editor of the [*Portland Daily*] *Press* appeared in a new role yesterday morning. He is trying to blarney the Irish, but he will have to do it more gracefully and adroitly to deceive the sons of the Emerald isle into any sympathy with the [Republican] party which has so frequently denounced the noble old Irish people as inferior in intelligence and all manly qualities to the negro race. Some of these radical writers of the *Press* school have gone so far as to declare that amalgamation has already commenced between the Irish and the negroes and that it will soon become general. Why, one of them said that "the fusion, whenever it takes place, will be of infinite service to the Irish!" and another that "if an equal number of negroes and Irish be taken from the city of New York, the former will be found far superior to the latter in cleanliness, education, moral feelings, beauty of form and feature, and natural sense!!"
>
> The miscegenetic [*sic*] editor of our cotemporary [*sic*] is doubtless making these soft approaches to the Irish under the delusion that they may be used to illustrate the revolting theory of amalgamation. He will find himself wofully [*sic*] mistaken. The Irish are the descen-

dants of as noble a race as have appeared in history and to insinuate that they have any sympathy with the negro loving fanatics is an insult that should cause their ancestors to rest uneasy in their graves and it will receive the scorn of every true son of Erin.[47]

This local editorial diatribe was not, in all likelihood, local in origin. Rather, it was part of a much larger political campaign focused on the presidential election of 1864 and on securing white, Irish American votes for the Democratic Party in that and subsequent elections. An Irish immigrant Democrat, D. G. Croly, together with coauthor George Wakeman, had created the concept of "miscegenation" and the word itself for this purpose. In 1863 they had anonymously produced a pamphlet titled, "Miscegenation: The Theory of the Blending of the Races, Applied to the American White Man and Negro." Their hope was that if antislavery leaders would endorse their theories, this would prove to be a major embarrassment to the Republicans in the upcoming national election. Croly even went so far as to denounce the very pamphlet he had secretly authored and the anonymity that had shielded its author, still unknown to the reading public.[48]

A local political broadsheet, probably from this same period, addressed "To the Irish Voters," spoke of the attempts of certain office holders to convince the Portland Irish to vote for "the Black Republican Ticket." It further stated that a Whig (pre–Republican Party) newspaper once called the Irish voters "Irish cattle."[49] Both the editorial and the broadsheet represented attempts not so much to drive the Irish away from African Americans as to lure them into the protective fold of the Democratic Party. There were, of course, many more Irish than African Americans in Portland at this time, and from a purely political viewpoint, this tactic would have been advantageous to the Democrats.

David Roediger concluded *The Wages of Whiteness* (1991) with a chapter titled, "Irish-American Workers and White Racial Formation." He stated that "what was most noteworthy to free Blacks at the time, and probably should be most noteworthy to historians, was the relative ease with which Irish-Americans 'elbowed out' African-Americans from unskilled jobs." Roediger, in a specific reference to the racial competition for longshore labor that appears to be highly relevant to the Portland model, concluded: "They had to drive all Blacks, and if possible their memories, from the places where the Irish labored. Frederick Douglass warned the Irish worker of the possibility that 'in assuming our avocation he also assumed our degradation.' Irish workers responded that they wanted an 'all-white waterfront,' rid of Blacks altogether, and not to 'jostle with' African-Americans. They thought that, to ensure their own survival, they needed as much."[50]

Roediger's study was followed four years later by a major work by Harvard lecturer Noel Ignatiev, who wrote that "on the docks, the Irish efforts to gain the rights of white men collided with the black struggle to maintain the right to work; the result was perpetual warfare." In 1850 the mainly Irish dockworkers in New York struck to force the dismissal of a black fellow worker. By 1852 the Longshoremen's United Benevolent Society, which was exclusively Irish, demanded that "work upon the docks ... shall be attended to solely and absolutely by members of the 'Longshoremen's Association,' and such white laborers as they see fit to permit upon the premises."[51]

This pattern appears to have been followed not only in New York but also in Philadelphia, where since 1835 the Irish laborers "proved their mettle" in union organizing. When necessary, or when prodded by the laboring majority, they would join with other ethnicities to help organize for the Knights of Labor or the Industrial Workers of the World (IWW). However, at other times the Irish also "proved their whiteness through their intense hostility toward African Americans."[52]

Despite the relative absence of any sizable black community in Portland, or certainly in Maine as a whole, there is no reason to believe that maritime laborers in Portland would differ significantly from those in other major Atlantic Coast ports.

Arrival of the Irish and Black Fades to Green

Certainly the United States in the nineteenth century was preoccupied with the questions of race and nationality. This was partially caused by the rapidly increasing famine-era immigration from Ireland after the 1840s and the slow but steady march toward the Civil War caused at least in part by the presence of chattel slavery in the southern half of the country. "The story of Americanization is vital and compelling, but it took place in a nation also obsessed by race. For immigrant workers, the processes of 'becoming white' and 'becoming American' were intertwined at every turn."[53]

New England, of course, was central to the nearly universal nineteenth-century concept of an Americanism that was white, Anglo-Saxon, and Protestant (WASP). Yankees, even in mid-nineteenth-century Portland, had rigid opinions of the Irish in their midst, particularly concerning their religious leaders, as can be seen in this excerpt from a Portland-based Protestant religious weekly newspaper:

> Prosperous Yankees knew the Irish only as servants and laborers. An Irish servant working in a well-scrubbed Protestant kitchen was forever a stranger, wilful, resentful and invincibly ignorant. They were, moreover, the stubbornest kind of Catholic. Most Yankees were prepared to pity the impoverished, ragged, and untutored Irish, but not even the most understanding could condone the 'cynical machinations' of the Catholic hierarchy.[54]

The New England Society was a nineteenth-century organization of native-born New Englanders and their children living in and around New York City. Dale T. Knobel has uncovered many references to the anguish and misgivings of these sons of New England that were caused by the ever-increasing levels of Irish immigration. Their home was becoming a far cry from the New England they remembered, "The blessed domicile of their ancestors [that] had, in its early years successfully guarded its character by 'repelling from its culture the idle, the ignorant, and the enslaved.'"[55] In mid-nineteenth-century New England, the Irish were clearly perceived as being undesirable. In the opinion of historian George Perkins Marsh, speaking in 1844 to the New England Society: "It may indeed be doubted whether it be possible now to construct a harmonious type of national character out of the discordant materials which have been assembled. . . . A nation, like an organic being, must grow, not by accretion, but by development, and should receive into its system nothing incapable of assimilation."[56]

The *Atlantic Monthly* reporting shortly after the failed Fenian invasion of Canada in 1866, just after the end of the Civil War, came to the xenophobic conclusion that perhaps the rebellious Celt was not fit to coexist with the Saxon in a democratic republic such as America: "All the qualities which go to make a republican, in the true sense of the term, are wanting in the Irish nature. . . . When anything comes in the guise of a law, there is an accompanying seizure of moral paralysis. . . . [The Irish rebel lives] in a world of unrealities almost inconceivable to a cool Saxon brain."[57]

In Matthew Jacobson's study of whiteness there is a very revealing analysis of the mid-nineteenth-century sea-faring classic, *Two Years before the Mast* (1840), written by Richard Henry Dana Jr., the son of a wealthy New England family. Dana dropped out of Harvard for the opportunity of sailing around Cape Horn to California. His observations of Latin America and its surrounding islands and of the natives and their customs, character, and religion (primarily Roman Catholic) were for many years on the required reading list of American schoolchildren. The book, first published in 1840 just prior to the Irish Potato Famine of 1845–48, went into multiple editions.

In a postscript to the 1859 edition, phrases like "English race" and "Anglo-Saxon race" appeared for the first time as a refinement of the standard "whites" or "white men" in the earlier editions. Jacobson believes this represented a sea change that reflected "a political revision of whiteness in Dana's New England during the two decades bracketing the famine in Ireland and the tremendous Celtic exodus to North America." In this same postscript, Dana's own prejudice surfaced when he wrote that "the Cathedral of St. Mary [where] the Irish attend, [was] more like one of our stifling Irish Catholic churches in Boston or New York, with intelligence in so small a proportion to the number of faces."[58]

In his autobiography, Portland writer Edward H. Elwell referred to Gorham's Corner, a well-known working-class Irish neighborhood adjacent to the waterfront, as "an unsavory locality of the town, in bad repute because of the turbulent character of its inhabitants, the center of sailor boarding houses, and the scene of street brawls and drunken rows." Later in the nineteenth century, Portland's mayor and prominent business leader, James Phinney Baxter, opined that it would be a good thing for Portland to limit its industrial expansion because industry tended to lure "ignorant and turbulent foreigners."[59]

At least three major factors could explain why in Portland in the mid-nineteenth century the Irish replaced African American longshoremen. First, the West Indies trade in molasses in exchange for Maine lumber declined. Second, the trade with Canada mostly involving the export of Canadian grain increased dramatically at the same time that dock work in this port was becoming mechanized. Third, the number of Irish immigrants in the pre- and postfamine period of the 1840s–50s also rose dramatically. Deeper analysis of these factors is required.

First, the importation of molasses declined at roughly the same time that new and more efficient methods of refining sugar were being perfected in cities other than Portland. This decline also coincided with strong prohibition measures initiated locally and throughout Maine by the temperance leader Neal Dow of Portland. Dow's prohibitionist "Maine Law" took effect statewide in 1851, although prohibition had been operational in many

Maine towns prior to that date.⁶⁰ The Maine Law became the prototype for national prohibition legislation that would eventually be enacted as the Eighteenth Amendment on January 16, 1920.

Second, mechanization allegedly was related to the diminished black presence on the waterfront. In Elijah Kellogg's historical novel, *A Strong Arm and a Mother's Blessing* (1880), a wealthy merchant in the West Indies trade, Mr. Jacob Knight, became the first to employ laborsaving techniques in Boston and Portland around 1833. This new technology reportedly had significant impact on the "negro" workers. This racially charged explanation seemed to place responsibility on its "negro" laborers for the seemingly voluntary abandonment of these maritime jobs in Portland:

> In the mean time [sic] Knight went among the shipping, and found cargoes there were discharged with a winch, that this required less men, and more work could be done in the same time for less money. He therefore bought a winch (windlass turned by cranks) and brought it home in the brig. The negroes would have nothing to do with it, because they could have no song, for this machine did not admit of it. There was neither poetry, music, nor pleasant associations connected with turning a crank, and the Irish filled their places; the lumber was cut off; the negroes gradually disappeared and sought other employments, and the entire course of trade changed.⁶¹

Kellogg's fictional explanation suggested that blacks were voluntarily leaving waterfront jobs because of a perceived marginal deterioration in working conditions and the introduction of technology. Maritime historian William Hutchinson Rowe, writing nearly seventy years later, appears to have accepted at least the possibility of this rationalization for labor displacement. Rowe wrote in nearly parallel if somewhat couched language that "it is said that after [winches] were introduced Negroes disappeared from the northern seaports, for they refused to work with a winch, as with that sort of labor their songs had no place."⁶²

Rowe, as late as 1948, may well have simply been passing along as fact earlier reported evidence of this phenomenon by Dana (1840) or Kellogg (1880), thus perpetuating this myth. At the very least, it represented an exaggeration or rationalization. In actuality, mechanization was inevitably linked to speed-up and expansion of work output for the primary benefit of the employing stevedores and their shipping bosses. This crucial factor should be considered together with the ethnic rivalries alongshore. Technology would remain a major issue of conflict between maritime employer and employee down to the present.

By the year 1853 Portland was linked by rail to Montreal and by transatlantic steamships to Europe. In 1853 the arrival of the SS *Sarah Sands* began the transatlantic connection between Portland and Liverpool, as well as other major European ports. The number of sailings by the turn of the century would swell to more than eighty per year, bunched mainly in the winter months of November through April when the Saint Lawrence River was normally frozen. From 1853 onward, the quality and quantity of work alongshore in Portland would be dramatically altered as Montreal supplied Portland with a nearly guaranteed heavy volume of exports that could never have been generated merely within Portland's hinterland.

Third, and most significant in explaining this racial–ethnic maritime labor transformation, was the factor of the rising number of Irish immigrants coming into America beginning in the 1840s, swelling during the famine years of the late 1840s and becoming a human wave after 1850.[63] Chronologically this peak in Irish immigration occurred simultaneously with the spike in maritime commerce out of Portland via the new rail link to Montreal. No longer would dock work be a black niche because the increased demand for cheap labor in construction, on the railroads, and along the waterfront was being answered by a growing supply of unskilled Irish immigrants who were attracted to Portland by the opportunity for entry-level employment.

In Maine in the year 1860, the foreign population was 37,453, of which 15,290, slightly less than half, were from Ireland. Many of the rest were Irish immigrants who arrived indirectly from other British provinces, mainly English-speaking Canada. Emigration from one British-owned territory to another was often subsidized, from regions of "congestion" to regions of opportunity. This practice gave rise to the term "two-boater," which described the emigrant who took one boat to Canada and a second boat from Canada to the United States.[64] This pattern held true in Portland as well where in 1860 nearly 15 percent of the population was foreign-born. In 1860 fully two-thirds of Portland's foreign-born population (2,627 out of 3,908) was Irish.[65]

Between 1860 and 1880 the population of this city rose by a healthy 20 percent from 26,341 to 33,810, and the percentage of foreign-born increased from less than 15 percent to more than 20 percent. There would be nearly 7,000 foreign-born persons in Portland by 1880.

14. *Jeanie Johnston*—replica of a "famine ship" used to transport Irish immigrants to North America, taken August 9, 2003, in Portsmouth, New Hampshire. From photo collection of the author.

Between 1860 and 1900 Portland's population nearly doubled from 26,341 to 50,145. The percentage of foreign-born remained at more than 20 percent, with fully 10,435 foreign-born persons in the city in 1900. Ireland was second among the top twelve countries in terms of contribution of immigrants to Portland in 1900: Canada (English) 3,968 (38 percent); Ireland 3,273 (31 percent); England 598; Canada (French) 408; Denmark 356; Russia 278; Norway 263; Sweden 231; Scotland 223; Poland 208; Germany 205; and Italy 148. It should also be assumed that a sizable number of those from English-speaking Maritime Canada, including New Brunswick, Nova Scotia, Newfoundland, and Labrador, were themselves first- or second-generation Irish.[66] The Irish population of Portland was increasing rapidly at the same time that the already small African American population was in decline, as seen in the earlier-reported statistics.

Passage to America for these Irish and other immigrants was quite dangerous. By 1864 the Montreal Steamship Company (the Allan Line) had lost eight of its first twelve steamers in the North Atlantic. Those who could afford to do so traveled via New York, but "immigrants and persons of moderate means" were left to ply the more dangerous "treacherous rockbound coasts." Therefore, it was not surprising but of great maritime significance locally when in 1901 the Montreal Steamship Company replaced Portland with the closer port of Saint John, New Brunswick, as its winter terminal.[67]

The loss of the RMS *Bohemian* off Cape Elizabeth on February 22, 1864, must have struck a special blow to Portland's Irish community because many of the deceased were themselves Irish. Within four days of the loss it was reported in a local newspaper that Hugh Dolan "in behalf of the Irish American League Association, put down $128 upon the subscription list, in aid of the *Bohemian* sufferers." The same edition reported the arrival of the British steamer *Hibernia* that had sailed to Portland from Liverpool via Londonderry.[68] Portland merchants, however, did not wait too long to find some profit in the loss of this ship. A little more than four months after its sinking, an auction was held by Henry Bailey and Company for "a small invoice of goods from the wreck of steamer *Bohemian*, consisting of broad cloths, cashmeres, linens, table covers, tailors' trimmings, carpets, carpet bags, waiters, etc."[69]

Portland newspapers around the mid-1860s offer a window into the difficult nature of the struggle for some local Irish to assimilate into their new

American home. In one edition alone of the *Portland Daily Press*, in addition to an announced meeting of the local Irish nationalists, the Fenian Brotherhood, at the Longshoreman's Hall, there were also three additional items of interest. The first reported that "the liquors seized a short time since on the premises of James McGlinchy, were declared forfeited to the city, no claimant appearing." The McGlinchys, James, Andrew, and Hugh, featured prominently in these years in the Portland newspapers because of their business in the manufacture and sale of alcoholic beverages. The second item detailed the charge of larceny of two hemlock piles from the property of J. N. Winslow by Michael and Ann O'Neal. "No person appearing to testify against them, [the charges] were dropped." Finally, there was this revealing, albeit humorous, report concerning an Irish plea for mercy: "An Applicant for Rations.—An Irish woman applied to the Relief Committee a few days since to be supplied with rations, stating that she had nine in her family, and no husband. A member of the committee took her name and residence and subsequently called at her house, where, to his great astonishment he discovered that she had told the truth; but, her family consisted of nine stalwart men *who were boarders!*"[70]

Early Longshoremen's Benevolent Association (Mid-1860s)

Much evidence exists by the mid-1860s confirming a considerable Irish presence along the waterfront of Portland of dockers who were looking to improve wages and conditions of work. Newspaper excerpts represent some of the first evidence of a formal Irish longshoremen's association, then referred to as the Longshoremen's Benevolent Association. Most likely it was similar to other self-help groups then forming in the mid-nineteenth century in larger seaports like Boston and New York for the protection of laborers.[71] This would have been a precursor of the modern maritime workers' union. Locally, the Portland Longshoremen's Benevolent Society (PLSBS) would formally incorporate within about sixteen years, by 1880.

In May of 1864, it was reported that the longshoremen who had previously been receiving three dollars per day "have struck for more pay. They demand $4.00 per day of 10 hours." It was subsequently reported in a local daily newspaper that "the merchants and Boss Stevedores of Portland are hereby notified that the longshore men feel the necessity on account of the unsteadiness of their work and high rates paid for every article of consumption, to strike for the following wages, viz: To men stowing cargo $.33

hour, To men on wharf $.30 hour. This is demanded for every hour they work."⁷²

Three days later the same newspaper reported that "on account of the high price that we have to pay for labor, the stevedores of Portland have been compelled to an advance on the rates of loading vessels." Six stevedores, i.e., those responsible for contracting dock laborers in Portland, signed the notice. "Stevedores were the hiring bosses. Shipping firms would contract with stevedoring firms to have cargo handled, and stevedoring firms would hire the longshoremen. Employers include ship operators, shipping agents, and stevedoring firms."⁷³

In July 1864, two months later, there was yet another report of a strike. One must speculate that wartime inflation and increased maritime shipping and demand for labor necessitated by the Civil War were the most likely causes responsible for this increased militancy on the part of the dockworkers. This scenario of a war-related boom followed by accelerated wage demands would become a general theme throughout the years for these Portland longshoremen. The threat of a strike and of violence against strikebreakers (scabs) was apparent in a subsequent newspaper excerpt: "Strike. The Irish laborers in discharging vessels have struck for higher pay. . . . We are informed that they threaten anyone who works for less than the price demanded. An appeal to the City Authorities would probably be attended to, and such measures would be taken as to secure laborers who choose to work for fair pay from interruption or danger."⁷⁴

The Civil War era appeared to be a fertile period for labor organization in Portland. Labor historian Charles A. Scontras reported that the first central labor union in Maine was formed in Portland in 1864 and that "the early 1860s marked the first discernible organized labor movement in the state."⁷⁵ Also, "in the summer of 1864, the Machinists and Blacksmith Union, the Longshoremen's Benevolent Society, and a local of the Molders International Union joined the labor movement."⁷⁶ The actual name and some details as to the nature of this fairly new dockworkers' association were more clearly revealed the following year when a funeral was covered by the local press: "William Dooly, a member of the Longshoremen's Benevolent Association, died Monday 27 February, 1865 [aged] 43, and his funeral, which took place yesterday, was attended by about 150 members in a body. He was one of the oldest and most respected members of that body and this was the first time it was called upon to pay the last tribute of respect to one of its numbers."⁷⁷

This announcement also revealed something of the difficulty and danger of this work along the waterfront if a worker of only forty-three years of age would be considered as one of the seniors of this group. One year later, two excerpts from a local newspaper give an organizational address to these maritime workers and serve to connect the Portland Irish longshoremen with the Fenian Brotherhood, a prominent Irish and Irish-American nationalist organization of this period:

> The members of the O'Donoghue Circle, Fenian Brotherhood are requested to meet at the Longshoremen's Hall this (Thursday) evening, at 7 ½ o'clock. Per order.
>
> There will be a meeting of the Roberts and Sweeney Circle [Fenian Brotherhood] at Longshoreman's Hall, No. 167 Commercial street, at 8 o'clock, Friday evening, 23d inst. It is hoped every member will be present, as business of importance will come before the meeting; also, all those wishing to join the Circle will have an opportunity to do so on that evening. Per order.[78]

These articles not only demonstrated that the Portland Irish longshoremen continued their nationalistic ties with Ireland but also that they were well enough organized by 1866 to have a permanent meeting place, a Longshoremen's Hall. This connection between the Irish longshoremen and Irish nationalism would continue over the next fifteen years and well beyond. The early records of the new Portland Longshoremen's Benevolent Society (PLSBS) would include several references in their earliest minutes from 1881 to the union's support for a significant new agrarian agitation movement in Ireland led by Michael Davitt and known as the Irish Land League.[79]

Founding the Portland Longshoremen's Benevolent Society (PLSBS) in 1880

By the end of the Civil War, the Portland Irish longshoremen through their benevolent association would have represented a powerful labor presence along the waterfront of this city. They had already demonstrated their militancy in their willingness to strike for higher wages. Soon they would be prepared to take the next important step in protecting their economic interests in this increasingly important North Atlantic maritime center. The longshoremen of Portland would formally incorporate as the Portland Longshoremen's Benevolent Society (PLSBS), which was officially chartered in 1880 just fifteen years after the end of the Civil War.

Between 1865 and 1880, Portland would undergo significant demographic, political, economic, and social changes. For some it was an exciting time that was full of opportunity for improvement and advancement. John Neal, a local author and art and literary critic, writing in 1874 just as the nation was entering the economic depression of 1873–77, was most optimistic about Portland's future, especially when he considered its maritime economic growth:

> Our tonnage is over 100,000; imports for '72, 23,000,000, exports 22,000,000—an increase of four millions both on the imports and exports of '71. . . . Sixty-five railroad trains enter and leave the city daily; and we have daily steamers to Boston, half-weekly steamers to New York, weekly and half-weekly ocean steamers for six months of the year, with lines touching at many ports eastward along the coast of Maine and the Maratime [sic] British Provinces . . . the intransitu [sic] and transshipment trade of the U.S. for [February, 1874] amounted to $6,851,768 of which Portland furnished $5,044,800 or about five-sixths of the entire sum. . . . With a population such as we have, busy, active, industrious, enterprising, thrifty and liberal, again, I ask, What have we to fear?[80]

John Neal was describing Portland from a Yankee entrepreneurial perspective. With Yankee capital and leadership, combined with cheap Irish manual labor, great commercial improvements might be realized and great wealth gained, at least for those in a position to so prosper commercially. However, for another group of the dominant Yankee community of Portland and Maine, those who would not directly profit from the employment of cheap labor, the influx of Irish Catholics into their essentially Yankee Protestant city must have appeared as less than reassuring.[81] The Yankee nativist social and cultural concerns led to a pessimism that was apparently at odds with John Neal's economic optimism. The increase in immigration in the mid- to late-nineteenth century must have been one further source of alarm for those older native Portlanders portrayed by William Willis as dreaming of the halcyon days that were forever gone: "In the circle of our little town, the lines were drawn with much strictness. The higher classes were called the quality, and were composed of persons not engaged in mechanic employments. We now occasionally find some old persons whose memory recurs with longing delight to the days in which these formal distinctions held uncontrolled sway."[82]

On the docks of Portland, Maine, the small African American workforce of the early to mid-nineteenth century had been forced to yield to the numerically superior Irish who formed a Benevolent Association around the time of the Civil War. After 1880, as a second wave of immigration to America was under way from an Ireland again in the grips of yet another devastating famine, some of these Irish longshoremen decided to formalize their association into the PLSBS. Between its founding charter on November 15, 1880, and the turn of the century, just twenty years later, the PLSBS would grow dramatically to more than 860 members.[83] The charter members of this union and their sons and grandsons would shape the nature of the PLSBS in terms of their own predominantly Irish heritage. This included their tendency to organize politically and economically to defend their rights, both in Ireland as well as in this new land of opportunity and challenge. Similar late-nineteenth-century unions in Maine and beyond also strongly influenced these longshoremen.[84]

Portland's Irish longshoremen would maintain their independence from larger longshore organizations throughout the rest of the nineteenth century and almost up to World War I. By that time, however, the shipping companies and their local labor contractors (stevedores) had consolidated their power, and the PLSBS would have to follow suit if they wanted to survive.

Much had changed in Portland since the mid-nineteenth-century rail link with Canada had been established in 1853, which led to a shipping boom based on Canadian grain exports. African American labor was no longer a presence on Portland's docks. One peripheral group had replaced another in this New England port city. This new longshore society would be exclusively white and predominantly Irish over the next century. It would strive, with a certain degree of success, to confront Portland's Yankee business elite to carve out for its ethnic membership a more secure maritime occupational niche along the waterfront of their newly adopted home.

3

A Mixed Blessing

Portland at the Turn of the Twentieth Century

The citizens of Portland, Maine, in 1900 lived in a city optimistic about its future. Portland's population stood at 50,145, a marked increase of nearly 39 percent over the last decade alone. As late as 1860 Portland had been the twenty-third largest city in the country, but even though it continued to grow throughout the Gilded Age, it was comparatively shrinking in size and importance relative to other faster-growing American cities.

The Irish numbered 7,644, representing 41 percent of the entire immigrant ethnic population. This was nearly double that of their closest potential ethnic and occupational rivals, the English-speaking Canadians, who numbered 3,976. Portland's nineteenth-century growth by decade was steady, if not dramatic. Irish labor in 1900 was dominant along Portland's waterfront and clearly a force to be reckoned with in other areas, especially within the field of manual labor.

Although Portland was now clearly outdistanced by Boston in the competition for northern New England's maritime trade, since 1853 the Grand Trunk link to Montreal had provided Portland with some insulation from its larger, richer, and more powerful southern neighbor. John A. Poor's grand dream of an international railway with Portland as its central hub had only been partially realized. The narrow-gauge line was a technique designed to end Maine's transportation dependence on Boston. This rail–maritime nexus envisioned by Poor now enhanced the commercial growth of Portland, a city that had been described as late as the early nineteenth century as a "deserted village."[1]

Portland jealously guarded this trade for the remainder of the nineteenth century and looked to its further expansion in the future. In these same years, especially following the devastating Great Fire of 1866, "Portland

Table 2. Total Population of Portland (1800–1900)

Year	Population
1800	3,704
1810	7,169
1820	8,581
1830	12,601
1840	15,218
1850	20,815
1860	26,342
1870	31,418
1880	33,812
1890	36,425
1900	50,145

Sources: Clayton, *History of Cumberland County Maine*, 167. Statistics for 1880–1900 taken from Barnes, *Greater Portland Celebration 350*, 111, 113, and 119.

bound up its wounds and settled down to serious business, and shipping and industry were soon vying with each other in the renewed commercial expansion."[2]

Elsewhere in Maine, outside of Portland, the Irish provided not only stereotypical brute force for this phenomenal growth but also, surprisingly perhaps in some cases, entrepreneurial skills and capital. In the late eighteenth through the early part of the nineteenth century, the Kavanagh and Cottrill families of Damariscotta Mills, Lincoln County, had created a maritime link with ocean schooners plying the Atlantic waters between Maine and the southeastern region of Ireland near their ancestral homeland in Inistioge, County Kilkenny, near the tidal limits of the River Nore.[3] Maine lumber was much in demand in Ireland, the original forests of which had by this time been largely denuded.

In the later nineteenth century, another Irishman, Edward O'Brien of Warren and Thomaston, became one of Maine's preeminent shipbuilders and importers of wood. O'Brien, the son of an Irish immigrant, had gone to sea before starting a career as an apprentice to a local shipwright. He built and owned ships for more than sixty years. O'Brien lived to be eighty-eight, and by the year of his death in 1882 he had become America's fourteenth millionaire.[4]

Back in Portland, millennial optimism was demonstrated in a year- and century-end New Year's opinion in a prominent newspaper. It stated that the previous year would be remembered with "pleasant memories" and went on to predict improving business and trade opportunities over the next year. It tempered its predictions by noting that "Portland is not a 'boom town,' its business is not of the spectacular and inflated order, but based on solid values and conducted along sound and legitimate lines."[5]

The renewed prosperity in Portland paralleled that of Maine as a whole. This same daily newspaper in 1900 reported, "Up to today the record of corporations organized during the year is the largest in the history of the State. There have been 695 organized under the laws of Maine."[6] Labor was in "good demand" throughout the state, and investment in factories, mills, and workshops soared, especially in the years 1899–1901. In 1899 alone, investment vaulted tenfold from $675,000 in the previous year to $6,800,700.[7]

The growth, especially in maritime-related business, did not come without cost, however. There had been many losses of Maine-based ships and their crews going back to the earliest days of marine commerce. During the Civil War alone, according to Yarmouth, Maine–based maritime historian William Hutchinson Rowe, eighty-eight Maine-built vessels were seized by Confederate raiders on the open seas.[8] One of the more spectacular seizures occurred within Portland harbor itself, bringing the Civil War to its very doorstep. On the evening of June 26, 1863, the U.S. Revenue Cutter *Caleb Cushing*, admittedly a governmental rather than a commercial target, was literally taken from beneath the noses of Portlanders by Confederate raiders led by Lt. Charles W. Read. The raiders were caught the next day, but only after their target had been blown up by the Confederates on the open seas to avoid its recapture.[9]

Ironically, after the Civil War the British government was held responsible for not exercising "due diligence" regarding the Confederate use of British-made ships for such seizures. Led by Caleb Cushing himself, a diplomat and U.S. attorney general from 1853 to 1857, the Americans eventually by 1871 compelled the British to pay the United States $15.5 million in damages arising from the so-called *Alabama* Claims.[10]

Between the Civil War and the turn of the twentieth century, among the many spectacular ocean disasters related to Maine shipping, three episodes stand out. These include the sinking of the Royal Mail Steamer *Bohemian* on February 22, 1864, with the loss of 42 lives, mainly Irish immigrant passengers in steerage; the wreck of the bark *Annie C. Maguire* off Portland Head Light on Christmas Eve of 1886; and perhaps the most profound maritime loss for Maine in this era, the sinking of the Portland Steam Packet

Portland north of Provincetown, Cape Cod, on November 26, 1898, with all 192 passengers and crew lost. The storm would forever be known as the "*Portland* Gale."[11]

"The greatest disaster, of course, was the loss of the *Portland*," one of the major assets of the Portland Steamship Company. This was a particularly heavy blow to the city's black community because many of the ship's staff, especially its pursers, were from Portland's black neighborhood. In the words of a maritime historian, "The loss of the second *Portland* in the great gale of November 1898 was the worst tragedy in the history of Maine steamboating." A total of 141 vessels were lost in the North Atlantic in this one storm alone with the loss of life totaling 456.[12]

All three of these disasters highlighted the dangers of maritime transport in this era, especially along Maine's rocky coastline. The loss of the RMS *Bohemian*, in particular, illustrated the perils of immigration because many of its victims were Irish steerage passengers. A Celtic cross was erected by the local Ancient Order of Hibernians at Calvary Cemetery in South Portland to commemorate the loss of these Irish lives and to mark the final resting place of twelve unclaimed bodies.

This same period, between the end of the Civil War and the turn of the twentieth century, marked an era of relative inaction on the part of the federal government regarding maritime interests. This would be especially true when compared with its enthusiastic support and promotion of railroad development such as the first transcontinental railroad that was completed in 1869.

Maritime historians point to these years as the period during which the United States lost its preeminence in maritime transportation, especially transoceanic (blue water) as opposed to coastal and inland (brown water) shipping, which remained quite strong. Maine, with its long coastline and historical connection to the sea and maritime activities of all types, was an exception to the rule. Maine congressional representatives such as John Lynch and Nelson Dingley Jr. continued to promote maritime development as a national security necessity. They were sometimes joined by other better-known politicians from Maine.

In 1866 James G. Blaine, a future Republican candidate for the presidency, championed the cause of New England shippers to "repatriate" American registered vessels that had previously registered under a foreign flag.[13] Later in this period Arthur Sewall of Bath headed the American Merchant Marine Association. Sewall was the 1896 nominee for vice president on the

Democratic ticket with William Jennings Bryan of Nebraska, the first of Bryan's three attempts to gain the presidency. Despite its lack of success nationally, "the maritime industry, moreover, had powerful allies—Maine's congressional delegation alone was a pantheon of national leaders."[14]

In 1900 the Spanish-American War had only recently ended on terms favorable to American expansionism. The British involvement against white Dutch settlers in South Africa's Boer War was also well under way, making daily news headlines. One consequence of the successful conclusion of the Spanish-American War was the confidence it seemed to restore to the American business psyche, shaken as it was by the deep economic depression of the 1890s. This confidence would have a positive, if indirect, impact on foreign-born, mainly Irish laborers in Portland.

The turn of the twentieth century appears to have been an opportune time to further consolidate the gains that the Irish had made in assimilation since the Civil War. John Higham noted in his major work on American nativism that "the brief struggle [of the Spanish-American War] raised no fears of disloyalty among the foreign-born. Nationalism, without abating a whit, grew heady and exultant. Anxieties over global dangers and rivalries diminished when the first test of modern American power gave the nation a fresh sense of vitality. Concern over internal dissention was engulfed in a joyous consciousness of national unity."[15]

For the Yankee natives, the halcyon days of a largely homogeneous, pre–Civil War Portland had long since disappeared. Ethnic harmony was crucial in a city like Portland, where nearly half of its fifty thousand residents at the turn of the century were of foreign parentage.[16] As time progressed, the social lines between native and foreign born were gradually blurred, especially as more foreign-born laborers, those "engaged in mechanic employments," as William Willis defined them, continued to arrive.[17]

Now, at the dawn of a new century, those so mechanically engaged in Portland were an increasingly large and essential sector of the community and its growing and diversified economy. Of Portland's labor force, many themselves being foreign-born or at least born of foreign parentage, the Irish were by far the largest component. The evolving national acceptance of the Irish, at least as an indispensable workforce, had many sources. These factors included the active role played by the Irish in the Civil War; the expanding postbellum industrialism of the late nineteenth century with its concomitant need for cheap unskilled labor; the current euphoria over America's recent victory in the Spanish-American War; and, arguably most

Table 3. Major Commodities Shipped to and from Portland (1895 and 1900)

Commodity	1895	1900
Grain	100,000	350,000
Miscellaneous	650,000	800,000
Coal	600,000	1,100,000
Total	1,300,000	2,200,000

Note: For statistics on increased shipping see Portland Port Commission, *Report of 1935*, Plate III, opposite 108.

importantly, the recent recovery from the economic depression of 1893–97. Economic security, it seems, often served to encourage domestic harmony, both ethnic and class.[18]

Meanwhile, the British involvement in the Boer War continued from 1899 to 1902, and the shipping of Canadian grain and other material through Portland thus increased. The daily headlines of Portland's major newspaper, the *Eastern Argus*, were preoccupied with the fighting in South Africa and were clearly pro-British, even though the sentiments of the Irish longshoremen would have been decidedly anticolonial, at least as far as British foreign policy was concerned.

The turn-of-the-century shipping boom, especially in exported grain and domestic coal, contributed to the flourishing activity along the local waterfront. This, of course, added to the demand for labor from Portland's Irish longshoremen. The growth in materials handled in Portland was substantial in the years 1895–1900, as demonstrated by a 1935 study showing commodity tonnages 1890–1934 (given in approximate short tons).

The shipment of both domestic (brown water) and transatlantic (blue water) cargoes was of special interest to the Portland Board of Trade, an influential group of Portland businessmen and merchants, and the predecessor of the Chamber of Commerce. This group published a monthly business magazine for statewide circulation known as the *Board of Trade Journal*. Given the dearth of significant primary sources on the city's commercial development after the mid-nineteenth century, this journal serves to partially fill the information gap that exists for this period.

The *Portland Board of Trade Journal* for January of 1900 boasted of the greatly increased steamship business in Portland as a boon to every city in the state. It proudly noted that four transatlantic steamships cleared Portland, all on December 23, 1899, bound for European ports "all taking out large cargoes and leaving enough to load as many more ships awaiting

15. Grand Trunk railroad yard and Portland Company (Munjoy Hill).

shipment, and millions of bushels of grain awaiting shipment by the same route."[19]

Canadian grain was shipped by rail to Portland where it was stored in one of the two massive grain elevators that dominated the waterfront near the Grand Trunk Railroad terminus. In Portland the grain was loaded by longshoremen directly onto transatlantic steamships, especially during the winter months of November through April when the Saint Lawrence River was frozen. The winter weather prevented direct Canadian shipment but provided Portland longshoremen with guaranteed work. By February of 1900 the second and newest of the Grand Trunk Railroad's grain elevators on the Portland waterfront was already insufficient to handle the increasing quantities of Canadian grain arriving by rail almost daily.

In March and April of 1900, the *Portland Board of Trade Journal* listed all the transatlantic winter sailings of major steamship lines from Portland for the years 1897–98 and 1898–99 with a total of eighty-five departures in the former season and eighty-nine in the latter. There were seven major transatlantic shipping companies operating out of Portland at the turn of the century, and the most common destinations were, in order of frequency, Liverpool, London, Glasgow, Bristol, and Hamburg. Transshipped cargo led to an increased demand for labor, so a meeting was held between the Board

16. Grand Trunk Station (1903–66), c. 1904. Note provocative street sign on nearby building on left, "Why Women Sin."

of Trade's Committee on Transatlantic Commerce and the Longshoremen's Association to address this challenge. They discussed the advantages and urged the development of year-round shipping out of Portland.[20]

This was clearly a sign of cooperation and shared interest between the forces of capital, mainly international shipping companies and domestic business interests largely owned by native-born citizens, and labor, mainly consisting of foreign-born Irish manual workers. These otherwise antithetical groups realized that they each could profit by cooperation during these years of maritime and commercial expansion. For example, two powerful business interests, railroad and steamship owners, fought against the American nativist impulse. At the turn of the century, this tendency was specifically represented by the many attempts of Massachusetts senator Henry Cabot Lodge, among others, to restrict immigration.[21]

In January of 1900 local representatives of the English steamship lines that made Portland their winter port were honored at the annual Board of Trade banquet. President of the board and future mayor Frederick E. Boothby introduced the guests by claiming that it was "to the development of the railroad, then, as well as the steamship, we owe much of our prosperity." Charles H. Randall, the former mayor of Portland, looked toward an even brighter future seeking "a gigantic trust formed to boom the old city of

Portland, and he hoped to see the day when there would be a dozen [grain] elevators in this city instead of two."²²

F. J. McClure who represented the Robert Reford Company, local agents for the Thompson and Donaldson Lines, chronicled the growth of Portland's transatlantic shipping for the year ending on January 18, 1900. McClure praised the "gradual but steady increase" of sailings from the arrival in 1853 of the *Sarah Sands*, the steamship that inaugurated the transatlantic commerce of this port, to the intermittent service which followed, to fortnightly service to Liverpool followed by weekly service to Liverpool, and finally to the point where "now six European ports are served by seven different steamship lines with an average of one sailing every other day all through the winter." Despite the obvious importance of this maritime trade, "most city leaders remained content to let the Grand Trunk Railway make all the effort and shoulder all the expenses; no plan was forthcoming and no city wharves or warehouses were built." In the absence of American maritime investment in Portland, the Canadians seized the initiative and "between 1900 and 1919 the Grand Trunk spent over $2 million on its Portland terminus."²³

F. J. McClure, however, also had a warning for the merchants of Portland. Joined by W. W. Wainwright, the local agent of the Allan Line, both were critical of the small volume of imports arriving into Portland. McClure admonished those present, "It must be remembered that all the vessels engaged in the North Atlantic trade which have a service to Portland

17. Commercial Street, Grand Trunk cars, and piers (c. 1875).

must depend on the east bound trip to pay the expenses of the whole voyage."[24] This imbalance, unfortunately, would remain a major impediment to the future development of Portland's maritime economy.

Although imports for the previous year of 1899, 24,028 net tons, were double those of 1898, they still represented less than one-fifth the volume of exports, most of which was in the form of Canadian grain. Yet another specific threat to Portland's shipping preeminence was noted at this meeting. Sadly lacking from this port's maritime shipping formula were exports emanating specifically from Portland or Maine itself. In the 1899 shipping season, these domestic products totaled only 3,202 net tons, a tiny percentage of the total volume exported through the port.

A perceived shift of emphasis hinted at a future contest for preeminence along Portland's waterfront between commercial and shipping interests on the one hand and the growing tourist industry on the other. Mr. Wainwright added that "while Portland does not yet occupy the position as a summer port that she should occupy, her position as a summer resort is certainly unequalled."[25] This observation would support the contention of Robert H. Babcock that tourism was replacing industrialism as the central focus of Portland's chief merchants, at least as reported by the *Portland Board of Trade Journal*. "Portland officials began to look at their own city with a tourist's eye."[26]

Thus, in 1900 we see a port bustling with activity, at least during the winter months. This activity obviously translated into jobs for longshoremen along the waterfront. But Portland's prosperity was precariously dependent upon exports generated, both produced and transshipped, from another nation. Unless a better balance could be achieved, as Wainwright strongly hinted to the Board of Trade, Portland's future development might be forced to turn away from maritime commerce in favor of tourism.

Babcock strongly implied that this decision evolved around the turn of the century and sealed the fate of Portland as a commercial and tourist city rather than an industrial or maritime shipping center. Despite the efforts of some members of the Board of Trade, the local shipping agents, and the PLSBS to develop the waterfront, Portland's entrepreneurs would continue to be diverted by the glittering promise of tourism.[27]

Another early indication that by the turn of the century Portland's maritime hegemony was under threat was the replacement of the graceful sailing ship, many of which were built on the coast of Maine, by the less esthetically pleasing but more functional steamship, which was especially

18. Schooner *Viking* at Brown's Wharf unloading southern pine.

suited for transatlantic voyages. Maine was not successful in making the shift from sail to steam, with the exception of the Bath Iron Works (BIW) and the New England Shipbuilding Corporation's South Portland shipyards. The former is an ongoing concern located in Bath, Maine, mainly concerned today with the construction of high-tech warships for the U.S. Navy. The latter remarkably launched 30 ocean-class freighters and 274 Liberty Ships between 1941 and 1945 alone.[28]

As long as the dominant form of maritime transport remained the sailing ship, Portland's location as the major American port closest to the large ports of Western Europe was one of its greatest assets. With the emergence of the larger and more dependable steamship in this period, Portland's proximity to Europe became relatively insignificant. Now the advantage would lie with the port that commanded the greatest hinterland, that was more efficient or technologically developed, and that was well connected by rail and closer to the major markets of North America.

In no way could Portland compete for the hinterland with Boston, New York, or even the major Canadian maritime ports. It is debatable as to whether a more concerted effort to follow through with John A. Poor's dream of Portland as a major international maritime hub could have forestalled the rise of these major competitors. At least it might have prolonged Portland's maritime shipping prominence by a few more years or decades.

The eclipse of the sailing ship seemed assured, however, and with its demise, the transport of goods to and from Maine would be one step closer to monopoly control by larger out-of-state shipping and railroad interests. The PLSBS would have to negotiate with major shipping concerns that had no links to Maine other than purely economic considerations and convince them of the most effective use of their capital resources, what is now referred to as a cost–benefit analysis.

In America the tipping point between sail and steam had almost been reached, as it already had been in Great Britain. The writing was clearly on the wall. The Bureau of Navigation reported that for the year 1899, 954 new vessels were built, with a gross tonnage of 267,642. Of this total, 533 were sailing ships and 421 were steam vessels. The steamships, of course, would always have the relative advantage of economies of scale, primarily because of their superior size. Simply stated, they more efficiently carried a larger volume of cargo. The vast majority of these vessels were built along the Atlantic and Gulf coasts (658), while the Pacific coast lagged far behind (114). As a comparison, it should be noted that Great Britain was still far in the lead with this form of modern transportation, constructing 744 steamships in 1899.[29]

Many sailing ships, of course, were still being proudly crafted along the coast of Maine. One such Maine-built ship was the *Snow and Burgess*, launched in Thomaston in 1878. This is of particular interest because the captain took aboard his young children, one of whom has given us a fascinating tale of life aboard such a vessel.[30]

The significance of Portland's coastal and transatlantic trade was clear from statistics of tonnage shipped into and out of this port. In these statistics for 1895 and 1900, the chief transatlantic commodity, Canadian grain, was handled in far less volume than miscellaneous cargoes, specifically the chief domestic commodity, coal.[31]

As opposed to blue-water or transatlantic shipping, the domestic coastal trade was often referred to as brown-water, so-named for the inland waterways they plied. Coastal shipping was of crucial importance to Portland's maritime economy. Here too, the surest means of transporting cargo and passengers to the larger cities to its south was increasingly by steamship. This domestic transport of goods has often been ignored, both locally and nationally. "For most of U.S. history, shipping on coastal and inland waters has exceeded oceanic shipping in both volume and value. America is a brown-water nation, with a blue-water consciousness."[32]

19. Deering Wharf—longshoreman sledding lumber.

Portland's maritime laborers were more than aware of this distinction. Larry Welch, one of several retired longshoremen with keen memories and, especially in his case a highly analytical mind, remembered that a major brown-water shipper in the early twentieth century was the so-called West Coast Boat of the Isthmian Line. He referred to these shipments of domestic goods to the West Coast via the Panama Canal as "coastwise" shipping. In later years he thought that, although coastwise shipping might survive in Portland, there was no future for "deep sea" cargo. Longshoreman Tom Mulkern used similar terminology to refer to these two distinct modes of maritime transport.[33]

Transatlantic commerce out of Portland appeared to be booming at the turn of the century, albeit with the major concern that the vast majority of exports were of Canadian origin. At the time, the future of the port appeared to be bright, and those who controlled shipping seemed generally content.

So too was labor optimistic in Portland and in Maine as a whole. Like the rest of the nation, Maine was emerging from the mid-1890s depression, and, with the exception of the once-booming textile industry, there was a swelling demand for labor. The commissioner of Industrial and Labor Statistics reported labor conditions in 1900 to be "very satisfactory," adding that "few persons have experienced any difficulty in obtaining employment at good wages."[34]

For the Irish longshoremen in Portland, this meant more work and a better living standard. By 1900 it was reported that "labor has never been so strongly organized in this city." Furthermore, according to the *Eastern Argus*, the city's largest daily newspaper, "Nearly all the people of Portland, union and otherwise, [had previously thought] that labor unions, so far as effectiveness and interest went, were really dead bodies. Since then their opinions of the labor men have changed. The cause of this, as many know, is the recent renewal of life among the different unions."[35]

Turn of the century Portland was increasingly a more ethnically diverse city, even though the racial composition would continue to be overwhelmingly white. Even though southern and eastern Europeans, such as Italians, Poles, Greeks, and Russian Jews, were beginning to make their way into the city, Portland's largest ethnic group continued to be the Irish. The source of origin for first- and second-generation immigrants in Portland (1900), with both parents born in specified countries, was as shown in table 4.

More than 40 percent of Portland's foreign population was Irish, either from Ireland itself or from English-speaking Canada. Many of the latter had benefited from "assisted emigration" from Ireland to the Maritime Provinces of Canada and Quebec in the famine and post-famine years.[36] Many of these would walk to America or take a ship to the south, thus becoming a "two-boater."

These were the immigrants who swelled union membership in the PLSBS. Membership peaked, at least for the time being, at 868 during 1900,

Table 4. Origin of First- and Second-Generation Immigrants in Portland (1900)

Origin	Number of immigrants
Ireland	7,644 (41.6%)
Canada (English)	3,976 (21.6%)
Mixed foreign parentage	2,100 (11.4%)
England	821 (4.5%)
Denmark	537 (2.9%)
Canada (French)	511 (2.8%)
Other	3,315 (18.0%)
Total	18,367

Source: *Twelfth Census of the United States (1900)*, Population, vol. I, 876.

20. PLSBS banner on parade, July 4, 1894, Cumberland Avenue (in vicinity of Preble and Brown streets).

the highest number since its formation in 1880 and as high a level as it would reach for another twenty years during the aftermath of the World War I economic boom. There were three peak periods for PLSBS membership: the turn of the century, 1899–1900 (868 members); the post–World War I boom of 1919–23 (1,366 members); and the World War II recovery of 1945–47 (745 members).[37]

The increasing level of membership was an indication of job security along the waterfront, and the Irish had maintained their strong numerical superiority within this union. Portland's Irish population finally held an occupational monopoly in an industry that was flourishing and seemed, apparently, to be secure well into the future.

The census of 1900 has made it possible to study the longshoremen of Portland in great detail. What follows is a very brief analysis of some of the characteristics of these longshoremen as depicted in the census for the month of June 1900. The following section is based on statistics from a computer analysis of data entered for 253 Portland longshoremen in the 1900 census.[38]

This brief narrative represents, at best, only a snapshot view of Portland and its Irish longshoremen at one specific point in time. It presents a lens through which one may view working longshoremen and their families as they were about to enter the twentieth century. The union and its members, unbeknownst to them, would suffer through a decade of decline at the start of this new century before entering into its period of greatest growth during and immediately after World War I. For Portland's maritime shipping industry and Irish longshore laborers, the turn of the twentieth century was a mixed blessing.

On the positive side, there was a real Irish community in Portland, their new home of choice, that centered on the working waterfront and that was served by the two major Catholic parishes, the Cathedral of the Immaculate Conception in the east end and Saint Dominic's Church, Portland's oldest Catholic house of worship, in the west end.

The Irish language was still commonly heard along the docks of Portland and in its working-class neighborhoods, especially the east end's Munjoy Hill and the west end's Gorham's Corner.[39] Portland was not atypical in that many of its Irish immigrants, especially in the famine and postfamine period, had come from the Irish-speaking provinces, such as Connacht, which included County Galway. Historian Kevin Kenny wrote that "between one-quarter and one-third of American-bound emigrants during the famine were Irish speakers." At the midpoint of the nineteenth century, Connacht and Munster, the two provinces from which most famine emigrants emerged, still were at least half Irish-speaking themselves. As the nineteenth century progressed and other famines occurred, the degree of western Ireland's depopulation increased. Connacht witnessed a 53 percent increase in emigration in the years between 1881 and 1910 while Ireland as a whole saw a 15 percent decline. "As many as half of these western emigrants were Irish speakers."[40]

Kenneth Nilsen's research into Portland's Irish speakers confirms Kenny's findings, as do the anecdotal memories of many of its longshoremen. Nilsen described Portland, even as late as the 1980s when he was conducting his research there, as "the United States city with the highest concentration of Irish speakers in its Irish immigrant population [and] all the evidence indicates that Irish speakers have been in the majority among Portland's Irish at least as far back as the 1880s."[41] The longshore industry, at least for Portland's first-generation Irish males, was the place where Irish ethnicity and Irish language often came together.

Larry Welch spoke colorfully of the reasons he thought the Irish were so plentiful alongshore: "They're the only mucks that would tackle it years ago before the union got any wages. It was not a good job, you know. They were driven in those days—no safety precautions, nothing! I imagine just like any immigrant class, they got the shit jobs. I suppose that's how it started."[42]

Phil O'Donnell, Portland's long-time harbormaster, remembered signs at the Grand Trunk piers written in Irish and Italian designating "No Smoking" zones ("Ná caitear tobac"). He further stated, "Some of the greenhorns [Irish immigrants] only had broken English." Tom Mulkern remembered that these Irish speakers would only talk it among themselves because "they figured it was ignorant to talk Irish in front of someone who didn't understand it." Mulkern further stated that the longshoremen spoke Irish in "Saint Dom's and India Street," designating, respectively, the west end and the east end of Portland. Roy Caleb recalled that Irish was spoken by "quite a lot, especially the real old ones," adding, almost sadly, that it "just went right over my head."[43]

Steve Concannon, who came to Portland in April 1921 at the age of twenty, was a native Irish speaker himself, having been raised in the townland of Derryloughane, near Furbo in County Galway, west of Galway city. He spoke only broken English when he arrived in Portland, but he was under the care of his uncle, Marcus Concannon. Steve remembered being called "Marcus's greenhorn" because his passage to Portland had been sponsored by his uncle. In describing the term "greenhorn" for a newly arrived immigrant, Steve said, in Irish, "Tá sé sách fada amuigh anseo tá na hadharcaí a' titim dhuit." (Literally—"He was out here long enough that the horns were falling off of you.") Concannon admitted, "We had an awful lot to learn to adjust to city life." He was formally educated back in west Galway only up to the age of about fifteen, and that was half in Irish and half in English.

Concannon worked two multiyear stretches as a longshoreman and fondly remembered the union in the early 1920s being at least 80 percent "Irishmen that came direct from Ireland—and they all spoke Gaelic. I felt right at home with them. That's all I cared to speak." Steve Concannon and other Irish speakers must have felt linguistically conflicted, however. At one point he stated, "Once you leave Ireland you can't speak [Irish] with anybody else"; but he later admitted, "If you tried to talk English among our crowd, they'd say you were trying to put on the airs, you know."[44]

Jobs in Portland at the turn of the twentieth century were plentiful, as attested to by the recent upsurge of new members into the union. Again, this was probably caused by the increased shipping due to the material demands of the Spanish-American War and the Boer War involving the United States and Great Britain, respectively. In many respects the first-generation longshoremen demonstrated traits that were neither purely Irish nor purely American. Rather, these "newly generated traits" demonstrated their ability to adapt to new surroundings while maintaining meaningful elements of Irish culture.

In several measurable areas, such as literacy and infant mortality, the second-generation Irish had improved over their first-generation forebears. These first-generation parents hoped that the children would be able to live in more comfort and security than they had found either in Ireland or in Portland. The successes of the Irish in Portland, especially of the second and subsequent generations, in terms of mobility, literacy, health, occupational security, and other areas, helped to dispel the stereotypical view of the immigrant as simply the "dregs" or "wretched refuse" of European society.

While measurable gains had been made, there were still important problems to be addressed. The geographical concentration of the Irish, especially the first generation, emphasized the limited choice of housing for these newcomers. Ninety-five percent of first-generation Irish longshoremen lived within the Irish waterfront neighborhood, defined by only three of Portland's twenty-five census enumeration districts. Precious few, only 5 percent, lived in the other twenty-two enumeration districts combined. As always, one is forced to guess as to the amount of choice versus compulsion in this starkly segregated occupational pattern. Limited housing mobility was compounded by the extremely low number of homeowners among the Irish longshoremen in Portland compared to other ethnic groups in other parts of the country.

This finding tends to support the thesis of several Irish American historians that the Irish in New England, and along the East Coast in general, were not representative of the Irish experience in the less restrictive, more fluid, and faster-growing environments of America, particularly the West and Midwest.[45] The families of Portland's first-generation Irish longshoremen suffered a high rate of infant mortality, over one and one-half child per family on average, although this rate was nearly halved among the second generation. Nearly 20 percent of the first-generation Irish longshoremen could neither read nor write. Although they were universally able to speak the English language, this represented for many of them, at best, a second language.

During the first quarter of the twentieth century, an economic slowdown was followed by the years of the greatest growth of Portland's longshore industry and the unionization of its maritime workforce through the PLSBS. In these years the generational dichotomy between the first- and second-generation longshoremen would continue. Portland at the turn of the twentieth century was indeed a mixed blessing, as seen through the experiences of this largely Irish maritime workforce. For better or worse, Portland was now their home. It had become a place of refuge for Irish immigrants, and a place of real opportunity for their children. In the words of playwright Kate Moira Ryan, taken from her play *Leaving Queens*, "The dreams of the first generation are lived by the second."

4

Lost Strikes and Union Affiliation

Early Twentieth-Century Labor Militancy Alongshore

During the first decade of the twentieth century, Portland's maritime dockworkers witnessed a steep decline in membership and work.¹ A weakening economy required fewer laborers to handle goods into or out of the port of Portland. Locally this was reflected primarily by a sharp decrease in the volume of Canadian grain being exported via Portland to Europe. Membership in the Portland Longshoremen's Benevolent Society (PLSBS) was cut in half to 425 between the years 1899–1910.²

With a recovery in PLSBS membership under way after 1910, however, a revived spirit of militancy also spread alongshore, nationally and in Portland. Portland longshoremen were not only crucial for the maritime transport of Canadian grain but also for other bulk cargo such as coal, necessary especially for helping to power the railroads, paper mills, and other manufacturing sectors in the state. Despite its relative isolation, Maine also experienced industrialization and urbanization, "both of which required the movement of large quantities of low-value but high-bulk raw materials."³

Traditionally, unions would seek wage and other concessions during times of growth and "rising expectations." The reverse of this could be true, as well, and pressures on longshore unions during times of economic slowdown were universal, such as in New York when in October 1874 the stevedoring companies joined forces to "humble the longshoremen's union." A five-week strike ended in defeat for the dockworkers and "the union's power on the docks was shattered [and] union wage scales did not again reach the levels of 1874 until 1916."⁴

In 1911 such a strike occurred in Portland amid less than favorable conditions. Again, in November of 1913, on the very eve of the outbreak of World

War I in Europe, the PLSBS, an independent and fairly isolated maritime union of Irish longshoremen in Portland, Maine, fought another unsuccessful struggle for increased wages with the agents of several major international steamship companies operating in this important North Atlantic port. Just three months following the loss of this second strike in two years, the PLSBS announced its affiliation with the International Longshoremen's Association (ILA) in February of 1914. These three major events were obviously more than simply linked by chronology.

Several questions emerge in attempting to analyze why a local union, technically a benevolent society, after nearly thirty-five years of independence, would choose to surrender its autonomy and affiliate with the fastest-growing longshoremen's union on the Atlantic Coast, the ILA. The following questions, along with efforts to provide answers to them, will compose the bulk of this chapter. How does this period fit into the larger context of the growth and decline of maritime development and commerce in Portland in the late nineteenth and early twentieth centuries? What had the PLSBS experienced in these early years, 1880–1913, and in particular what had been the reaction locally to an earlier failed attempt to raise wages in 1911? What were the primary contentious issues involved in these strikes, and were they "pure and simple," that is, primarily wage-related, or did they involve work rules and conditions of labor? What was the impact of the arrival of Italian laborers on the Portland waterfront, and what was the associated threat of strikebreakers, or "scabs," during the strike of 1911? How did these demographic changes challenge the ethnically homogeneous Irish longshoremen of Portland? What labor actions were occurring in the other major Atlantic ports, primarily Boston and New York, at this time? How was this strike reported in local newspapers and what were the concerns of the business and financial interests of the city? What had been the role of the ILA in other major Atlantic ports in this period, and why was their offer of affiliation with Portland finally accepted in early 1914, only two years after being rejected by this same group? Finally, what were the immediate consequences of the major strike in 1913, and of the subsequent drive by the ILA "to make this port Union all over?"

The emergence of Portland as a major Atlantic port could be dated from the previously discussed mid-nineteenth-century linkage by rail to Montreal and, by extension, to the productive grain-producing regions of Canada's western provinces. Before this Montreal connection, work along

Portland's waterfront had been unpredictable, seasonal, and casual. The nineteenth-century West Indies trade in molasses and rum had provided work for a small group of African American dockworkers, but they were largely displaced by the more numerous Irish who arrived in Portland by the mid-nineteenth century and were hungry for work at almost any wage or condition.[5] By 1880 this group of predominantly Irish longshoremen, seeking a greater level of occupational security in their newly chosen home, formed the PLSBS.[6]

Membership in the union varied widely during its first two decades, but by 1899 it had reached its highest level of membership up to that point, at 868 members. How would these predominately Irish maritime laborers respond to the significant threat to their livelihood posed by a decade-long decline in work that had halved their membership by 1910?

Maritime Strike of 1911

Two of the most significant maritime strikes along the Portland waterfront occurred in 1911 and 1913, just prior to the outbreak of World War I in Europe. These work stoppages were not limited to Portland. Boston and other Atlantic Coast ports were also affected.[7] Just two years prior to this, in 1909, a longshoremen's strike occurred in Boston during which the mainly Irish laborers there asked for an increase in pay for handling bulk cargo. The steamship agents and stevedores were reluctant to grant pay increases or other "ill-timed" concessions and observed that they were "facing one of the worst periods of depression they have known for years."[8]

Two years prior to the Boston longshore strike of 1909, nearly all the waterfront workers of New York united in 1907 for a remarkable, if unsuccessful, display of solidarity also concerning the question of stagnant wages. Although these largely immigrant or second-generation workers had been "virtually unorganized" and largely lacked the experience of trade unionism, they attempted to overcome the united forces of the shipping companies. They demonstrated the commonsense notion that one must be united to prevail against a united adversary. "The success of industrial unionism by definition involved overcoming occupational separation, but it was also determined by the degree to which racial and ethnic divisions, potentially fatal to workers in struggle, could be overcome."[9]

On December 28, 1910, the Portland longshoremen's records reveal that the stevedores had based their contract on a gang of ten workers rather than the standard-sized gang of sixteen. Although the term stevedore is often popularly used interchangeably with longshoreman, a stevedoring company is "a firm that contracts to load and unload ships." In this case the conflict of interest between the stevedoring company (employer) and the longshoremen (employees) was quite apparent.[10]

The size of a gang was one of the principal methods of determining the quality and safety of working conditions alongshore. This issue was, together with the weight of a sling load, one of the essential elements of work rules alongshore. Work rules were unique to each port and were the method by which local unions negotiated their own basic working conditions. Nearly universally, "smaller gangs, according to the longshoremen, meant harder, more dangerous work."[11] This local anomaly concerning gang size late in 1910 occurred because some Grand Trunk employees had unloaded the last pulp ship using only a ten-man gang. Pulp was a commodity that was both imported into and exported from the port of Portland. Locally, it was used in the production of paper at one of several mills, the largest and closest to Portland being the S. D. Warren Paper Mill in Westbrook.

As a result of this one-time exception to the work rules, early in 1911 the stevedoring firm of Trefethen and Dugan became embroiled in a serious dispute with the PLSBS over the handling of wood pulp. Although the society briefly discussed but dropped the proposal to suspend any man working for Trefethen and Dugan, it did vote on January 3, 1911, to hereafter use the standard gang of sixteen. The coal shovelers employed by that same contracting firm were also a source of much contention. The PLSBS coal shovelers brought up the question of gang size again at the January 10 meeting and requested the labor committee to intervene on its behalf. Coal work was usually seen as one of the "least desirable jobs in the harbor," and, at least on the New York waterfront, it was often done by special gangs, mostly composed of Italian laborers.[12]

The following week a committee invited Trefethen and Dugan to appear before an imminent special meeting of the society. Not surprisingly, neither owner appeared on such short notice. Society president John Caselden was therefore appointed to request Trefethen's appearance at the next regular union meeting. Still no representative of the firm attended, however, and the matter was laid over until January 31, 1911.

Union recognition was another central issue. By this time the PLSBS, clearly out of patience, threatened that "if Trefethen and Dugan do not come to our Hall Tuesday night or before and settle the grievance between [the]

Society and the firm, the Society will call the men out on strike again."[13] Tempers were high at the next meeting on February 7, 1911, as noted in this graphic yet somewhat comical excerpt concerning one member's free use of the English language: "In arguing the way Trefethen and Dugan did not come and explain how the last strike was settled to [the] Society, Patrick Gorham made a little blunder in swearing twice [for] which he was fined 50 cents for each offence totaling one dollar, though he was warned beforehand not to say so much."[14]

When no reply was received by the union's labor committee from either Trefethen or Dugan, the recording secretary was asked to request a signed agreement from the former. When, apparently, he did not sign, the PLSBS voted on February 14, 1911, to strike against Trefethen and Dugan "until our Society be recognized by the above named firm."

The firm was notified that work that had started aboard ships before this strike vote would be finished.[15] This appears to be one of the earliest bona fide strikes by the Portland longshoremen since the Civil War period, and as such it demonstrated the rising level of frustration and militancy within this union, and unions in general, in this period.

This was a time of labor militancy nationally as well, and before the year was out, longshoremen in both Portland and Boston would be on strike for higher wages and better working conditions, especially regarding the limited sling load. The limited sling load, that is, how much weight or volume could be placed on each load taken from or loaded onto a ship, was perhaps the central issue of safety and work rules for all American maritime dockers, whether Atlantic, Pacific, Gulf Coast, or Great Lakes. The actual weight would vary from port to port and over time depending upon such factors as the commodity being handled, the technology being employed by the longshoremen, and local tradition.

The PLSBS, and nationally the ILA, would consistently fight for greater limits on the maximum sling load, and this would remain the hallmark of a strong union well into the twentieth century. The late twentieth century would witness the gradual replacement of this issue of the sling loads with "roll-on/roll-off" cargo ships and eventually container technology. As late as 1945, however, the inability of New York longshoremen to get the desired limit on the sling loads was mentioned as a precipitating cause in a longshore walkout there.[16]

The strike vote was certainly the action needed to show Trefethen that the union meant business, as he was personally in attendance at the very next society meeting on February 21, 1911. Probably realizing that the union would not back down, he made a formal capitulation to the society. Although the debate that followed "took considerable time," Trefethen's concessions were accepted by a standing vote of twenty-eight in favor and six opposed.[17] Trefethen's firm had recognized the PLSBS, a symbolic but important victory, but the peace that followed along Portland's waterfront was short-lived, remaining only through the rest of that work season.

The busiest work season for Portland's longshoremen effectively ran from November through April. It commenced with the anticipated freezing of the St. Lawrence River, thus idling the port of Montreal throughout the winter. It largely ended with the coming of spring weather and the opening of the St. Lawrence down to Quebec and Montreal. Weather, of course, thus contributed to the transient (irregular or seasonal) nature of longshore work, both in Portland (winter season) and Montreal (summer season).

The transient or casual nature of longshore labor created seasonal migrations in both directions as dockworkers, especially those who were unmarried or were without families, searched for venues where their labor would be needed. Portland longshoremen had long migrated northward in the idle summer months, aided, of course, by the Grand Trunk Railroad connection. Many Quebec and Montreal longshoremen would often migrate southward in the winter months. The Canadian laborers, apparently, were a little more adventurous and had many more work options than their American counterparts. Evidence demonstrated that they would travel as "snow birds" as far south as Savannah, Georgia, or even to New Orleans, Louisiana. In the latter port, perhaps they would work with their Cajun (Acadian) brothers on the piers of the Crescent City. These "seasonal migrations" were more well planned, rational, and predictable than the word "transient" would seem to imply.

These migrations had become "an established practice as early as 1853," and evidence exists of even slightly earlier wanderings. By 1861 "several hundreds [of Canadian longshoremen] spent the winter months in the southern United States." Daniel Kane, a stevedore, glowingly reported to a Canadian Royal Commission studying labor conditions: "I worked for eighteen or nineteen winters, down south, in connection with stevedoring with Quebec Ship Labourers, and I tell you gentlemen, there is no occasion for a stevedore to talk to them. Instead of a stevedore driving them, they, in fact, drive the stevedore, and wherever a Quebec man shows himself, down south, he can always get a job, if a job is going."[18]

The presence of longshoremen from Canada on the Portland waterfront during the busy winter months was ongoing, as could be witnessed in a newspaper clipping from around the turn of the twentieth century: "Thirty-seven longshoremen, including three bosses, arrived on the noon train Tuesday from Montreal to work on the English steamers."[19]

The wage schedule in effect since the turn of the century called for thirty cents for general cargo (day) and forty cents for general cargo (night). Apparently, the Boston longshoremen had a similar wage structure. They were also making a demand for a ten cents increase across the board, although they later compromised on the five cents increase that the Portland longshoremen were demanding at this same time.

In Portland, a new wage scale was reported out by the committee on longshore wages in September, near the end of the 1911 work year (November 1910 through October 1911). It called for an increase of five cents per hour over the previous year's wages and an additional night work differential after midnight:

Day work	—35 cents per hour
Night work (7 [P.M.]–12 [A.M.])	—45 cents per hour
Night work (1 [A.M.]–6 [A.M.])	—50 cents per hour[20]

This new scale was approved by a unanimous standing vote. These increases were in line with those demanded by the Boston longshoremen also late in 1911, and the failure of the latter to achieve these increases led to a bitter strike in Boston between January 5 and February 14, 1912.[21] Other specific issues also were discussed in Portland, and the implementation of the wage package was set for no later than the start of the new work season on November 1, 1911. All stevedores doing business with the PLSBS would be informed of the new wage scale by typewritten notification from the recording secretary.

By late October 1911, responses had been received from some steamship companies, and a meeting between these companies and the top four officers of the society was scheduled for October 28, 1911, at the rooms of the Portland Board of Trade.[22] The Portland Board of Trade as mentioned before was a precursor to the Chamber of Commerce and had played a very active role, and would continue to, in the maritime development of the port of Portland. Its members were concerned with the port's continued dependence on Canadian grain, and with the continuing inequity between lagging imports and booming exports. They wondered what would happen if that one export commodity should somehow disappear. Could Portland survive on its own hinterland? Some warned that "powerful interests [were working to divert Portland's trade] to other ports showing greater local interest."[23]

The final meeting of the society in fiscal year 1911 was disappointing. Management refused to accept the union's wage proposal, and now it was again up to the Portland longshoremen to act. A standing vote was called to reaffirm the new wage proposals, and the results were 155 in favor and 1 opposed. It was further voted that "to make a showing of the members" the society would implement a selective strike by refusing to work either woodpulp or china clay boats. China clay is a product imported from England or domestically from Georgia to assist in the making of fine-quality paper products. This threatened work refusal occurred in Portland at the beginning of the period that has been referred to nationally by labor historian David Montgomery as the "strike decade," with work stoppages and job actions in New York and, closer to home, in Boston, Lowell, and Lawrence.

Workers were frustrated and saw no other recourse. A local newspaper reported that the three hundred men then out on strike "will be increased when the steamship season closes at Montreal as about 300 members of the Portland society are now employed at the Canadian port." A local newspaper stated that this conference "did not result in any satisfactory arrangements being made."[24] In most ports, as in Portland, longshore work was both casual, that is, dependent upon the irregular arrival of ships, and seasonal. In New Orleans "longshoremen encountered prolonged periods of unemployment [and] work was practically nonexistent during the off season," spring and summer. Because of this seasonal or casual nature of the work, "they also had to labor in other fields, on and off the docks."[25]

It was decided that the New York boat, primarily a regularly scheduled passenger carrier between Portland and New York, would remain unaffected by the strike action. Goods continued to flow into the port, however, as demonstrated in a statement made by the Maine Central Railroad that they soon expected the arrival of seven thousand tons of coal from Baltimore, most likely for domestic heating or for use in local paper mills.[26] The mere announcement of the grievances of the dockworkers was clearly insufficient. Therefore, the intention of the union to go on full strike as of November 1, 1911, was formally reported to the steamship companies.[27]

Steamship officials reacted forcefully to the strike announcement, claiming that local longshoremen were already overpaid. They stated that local wages "are larger than at Montreal, Boston, Saint John and other leading ports," and that the increases demanded by the Portland longshoremen would add 25 percent to their local payroll. They admitted—somewhat contradictorily, however—that the wage schedule had remained unchanged "for a number of years." Nonetheless, rather than submitting to such a pay increase, these steamship officials threatened to discontinue steamship service to Portland.[28]

The advantage was clearly on the side of the employers. These steamship agents and international companies could negotiate for competitive advantages of one port over another, and threaten to use alternative ports or alternative forms of transportation, such as rail, if a strike was threatened. In Boston, at this exact same time, the longshoremen were being told by the steamship officials that their similar demands would increase local payrolls by 24 percent and thus "seriously damage Boston's competitive position."[29]

Now the lines were clearly drawn, and the PLSBS was fully on strike for higher wages as of November 7, 1911, when the new fiscal year commenced. Coincidentally, the local press reported that a new so-called Portland Longshoremen's Union, which hoped to incorporate within two weeks, was in the process of being organized.[30] The group claimed to have one hundred names already on its roster and was open to "any person familiar with stevedore work, regardless of place of residence."

Without doubt, this new longshore group was, in fact, a creation of the steamship companies. Strikebreakers were also widely used in Boston's longshoremen's strike just two months later.[31] One week earlier the employers had threatened to refuse to send steamships to Portland or to "secure labor from other cities" unless the strike was settled soon.[32] This scab or strikebreaker union reportedly expected to eventually have two hundred members, which officials felt would be sufficient to "handle with ease all the transatlantic steamers due to arrive here the coming winter."[33]

Then, as quickly as the newly announced phantom union had appeared, it disappeared, presumably because in fact there never had been any such entity. The steamship companies had surely used scare tactics against the PLSBS. Most of these steamship companies were European. Together with the railroads, which locally employed the predominately Italian freight handlers to load and unload rail cars, they represented the nexus of power in all major American ports. "Because these foreign-owned lines floated huge fleets engaged in intense competition with one another in price and in scheduling, their managers [were interested in] getting their ships unloaded and loaded quickly."³⁴

In the earlier 1907 New York strike, the Irish labor leader James Connolly, then in residence in the United States, had referred to the "old, old story, empty stomachs [against] concentrated capital."³⁵ The agents also knew that the longshoremen in most Atlantic ports were not coordinating their efforts or, for that matter, even aware of conditions outside their own local domain. There were reports that "freight being transported by rail to Boston from the west would be rerouted to New York, Baltimore, and Portland, and New England bound ocean freight would be re-routed to New York. Employers knew that Boston longshoremen were organized independently of longshoremen elsewhere, and had no previous contact, or record of past cooperation, with them."³⁶ Calvin Winslow also analyzed the competitive disadvantage of capital over labor. He described the shippers as possessing tremendous advantages such as organization and wealth behind them, and he even doubted their interest in reaching a settlement on anything but terms highly favorable to their interests. "The estimates of the cost of the strike to the shippers were staggering, as were estimates of the costs to [the] economy, yet the shippers were able to absorb them."³⁷

The scare tactics employed by management included the threatened use of scab labor to form a "company union." It is difficult to estimate the exact significance of the threatened scab longshore union in this labor action although it clearly must have had a chilling effect on the PLSBS in its negotiations.³⁸ Whether this involved the use of newly arriving Italian immigrants into Portland is also a matter of conjecture, but evidence does exist to show that it was a distinct possibility.

Strikebreaking and Ethnic Tension with Italians

In the late nineteenth and early twentieth century in America, Italians occupied a social and racial niche between whites and blacks. When asked if an Italian was a white man, a West Coast construction boss in the 1890s answered, "No sir, an Italian is a Dago." Some went as far as to racially refer to an Italian as a "white nigger."³⁹ As early as 1887, Portland longshoremen had shown pessimism about their future because of competition from these and other newly arriving immigrants. This was clearly demonstrated in an 1887 report from the Maine commissioner of industrial and labor statistics: "The condition of longshoremen in Portland is not as good as it was fifteen years ago. We do not get half the work now that we did then. We number in Portland between 300 and 400 members. The future of the longshoremen looks dark; we have to compete with Italians and other cheap imported help, who work for $1.00 per day. In former years two-thirds of the longshoremen were Irish."[40]

Prior to World War I, nearly 60 percent of the industrial workforce in America was foreign born.[41] In Portland, as with the rest of the United States, the composition of this ethnic labor pool was changing, marked by a dramatic shift, roughly between 1890 and 1910, in the sources of immigration into the United States. The "old immigrants" had been mainly from the northwestern parts of Europe, including Ireland, Great Britain, Germany, and Scandinavia, while the "new immigrants" of the early twentieth century increasingly came from southern and eastern Europe, including Italy, Greece, the Balkans, Poland, and Russia, the latter two including large numbers of Jews. Simultaneously, there were also significant numbers of Chinese and Japanese immigrant laborers coming into the Pacific ports.

Irish-born historian Kevin Kenny writes, "Largely because of the arrival of the 'new' immigrants, the Irish were now less concentrated in manual labour than they had been; but many Irish-Americans, especially recent immigrants, continued to work in unskilled labour and rates of social mobility varied widely from region to region." Of significance for Portland's Irish longshoremen, the Irish rate of economic progress in America was reportedly "least in the relatively static and socially stratified states of New England."[42]

Ethnic cohesiveness was one method to ensure union solidarity. The reverse would also, unfortunately, be logically true. These changing patterns of immigration into Portland in the early twentieth century were bound to have an impact upon this largely Irish union. The newly arrived Italians in Portland took jobs at the lowest rung of the economic ladder on the docks, as freight handlers. David Montgomery reported that "in both [New York and New Orleans] freight handlers' hourly wages were consistently lower than those of longshoremen proper."[43] This was true for Portland as well, as retired longshoreman Phil O'Donnell confirmed, albeit with a mitigating twist: "Freight handling paid thirty cents an hour less than longshore [but] you were out of the weather."[44]

In Philadelphia, "once Southern Italians, almost entirely of peasant stock, started arriving in America in large numbers, they also vied for unskilled jobs. Generally, Italians, despite their own dark complexions, were favored over blacks for [Philadelphia's] unskilled work." This racial preferential system was also chronicled by historian Bruce Nelson, who reported that "one New York waterfront employer who, when hiring, distinguished between Poles or Italian versus 'white men.'"[45]

These racially charged stereotypes would apply on the New York waterfront as well. By 1907, Italians in New York represented nearly one-third of the workforce, approximately equal to the Irish. However, blacks and Italians were also well represented in the scores of strikebreakers used at this time. "The Italians also came in invasions, that is, as strikebreakers, though in far larger numbers [than blacks]."[46]

Racism within the field of labor was also the case throughout most other American cities in this period, and even more so concerning African Americans who were routinely excluded from the American Federation of Labor (AFL) and other nonaffiliated unions. The frustration of black United Mine Worker organizer Richard L. Davis at the exclusion of blacks from the AFL, which he referred to as "rottenness," was also apparent at the turn of the century in most regions and in most occupations.[47]

The Portland Irish longshoremen seemed to have had a complex relationship with Italians. Although originally seen as potential competitors, at best, or strikebreakers, at worst, Italians slowly but steadily entered the PLSBS. Steve Concannon remembered that "most of the Italians worked the freight sheds [but] one gang of longshoremen was practically all Italians." He reasoned that the early ethnic friction was possibly because of cultural suspicions. "The Irish were great for unions. They were afraid probably that the Italians would not cooperate with them when it came to unions." Ultimately, however, attractions proved stronger than suspicions. Close demographic proximity, common worksites and schools, and, in most cases, a common Catholic religion, led to the inevitable. Roy Caleb spoke of what many Portland longshoremen would eventually acknowledge, especially after World War II: "Italians and Irish here intermingled and intermarried."[48]

During a period of labor unrest less than three years after the Portland longshore strike of 1911, and after affiliation with the ILA, a PLSBS member spoke of his success "in keeping the non-union Italians from strike breaking." The PLSBS was counseled at that time about the necessity of "asking the Poles and Italians to join [the] Society as soon as possible." This warning was made on September 15, 1914, by the ILA Atlantic Coast secretary, Brother William Dempsey.[49]

The potential use of Italian, Polish, or other recently arrived immigrant groups as strikebreakers must have concerned the union as the strike of 1911 continued with no end in sight. In a sense, the Irish longshoremen partly brought this situation upon themselves by maintaining such an ethnically segregated union. When Italians arrived in Portland and were not welcomed into the union, they had few alternatives besides scabbing or forming an independent union, such as the Italian Freight Handlers (ILA Local 912), both of which they did. The records of this largely Italian union are intact today.[50] Knowledge was widespread of the historic use by employers of ethnic strikebreakers, especially along the Atlantic Coast. As early as 1887, in the aftermath of a massive New York dock strike, "employers brought in legions of Italians to weaken that Irish-dominated workforce."[51]

In Baltimore two major strikes occurred in 1900 and 1912 pitting "black and white strikers against immigrant Italian strikebreakers." The New York waterfront was "remarkable in the degree to which it was divided along racial and ethnic lines." In the 1907 New York longshore strike, there was a major confrontation between black longshoremen and Italian strikebreakers. The first casualty, however, was reported to be an Italian scab who was seen leaving the White Star Line piers and was "attacked [and killed] by a crowd of Irish."[52]

Portland's Irish longshoremen did not appear to be unique in this issue of racial and ethnic divisiveness at the turn of the twentieth century. Earlier, in the previous century, they had effectively eliminated any competition from African Americans who, until the middle of the nineteenth century, had played a major role in the stevedoring labor of Portland. This small group had been specifically forbidden membership in the PLSBS by its original bylaws in 1880.

Now that Italians, Poles, and other "new" immigrants were arriving in larger numbers especially since 1880, the first instinct of the Irish longshoremen was apparently similar, exclusion. However, they were now slowly beginning to see that such exclusivity could ultimately be counterproductive to the union in its fight against the steamship companies. The employers had not only capital on their side but also the option of using many other ports if local costs and working conditions were seen as uncompetitive in the relatively small and isolated port of Portland. The question appeared to be could the Portland Irish longshoremen put aside their racial and ethnic prejudices to secure their precarious occupational advantages?

Under the threat of the possible use of scab labor late in 1911, the Portland longshoremen were in a difficult position. Contemporaneously, in Boston, the steamship agents also threatened widespread use of strikebreakers. The January 6, 1912, edition of the *Boston Globe* carried an advertisement: "Wanted 500 Able-Bodied Men To Work on Piers and Steamers . . . a strike being now in existence." Two days later it was reported that the five hundred strikebreakers had arrived and that this was only the "advance guard" for three thousand more expected soon.[53]

PLSBS president John Caselden next met in conference with John A. Torrance, the Portland-based agent of the White Star-Dominion Line, and Charles F. Flagg, the chairman of the Portland Board of Trade. In no uncertain terms, the steamship companies and their agents refused to budge. One week later at the regular meeting, "the President expressed his feelings in regards to getting more wages, stating that there was no possibility of getting any more than the present scale as the steamship officials would not pay any more under any circumstances."[54]

In addition to the threat of strikebreakers, the steamship agents could reroute cargoes to other ports, thus avoiding the striking longshoremen altogether. Portland, before its own strike action, was reportedly "expected to benefit by an increase in the volume of perishable goods shipped through that port" instead of through striking Boston. This was a strong argument in favor of possible affiliation with a larger body, one that would represent longshoremen regionally and not just in one port, thus preventing shipping companies from playing off one port against another. For the shipping agents, this tactic of rerouting "certainly reduced the pressure on the employers to accede to the longshoremen's demands."[55]

By late in 1911, the PLSBS was defeated and they knew it. Shortly thereafter, Portland's longshoremen were forced back to work under the conditions that had prevailed before their strike action began. However, when it was moved to disband the strike committee at the PLSBS meeting of January 9, 1912, the motion was withdrawn in favor of a vote to keep the committee in force an additional six months, a further indication of discontent.

Maritime Strike of 1913

The major contentious issues remained unsolved. As the transatlantic season was about to commence nearly two years later, in the fall of 1913, the PLSBS again challenged the wage structure along Portland's piers. The defeat of the union in late 1911 was still fresh in the minds of most members at a meeting in mid-September of 1913 when "it was considered near time to raise wages per hour along the waterfront and especially on transatlantic steamers." This call resulted in the first reading of a new wage proposal on October 14, 1913, calling for thirty-five cents per hour (daytime), double time for Sundays and holidays, and forty cents an hour for handling coal.[56]

The new wage scale had unanimously passed its third reading by the meeting of October 28, 1913, and it was voted effective as of November 1, 1913. The society had apparently learned some important lessons from their recent labor defeat at the hands of the major shipping companies. Therefore, it was decided to pressure management and, simultaneously, to favorably influence Portland's general public opinion by advertising the new wage scale in the three daily newspapers: the *Portland Press*, the *Daily Eastern Argus*, and the *Portland Express*.[57]

All steamship officials would be notified "in type written letters," and a committee of seven was chosen "to wait on steamship officials in case of future trouble." The attention given to formally notifying the steamship officials is ironic because regardless of the method of notification, the officials were apparently given only three days official warning of the new wage scale.[58]

Of the major Portland daily circulation newspapers then operating, the *Daily Eastern Argus*, with its Democratic Party leanings, was most likely to be sympathetic to the union's cause. An analysis of this paper during the strike period of November 1913 was most revealing. Notice was given and signed by PLSBS president Michael McDonough of a meeting to be held on November 11, 1913, with "business of importance to come before the meeting."[59] The steamship officials again balked at the society's demands. As a result, at the November 11 meeting the union members voted to stand by their demands, and the following call to strike was issued: "That the longshoremen be all called out from Fish Point to Rolling Mill, including men working on coastwise as well as transatlantic steamships."[60] The next day's newspaper reported that "about 30 Polacks who had refused to work on Monday unless paid the new wage scale of 35 cents an hour having changed their mind and concluded to accept the old rate of 30 cents. None of them were members of the [PLSBS]."[61]

At a special meeting held on November 13, 1913, the strike committee reported that local steamship agents refused to pay any higher than the rates in Boston, thirty-three cents per hour (daytime), thirty-three cents for coal, and fifty cents for Sundays and holidays. By a vote of seventy-nine to thirteen, the society lowered its demands and amended its original wage schedule to now read thirty-five cents per hour (daytime) for general cargo, forty cents per hour (daytime) for coal, and time and a half on Sundays and holidays, a drop from the double time they had hoped for and originally proposed.

Because there were more than six hundred members in the union at that time, this vote, which represented fewer than one hundred members, indicates that they were perhaps already a discouraged body that recognized their own weakness in acting alone. The counteroffer had come from a group of steamship representatives including John Torrance, White Star Line; William Bailey, Canadian Line; Robert M. Smith, Dominion Line; and William Leavitt, china clay steamers. These representatives characterized the offer as "the same scale for steamer and coal work as now paid in Boston." They further maintained that "for years the most harmonious relations have existed between the steamship companies and the men."[62]

In an attempt to gain public support among Portland's citizenry, the members again determined to deal with public opinion by advertising their "fair deal" in the three daily newspapers but, simultaneously, also to check on the agents' assertions concerning nearby Boston's scale of wages.[63] They wanted the public to see how underpaid they were, and how long they had worked without an increased wage. This resulted in perhaps the fullest reportage of the union's position in this strike in a long, articulate exposition defending the society's demand for increased wages. A front-page promotional piece, almost like an op-ed by the PLSBS itself, in the *Daily Eastern Argus* gave the union's perspective on issues such as inflation pressures, the short work season, and the irregular (casual) work schedule: "Since the Society was organized in 1880, from then to the present time we have received 30 [cents] per hour for day work for a period of 33 years. . . . Our demand for an increase in wages is an honest one and we ought to have it in order to live, not exist. . . . The wages received from this work as will be readily understood will go but a short ways in taking care of a family."[64]

Deadlock resulted, as reported at the next regular meeting of the society on November 18, 1913, with both sides sticking to their offers and with little movement toward compromise. The financial secretary, John Caselden, reported on the Boston wage scale and conditions. Boston's longshoremen had gone on strike in early 1912 to gain a raise from thirty cents to forty cents per hour (daytime), but "returned to work at the same wages and conditions as had existed prior to the strike."[65]

A historically significant development within this meeting was the report of a renewed effort by the ILA to organize Portland within its ranks. Boston and other North Atlantic ports had been affiliated since 1912, but the efforts to include Portland into the ILA's Atlantic Coast district had failed late in that year. The ILA controlled nearly the entire Atlantic Coast, and Portland would add to their hegemony, thus giving them even more leverage to negotiate a coast-wide agreement with the major shipping companies.

Now one year later, the time appeared to be ripe for another organizing drive. The receipt of a letter from the ILA directly on the heels of Brother Caselden's return from Boston was, therefore, all the more significant. The ILA did not instantly succeed, but now, perhaps for the first time, the Portland longshoremen apparently realized that they were in trouble and needed additional support.

As the maritime labor impasse continued, there was concern expressed by the "business and shipping circles" about this deadlock. "If [the steamship companies] cannot get their boats loaded here they will make other arrangements." There followed calls for the board of trade to arbitrate.[66] Interestingly, a "Montreal Wage Decision" was reported in this same period in which the longshoremen of Saint John, New Brunswick, who like their Portland counterparts had asked for the equivalent of forty cents an hour in winter (and, unlike them, for forty-five cents in summer) had been granted five cents less in each category by the Canadian minister of labor's arbitration board.[67] A lengthy article titled "Portland's Shipping Crisis" also contained a statement directly from the PLSBS and further reported that the board of trade was "Trying to Avert Disaster."[68] Other threats followed in the local newspapers: "Unless the labor troubles here are settled very soon [the White Star-Dominion liner *Canada*] may be held at Halifax on arrival and make that her port of departure [instead of Portland]."[69] "Unless the longshoremen at Portland, Maine moderate their demands Portland will be withdrawn from the itinerary of the [Allan Line's] Glasgow-Portland-Boston services."[70]

This latter report came from Montreal, directly from Andrew A. Allan. It was stated that Hugh Allan of London was already preparing for this withdrawal. If the stick was already being applied, could the carrot be far behind? The same edition of the paper reported that "exports of grain from here during the coming winter will be the heaviest on record unless labor matters interfere with the business."[71]

After intense negotiation, a second special meeting on November 21, 1913, signified a changed atmosphere and gave hint of a possible settlement. The local press, undoubtedly impressed by the union's candid reportage on their interpretation of events, favorably characterized the dockworkers' leadership as having "shown a willingness at all times to discuss the strike situation, believing that they are demanding wages that they are entitled to receive."[72] Union president Michael McDonough, clearly beaten by the intransigence of management, admitted to his members that "it was necessary that we should reconsider our trouble."[73] McDonough reported a proposal from the Portland Board of Trade that suggested binding arbitration for the wage dispute.

This conference on the wage dispute was attended by the British vice consul, John B. Keating, and called for binding arbitration with two representatives each from the union, the shipping companies, and the board of trade.[74] A meeting was tentatively scheduled for 10 A.M. the next morning at the board of trade hall. This binding arbitration proposal heavily favored the steamship officials who, of course, could anticipate the support of the board's two delegates. The shipping agents were reportedly "satisfied with the action taken by the Board of Trade." The Portland Board of Trade, represented by its president, Silas B. Adams, and its secretary, Maurice G. Rich, had tipped its hand when it was reported that they concluded that a continued longshore "disagreement" was "likely to cause serious inconvenience and loss to other citizens of Portland."[75]

At this special meeting of the PLSBS, and at the invitation of society president McDonough, Roy C. Burns, a representative of the board of trade, offered his solution to the deadlock. A local newspaper identified Burns as the chairman of the board of adjustment of the Boston and Maine Railroad, Portland Division, for the Railway Trainmen. He was also a member of the board of trade. Burns, before addressing the audience, showed his credentials by displaying his union card, that of the Railroad Brotherhood of Trainmen. His union membership would have made Burns unique among board of trade members, and this was highlighted as he addressed the members assembled as "Brothers."[76]

> Mr. Burns spoke lengthily on labor though he being a representative of the Board of Trade. He explained that it was a hard thing for labor to fight capital. He also gave us to understand that the steamship officials were determined not to pay any more than the previous figures and further he said to be sure and send a committee of two of our best men at the arbitration to fight our cause and try and get all they could before they would give in. He gave us lots of logic and good advice accompanied with all the information that was needed. He was a thorough, good speaker and we paid strict attention to him with one exception, he being interrupted by John Brown, which cost Brown one dollar for disturbing our interested friend and also the meeting.[77]

The union records report that Burns "cheered the boys" and was cheered, applauded, and given a vote of thanks upon retiring. Although a board of trade member, he had shown his sympathy, at least outwardly, with Portland's longshore laborers. It seems quite likely that Burns was attempting to counsel the union as to the inevitability of its second defeat in as many years, and to soften the blow of their return to the docks under conditions far less favorable than those that the union had demanded.

With all the preliminaries now over, John Caselden and Stephen Mulkerrin were chosen to arbitrate for the society the following morning at the board of trade. The press spoke again of the pivotal role of Roy C. Burns and opined that "labor trouble on the steamer docks cannot fail of proving most disastrous to the business interests of the city."[78] The arbitration went less than well, as had been anticipated, and Brother Caselden reported this to the society meeting of November 25, 1913. The settlement was thirty-three cents per hour (daytime) for general cargo and thirty-five cents per hour (daytime) for coal.[79]

"Happily Settled" was the headline. A last-minute glitch was avoided with the china clay lines when board of trade president Silas B. Adams took a train to Boston to ensure their compliance with the deal.[80] Although Sunday and holiday rates were not mentioned, this represented a slight compromise by both parties but with the society giving up more than the steamship companies. The union had gained a raise of only two cents per hour for handling coal, to thirty-five cents rather than the forty cents per hour as proposed. Roy C. Burns had given an accurate warning about conditions in 1913 as America was experiencing a prewar economic recession—"it was a hard thing for labor to fight capital."

In the next two meetings after the strike, seventy-two new members joined the PLSBS.[81] This was perhaps the best indication that maritime work as usual could now return to the Portland docks. As with any protracted dispute, however, there were bound to be ill feelings that lingered, especially on the part of the defeated longshore workforce. This could be seen at the December 30, 1913, meeting where the society advised the stevedore, Mr. Dugan, to keep Mr. Fred Norton, his foreman, "away from where Union men are working." On January 20, 1914, just three weeks prior to ILA affiliation, a dispute was reported again over the handling of china clay, and it was moved that no union men would work "unless all union men are hired first."[82]

The strike of 1913, which had lasted two weeks, was now over. Undoubtedly, its greatest legacy was not the few cents gained per hour but rather the organizational lessons learned. Clearly, in taking on the amalgamated power of the united steamship companies, a small independent benevolent society, even with a united, determined, and militant membership, was at an inherent disadvantage.

Almost predictably, within two months of the conclusion of this strike, the PLSBS joined the ILA fold from which all future wage and work conditions would be negotiated. This was the true legacy of the "failed" strikes of 1911 and 1913. A strikingly similar conclusion was reached in analyzing the Boston longshoremen's strike of 1912 that had occurred directly between Portland's two major labor stoppages. The Boston longshoremen had lost the strike of 1912, but in the process of losing, they "learned some important lessons from it." Francis McLaughlin logically concluded, "They must certainly have been impressed by their vulnerability in a portwide strike in the absence of cooperation with longshoremen in other ports and in the face of employer ability to hire strikebreakers."[83] These same two major disabilities existed just one hundred miles east along the Atlantic in the smaller maritime port of Portland.

Affiliation with the International Longshoremen's Association (ILA) in 1914

The International Longshoremen's Association (ILA) filled the vacuum created by isolated and disunited dockworker organizations around the turn of the twentieth century. The ILA had been preceded along the Atlantic Coast by a series of less formally organized groups known collectively as "benevolent societies." The PLSBS, organized in Portland in 1880, was a prime example of this type of society. In New York City the Alongshoremen's United Benefit Society, founded in 1853, and the Longshoremen's Union Protective Association, No. 2, incorporated in 1866, fit this pattern. In the 1880s many longshore societies also cooperated, to varying degrees, with the Knights of Labor (KOL), which had blossomed in the later years of that decade.[84]

As early as May 14, 1901, the PLSBS had received entreaties from the AFL to join with the ILA, its maritime affiliate. Between 1901 and 1913, Portland's local longshore society had resisted these overtures. Perhaps this resistance came from the fact that the Portland dockworkers felt a sense of isolation from the major Atlantic Coast ports to their south, or perhaps they never had experienced such a clear incentive for them to affiliate. The benevolent society concept had, for a time at least, seemingly satisfied most of their needs.

The PLSBS would need a stronger argument in favor of such an organizational change and the relinquishing of local autonomy that it would entail. A similar evolution was under way on the docks of Boston where a longshore "mutual aid society" eventually matured into an ILA-affiliated longshore union in 1913.[85] The ILA envisioned that such a federation would enroll longshoremen in all ports between Portland, Maine, and Galveston, Texas. Thus collective action could be employed and all these ports could strike, if necessary, in sympathy with any one of the ports that may have been in conflict with the shipping agents.[86]

A mere two months after losing the strike in Boston, its longshoremen had largely affiliated with the ILA by April 1912. By February 1913 they had essentially won the wage increase they had independently failed to gain during their recent strike. Under the leadership of ILA International president Terrence V. O'Connor, the Boston longshoremen ratified a new 1913 contract by which "the issues that had caused the strike of the previous year were finally resolved."[87] Gaining these wage increases was an immediate and tangible proof of the benefit of collective action. What had become apparent in Boston would not have been lost on their fellow longshoremen just one hundred miles Down East.

The Portland longshoremen must have marveled at the success of their Boston counterparts, and it was not long before they put into motion similar tactics concerning a coastwide federation of dock laborers. In November 1913, the ILA resumed its organizing effort in Portland at a time when the PLSBS, then in the midst of its difficult and ultimately unsuccessful strike for higher wages, appeared much more receptive to the international union's message.

The first of these communications was noted in the minutes of November 18, 1913, directly in the midst of their bitter strike. A call was made in the record book to stand firm on the new wage demands. The new environment of labor unrest and the perceived intransigence of the shipping companies clearly had an impact locally. On December 16, 1913, little more than one year after rejecting affiliation but only three weeks since losing their second strike in two years, the membership reversed itself:

> Moved and seconded—We should belong to the I.L.A.
> Moved and seconded—We tender Mr. O'Connor an invitation to come and address our meeting, he being President of the I.L.A.[88]

ILA president Terrence V. O'Connor spoke to the Portland union on January 8, 1914.[89] The proof that he made a convincing case came at the next regular meeting when the motion to affiliate passed its first reading.[90] The installation of the PLSBS into the ILA occurred at the meeting of February 10, 1914: "Brother William F. Dempsey then installed the officers of [the] P.L.S.B.S. into the I.L.A. and also pledged them to the faithful performance of their duty while in office. And afterwards installed all the members present and enlightened them on the great combined organization [to which] we now belonged. He also gave the current password 'Educate.'"[91]

William F. Dempsey of South Boston, the ILA Atlantic Coast District secretary, would become the key contact person for the PLSBS. His presence in Portland, especially during periods of labor turmoil alongshore, was noted with regularity in the union minutes throughout the next decade. Portland, in its affiliation with the ILA, was typical of other Atlantic Coast maritime ports. What had just occurred in Portland was similar to what had only recently transpired in other Atlantic ports such as New York where, "by 1914, when New York's various dockers' unions had almost all

INTERNATIONAL LONGSHOREMEN'S ASSOCIATION

ORGANIZED AUGUST 27, 1892
REG. U. S. PATENT OFFICE

Whereas, An Application in due form has been received, asking for a charter to be granted to *Longshoremen and Handling of Ship Liners* to be known as International Longshoremen's Association Local Union, No. **861** Located at *Portland, Maine*, and by authority of the Laws and usages of the INTERNATIONAL LONGSHOREMEN'S ASSOCIATION, we do grant this

CHARTER

TO SAID LOCAL UNION:

By Virtue of this Charter, Said Local Union is empowered to perform such acts and enjoy such benefits as are prescribed in the laws and usages of the INTERNATIONAL LONGSHOREMEN'S ASSOCIATION, and the members thereof are strictly enjoined to bear constantly in mind the cardinal principles of the Association.

The INTERNATIONAL LONGSHOREMEN'S ASSOCIATION reserves the right to suspend this Charter and annul the rights and benefits therein conferred, for any neglect or refusal to perform the duties required by the laws and usages of the INTERNATIONAL LONGSHOREMEN'S ASSOCIATION.

In Witness Whereof, We have subscribed our names and affixed the seal of the INTERNATIONAL LONGSHOREMEN'S ASSOCIATION.

this **2nd** day of **February** 19**14**

Thomas W. Gleason
International President

Harry R. Hasselgren
International Secretary-Treasurer

This Duplicate Charter issued June 14, 1978.

21. ILA Charter Local 861, Portland (February 2, 1914).

entered the I.L.A., that organization had twenty-one locals in the port." The minutes of the next meeting, February 17, 1914, began with the heading, "I.L.A. Local No. 861," the first time this description was officially used. On February 24 the society sent for an ILA flag.[92]

A local newspaper detailed the affiliation ceremony and the installation of officers, and, anecdotally by the surnames reported, the continuing Irish domination of the ILA at both the national and local level:

> An enthusiastic meeting of the Portland Longshoremen's Benevolent Society was held last evening at their hall on Fore Street. This society after many years of independent existence recently voted to affiliate with the International Longshoremen's Association and William F. Dempsey of Buffalo, N.Y., the secretary-treasurer and organizer of that organization, was present last evening to install the officers of the local branch.
>
> The officers installed were as follows:
>
> | | |
> |---|---|
> | President | Michael McDonough |
> | Vice President | Patrick Barrett |
> | Financial Secretary | Patrick O'Donnell |
> | Treasurer | Thomas Mulkern |
> | Chairman of Trustees | John Thornton |
> | Sergeant-at-arms | Coleman Lee |
>
> The international body of which the local organization has become a part numbers over 50,000 members and embraces both the Atlantic and Pacific coasts as well as the Great Lakes. The international convention will be held at Milwaukee in July and the district convention at Saint John, N.B., on the 25th of May. Secretary Dempsey reports the past year as having been the most prosperous in the history of the association, both as regards membership and in its financial results.[93]

The answer as to what Portland's longshoremen were seeking through affiliation with the ILA could be summarized in one word: security. The search for security by union members to control the docks of Portland was in evidence in the months that immediately followed affiliation. On the issue of nonunion workers, a resolution was passed on April 14, 1914, "that all bosses along the waterfront give the preference of work to Union members before non-Union men."[94]

Job security and union preference was also the case in the port of New York at this time. International steamship (deep-water) companies were willing to pay higher wages to experienced longshoremen in return for a faster turnaround time. "In return for spasms of intense toil, those men received a good 30 percent more per hour than longshoremen on coastal shipping. Of the forty-five thousand workers in New York harbor in 1914, only three thousand then belonged to the ILA and most of them worked the piers of European fleets."[95]

Again on May 19, 1914, this time specifically dealing with pulp wood, it was moved that "all Union men will get the preference of the work hereafter," and further that if union bosses and walking bosses, the equivalent of gang foremen, were not hired, "union men will be called out." Finally, on July 7, 1914, the coal concerns were directed "to give the first privilege to the Union men."[96] With each of these separate commodities, the concern for union workers was central. In the wake of a protracted and difficult strike, followed within two months by affiliation with the ILA, the PLSBS was feeling the need to reassert its prerogative with local business concerns, individually if necessary.

Similar activities were going on in most major Atlantic ports. The success of the ILA in these years assured the workers that the threats of steamship agents—employed by them at all previous work actions—to divert Portland-bound ships to other Atlantic ports would no longer be effective. At this very time, for example, the ILA was attempting to consolidate the port of New York where the Longshoremen's Union Protective Association (LUPA) locals had existed since 1866. This consolidation finally occurred in 1914 with LUPA locals joining with the ILA. New York achieved a portwide collective agreement two years later, in 1916. That contract provided not only wage increases but—arguably more importantly—it also provided preferential employment opportunities and thus more job security for ILA union members along the New York waterfront.[97]

On the docks of Philadelphia at what had once been the "chief commercial city of the country prior to 1830," a very different racial and social phenomenon was developing in these same years. There, at the meeting of the Schuylkill and Delaware rivers 120 miles from the Atlantic, a biracial workforce was emerging. In 1896 there were only 164 black longshoremen in Philadelphia. By 1910 this number had increased tenfold to comprise nearly half of all dock labor. Majority black status was achieved before World War I, and by 1920 blacks accounted for nearly 60 percent of the labor force. By contrast, in Massachusetts blacks made up only 4.6 percent of dock laborers in 1910 and still less than 10 percent by 1920; in New York blacks numbered 6 percent in 1910 and 15 percent by 1920.[98] Despite their notable presence on the Portland, Maine, waterfront in the early nineteenth century, before the arrival of significant numbers of Irish laborers, blacks were now all but totally eliminated as dock laborers since the mid- to late nineteenth century.

Despite continuous efforts by the ILA to organize the Philadelphia docks, the racial nature of its labor force trumped the ILA efforts there. Blacks were attracted to the Philadelphia waterfront despite the dangerous, strenuous, and poorly paid nature of the work. Probably because of these difficulties, blacks were in a position to dominate other groups in this low-skill, low-wage workforce, thus avoiding the overt discrimination then found in most other better-paid occupations.

The Industrial Workers of the World (IWW, or Wobblies) practiced more radical and racially inclusive policies. Their reputation of interracial unity and nondiscrimination, in contrast with the ILA's tradition of racially separate locals, gave them a distinct advantage in organizing the Philadelphia waterfront. Prime examples of the ILA's exclusivity would be found on the ILA-controlled New York docks that were perceived as largely being open to blacks only as strikebreakers, and the Boston and Portland waterfronts where "Irish dominated unions excluded blacks from entry to the trade."[99] In Philadelphia there were tangible proofs of the rewards for racial solidarity. These included a doubling of wages in just four years, a ten-hour day, and time and a half for overtime and double time for Sundays and holidays. In the post–World War I period, this Philadelphia union, IWW Local 8, became the second-largest Wobbly local in America. On the crucial question of ethnic and racial harmony, "It brought together black and white workers forging one of the strongest and most successful interracial alliances in the first quarter of the 20th century."[100]

Back in Portland, on April 7, 1914, the union membership discussed the upcoming ILA convention in Milwaukee scheduled for July, and at the meeting of May 5, 1914, James E. McGrath was elected as the local delegate. Part of the reason for sending a delegate to the annual ILA convention was to help to enhance union security and preference along Portland's waterfront as part of this powerful international union with affiliates along the Atlantic Coast, the Gulf Coast, the Great Lakes, and in Canada.

The ILA could trace its history back to its origin in Detroit in 1892 as the International Association of Lumber Handlers. By the early twentieth century, they were involved with a number of maritime-related jobs, thus creating friction with the International Seamen's Union, among others. By 1907, AFL president Samuel Gompers ordered them to limit their scope to "shoreside" labor and to reclaim their earlier name, ILA. The year 1914 was a banner year for the ILA, especially in the port of New York where they brought most of the competing dockers' unions and factions together under the banner of their union.[101]

It was clear to the majority of PLSBS members that the ILA would now give them significant leverage in their local struggles with the international shipping companies and their agents. Their instructions of June 30, 1914, to James E. McGrath were that "the delegate [should] have power to use all his influence while in Milwaukee to make this port Union all over." At the next meeting on July 7, the local voted thirty-three to one to support this resolution. One month after the Milwaukee convention, Local 861 had still heard no word on the fate of the resolutions offered by Brother McGrath. Regarding the issue of the closed shop, making Portland "Union all over," something eventually came of this proposal. The minutes of February 6, 1917, announced the position of port organizer that would be held by the current PLSBS president.[102]

Effectively, the PLSBS was now part of a much larger labor pool. Although many of their unique, particular issues regarding work rules and conditions could still be negotiated locally, "in practice, the master agreement between these parties [the ILA and the New York–based employers' association] became the standard contract for all ports from Portland, Maine, to Norfolk, Virginia, by action of the employers' associations and the ILA locals in those ports."[103]

Now within the protective fold of the ILA, the Portland longshoremen once again turned their attention to the enforcement of local work rules, especially the limited sling load. The type of technology available on the docks and the commodity being handled would clearly influence the potential weight of the sling load. As early as October 6, 1914, the union minutes revealed the type of technology then being used alongshore in Portland when it was reported that the society set a rate of fifty cents per hour "in regards wheeling coal, salt, sand, sulfur and clay or anything hoisted by quick steam."[104] Quick steam was the name given to the most modern form of hoisting large sling loads then employed on the Portland waterfront.

Local longshoremen well into the twentieth century still regarded the limited sling load as the litmus test of a strong, progressive longshore union. One retired longshoreman in a 1982 interview proudly maintained that Local 861 defended the limited sling load long after it was given up at other Atlantic Coast ports. The records seem to confirm his memory on this issue.[105] It was primarily a safety issue, but also one that regulated the pace or quality of the work to be performed.

The concern for safety increased with the doubling of work during the World War I boom. Accidents, always a hazard for longshore workers, would take a higher toll during such periods of speedup. Throughout American ports the dangerous working conditions and long hours, together with the greater sling loads and increased pace of work, led to an increase in maritime-related accidents. Nationally, it was reported that "first-aid facilities on the piers were usually limited to fruit crates to remove the dead or disabled, and hospital emergency staffs regarded their filthy patients with contempt."[106]

Just as the United States was about to enter the Great War, two serious accidents to longshoremen in Portland were reported within a three-day period. In the first case, James A. Norton was "badly hurt" when he caught his right arm in a steam winch at Grand Trunk Wharf #8. Three days later Michael Mahalia's right foot was "badly crushed" when a crate of ammunition shells weighing a half ton, which he was attempting to load from a truck to the ship, dropped onto him.[107]

Two retired longshoremen remember well the difficult and dangerous nature of the work on Portland's docks. Tom Mulkern noted that the fathers of two future Portland policemen, Joe Coyne and John Davis, lost their legs working longshore, and that longshoreman Pat Joyce was crushed against a ship. Mulkern remembered that specific doctors would work almost exclusively with these maritime laborers, Dr. Drummond in the earlier years of the twentieth century and Dr. Monkhouse in the later years. It was useful for the union to have the professional services of such doctors on call when needed. Phil O'Donnell recalled "quite a few deaths in my days." He reported one harrowing case in which Jack Connolly, a foreman on china clay, seeing the boom break, pushed his nephew out of the way only to lose his own life. O'Donnell, displaying his dry Irish wit, noted that he met his future wife, Thelma, a nurse in training, while visiting an injured longshoreman in the hospital. His take on this: "The Good Book says visit the sick and bury the dead. I went to visit the sick—that's how I met my wife."[108]

The first fourteen years of the twentieth century had been tough ones for the PLSBS. It had weathered many storms such as the dramatic decline in longshore jobs after the turn of the century and the loss of two major strikes in 1911 and 1913. While the PLSBS had not always come out on top, it had survived. Following its affiliation with the ILA in 1914, ILA Local 861 was about to enter into its greatest decade of growth in the context of the shipping boom during and shortly after World War I.

During these years membership would swell to 1,366 by 1919. This marked the historic highpoint of this union's membership in Portland. Historian Robert H. Babcock, however, contends that Portland was squandering its potential as a major Atlantic port. Thus, through political and commercial indifference and inactivity, Portland enabled much larger cities, such as Boston or Halifax, but also comparably sized cities, such as Saint John, New Brunswick, to emerge after the early 1920s with the lion's share of the region's maritime-related trade.

It seemed to be another ironic case of bad timing. Just as these economic facts seemed to dawn on Portland's business and political community, "the Maine State Pier opened too late to affect the outcome. [Public] and private capital in Saint John were coordinated and integrated; in Portland they were diffused and scattered."[109] Although future trouble would soon present itself, the best years for Portland's Irish longshoremen appeared to be within sight on the immediate horizon.

5

Apex of the Union and Catholic Hierarchical Influence

Members of the PLSBS in the late nineteenth and early twentieth century were primarily first- or second-generation Irish, many tracing their ancestry to County Galway, located on Ireland's western Atlantic coast.[1] There were bound to be strong ties between these laborers and the Roman Catholic Diocese of Portland. This chapter will look at this ethnic union through the lens of the Catholic episcopal influence of three bishops in these years: James Augustine Healy, William Henry O'Connell, and Louis Sebastian Walsh, who served during the maritime strike of 1921.

The Catholic Church, of course, would wish for the financial success of its members, but not at the price of radicalism or secularism. While many of the clergy largely ignored the issues of labor altogether, some of even the more liberal of the Catholic hierarchy, such as James Cardinal Gibbons, benignly urged their flocks to "foster habits of economy and self-denial [and shun] the slightest invasion of the rights and autonomy of employers."[2]

Despite this seemingly proemployer position, Cardinal Gibbons and others within the liberal "Americanist" wing of the Catholic episcopal hierarchy would constantly worry about any possible estrangement between Catholic workers in America and their Church, as had occurred in Europe. Gibbons, as bishop and later cardinal of Baltimore (1877–1921), would later become strongly identified with the policy of assimilation sometimes referred to as "Americanization." This policy would lead to strains within the Maine Catholic Church, especially between its largely Irish hierarchy and its significant and rapidly growing French-speaking congregations.[3] Gibbons and others wished to avoid ethnic divisions and prevent the rift between labor and the Church that had become all too common in Europe. He would eventually argue successfully to Pope Leo XIII that "the working class would be lost to the Church if the Pope did not take a strong moral stand in defense of them."[4]

During the last quarter of the nineteenth century, however, the bishop of the Portland Diocese seemed to be headed in quite another direction regarding the rights of labor to organize, at least in what he claimed as "his" state. The second bishop of the diocese of Portland would remain, on labor and other questions within the last quarter of the nineteenth century, firmly within the more conservative and traditionalist "ultramontane" wing of the Catholic hierarchy in America. This wing looked directly to the Vatican for guidance on labor and other vexing questions.

Bishop James A. Healy and Opposition to the Knights of Labor (KOL) 1875–1900

James Augustine Healy remains one of the more interesting and compelling characters in Portland's rich social history. Born in Georgia on April 6, 1830, he was the son of an Irish father, Michael Morris Healy, and a black slave mother, Eliza Clark Healy. His father claimed his roots to be somewhere in the vicinity of the central Irish town of Athlone. James was the eldest of ten children born to these parents who married in the direst of conditions for any interracial couple in the Deep South in that era. They decided to send their children north for education, and for safety. The family as a whole is remarkable. One brother, Patrick, became an early president of Georgetown University. Another, Michael, became a pioneering Coast Guard captain in Alaska, serving much of his time above the Arctic Circle.[5]

James A. Healy, like many of his siblings, would be educated at the College of the Holy Cross in Worcester, Massachusetts. Located forty miles west of Boston, Holy Cross provided a quiet and secure place from which the Society of Jesus (Jesuits) could train the sons of Irish and other immigrant families into the priesthood, or in other religious or secular fields. He moved up rapidly in the priesthood and, like most of his siblings, successfully "passed for white" during the greater part of his life. By the relatively young age of forty-five, James A. Healy became America's first African American Bishop, and his diocese would be that of Portland, Maine.

Healy's episcopal influence in the area of labor relations in Portland became historically significant. Just one year into his tenure, the new bishop of Portland, in a pastoral letter dated 1876, referred to secret societies and warned, "the ordinary subterfuge that the members are allowed to tell their confessor is only a subterfuge making more plain the character of the society." By 1885 Bishop Healy had condemned the Portland local of the Brotherhood of Locomotive Engineers, which had been founded in 1865 and reorganized around 1871, on the grounds of secrecy. On the same grounds, he had earlier condemned the Ancient Order of Hibernians, the Odd Fellows, and even the Grand Army of the Republic, a seemingly harmless Civil War veterans' organization. Healy at least appeared to be consistent in issuing these condemnations.[6]

During the spring of 1885, there was a fascinating confrontation between Bishop Healy and Terence V. Powderly, the Irish-Catholic leader of the Knights of Labor (KOL), America's premier labor organization before the emergence of the American Federation of Labor (AFL) in the 1890s. Bishop Healy has been referred to as "the foremost episcopal opponent of the Order [KOL] in the United States." A biographer stated that "secret societies became Bishop Healy's *bête noire*. He believed they were the termites of the social order. He saw in them the most sinister enemy of the Church both in Europe and America."[7]

In his memoirs, Powderly recalled that the bishop summoned him while on a speaking tour in Maine, most likely in May 1885. After forcing Powderly to wait for nearly two hours, the bishop allegedly began their meeting by asking the leader of the Knights if he were a Catholic. Upon receiving a reply in the affirmative, Healy asked, "Then what right have you to speak in my state without my permission?" Powderly strongly defended his right to speak with or without the bishop's permission and later recalled his own heated reply to Healy: "I speak only on the labor question, I do not meddle with religion, I do not interfere with the faith or morals of any man, I am a freeborn American, and do not acknowledge your right, or the right of any man no matter what his religion or position in society may be, to question me for doing that which I have a right to do under the laws of my country."[8]

The stated concern of many conservative members of the Catholic hierarchy in this period seemed to focus on the rights and interests of the employers, as a class, as the providers of employment. This focus seemed only to increase with the growing prosperity of individual Church members and, by extension, of the Church itself. There were, to be sure, unmistakable countervailing influences for many of these Irish working-class immigrants with trade unions and, politically, with the Democratic Party. Even conservative members of the clergy and Catholic hierarchy, however, could see in these connections potentially useful tools. The leadership of the emerging AFL contained many Irish and German Catholics who might have many "cultural values to which clerical leaders could effectively appeal against the rising tide of socialism."[9]

The rancorous meeting and continued hostility between Healy and Powderly—both Irish and each representing a crucial aspect of the Irish American community in America, the Church, and organized labor—were instructive concerning the conflicting loyalties of this group in the late nineteenth century. Perhaps Healy disliked Powderly's title, "Grand Master Workman," and as some have suggested it may have sounded too Masonic or too pompous. Perhaps it was simply true, as is often written, that Healy believed that the ritual of the Knights "contained an oath of secrecy and obedience which made the society forbidden to Catholics."[10] It is clear that this rift was never mended, however, and in his memoirs Powderly probably had Bishop Healy in mind when he scornfully wrote: "Some of the best men I ever knew were Catholic priests [but] some of the most vindictive, revengeful, arrogant, and intolerant men I ever met were [also] Catholic priests and bishops."[11]

It is fascinating to conjecture as to why Bishop Healy chose to play such a prominent role in opposition to the Knights of Labor in America in the late nineteenth century. Indeed, "the non-industrial character of his diocese would not seem to have warranted such concern."[12] One possible explanation would be his perceived need to protect his minority Catholic flock in an overwhelmingly Protestant city, state, and country. Healy argued, for example, against the Americanist position on public versus parochial education, and in the early 1890s he complained that he had "lost nearly a fifth of the students in his cathedral's school because of this Americanist 'confusion.'"[13]

Previously, the bishop ruled that if any Catholic parent were to remove their child from a parochial school, "that father or mother is excluded from the sacraments." In this same decree in March 1883, addressed to the Sisters of Mercy in Portland, and specifically mentioning Saint Dominic's Church, Healy added unequivocally that "no child is to receive corporal punishment from one of the Sisters."[14]

Eventually, the papal encyclical *Rerum novarum* (*Of New Things*) in 1891 apparently gave unambiguous guidance on the labor question, much more supportive of Cardinal Gibbons' earlier stated prolabor position but contrary to Healy's strongly held views. Bishop Healy, who had always desired the condemnation of the Knights and other "secret societies," reportedly "dutifully accepted the Vatican's resolution of the issue once it came."[15] An earlier biographer, Albert S. Foley, agreed that Healy automatically withdrew his objections once the matter was made clear from the Vatican, and added that Healy "wrote to Rome to explain that his opposition to [the KOL] was on the basis of their condemned secrecy of oath and ritual, not their constructive efforts to better the condition of the workingman."[16]

In his major study of the Catholic Church in Maine, William Leo Lucey seemed to concur with Foley's sentiment, published only three years before his own work and perhaps dependent on it in this regard. Lucey added, in an editorial fashion, "Fortunately the saner view of Cardinal Gibbons prevailed." He further reported that Healy's strong positions on the question of labor were unusual given his lack of experience in this field. Lucey also largely accepted Bishop Healy's disclaimers, after the fact, that his motivation "appears to have been dictated more by his over-cautious attitudes toward secret societies . . . than any lack of sympathy for the struggling workers."[17]

Near the turn of the twentieth century, in 1899, and in the last full year of Bishop Healy's tenure, the leadership of the American labor movement protested against new immigrants entering the United States. In one case, at least, specifically named were Finns, Slavs, and Sicilians, so-called brothers to the ox, who were seen as being brought to America by employers to undercut workers' wages. In racially charged terms that would be repeated well into the twentieth century, labor leaders contended that because business interests were "not content with the negro, we call these hordes into our beloved land to hinder the growth of democratic and social justice."[18]

A local maritime example of these xenophobic pressures could be seen in a newspaper article from late 1897 that reported on a strike ending at the Maine Steamship Company freight sheds on the Portland waterfront. "All the old hands were back at work and they were hustling in great shape in their endeavors to straighten out the general chaos left by the Italians." This specific ethnic reference to Italian strikebreakers was revealing, as was the demand that they be discharged before the regulars returned to work. The union would "take action [against] our own men who did not stick to us." This article optimistically concluded, "the Italians mixed everything up and we are now trying to straighten matters out. There will be no trouble after this and all the steamers will get away on time."[19] Tensions between the largely Irish Portland Longshoremen's Benevolent Society and the significant and growing Italian community in Portland, as was analyzed in the previous chapter, would only increase in the first quarter of the twentieth century.

Ethnic divisiveness was rampant both in the labor movement and in the Church at the start of the twentieth century. In each case, the disunity damaged these institutions and hurt their missions, especially considering the rapidly expanding immigrant population in America by the turn of the twentieth century that greatly reshaped both labor and the Church. It was in the field of labor where these two highly influential bodies intersected.

Any conclusions concerning Bishop Healy's motivation for his stance on the Knights of Labor specifically, and on labor unions in general, should keep in mind his consistent association with the conservative wing of the Catholic hierarchy. James M. O'Toole, after extensive research into Healy's archives, including diaries, letters, and decrees, unambiguously yet simply stated his opinion that "Healy's conservatism on issues was rooted in a deeply conservative personality."[20]

The Portland longshoremen, largely Irish and Catholic, had founded their society in 1880, just five years into Bishop Healy's tenure, and it grew enormously in the final twenty years that he served as Bishop. The records of the PLSBS demonstrate only a minimal contact between themselves and the Knights of Labor, although they were contemporary labor organizations in Maine in the 1880s. The first recorded correspondence between the KOL and the PLSBS occurred in 1883. On November 11, 1884, longshore records dismissively reported that the "document received from [the] Knights of Labor be not entertained."[21]

There is also no apparent evidence to suggest any conflict between the PLSBS and any ecclesiastical authorities in these years leading up to the twentieth century. On the contrary, Catholic hierarchical influence with the PLSBS would only increase during the first quarter of the new century under Bishop Healy's two successors, William H. O'Connell and, especially, Louis S. Walsh.

Bishop James A. Healy was America's first black Roman Catholic bishop, but his black ancestry was largely unmentioned, especially by the bishop himself, during his tenure in Portland. Healy shepherded a Catholic flock in the Portland Diocese that had originally been largely Irish, especially in the cathedral city of Portland itself, but was becoming more ethnically diverse. This change in ethnic composition was specifically caused partially by the arrival of Italians and other eastern and southern Europeans into

Portland. More numerically significant, however, was the steady influx of French-Canadian workers and their families in many of Maine's and New England's burgeoning factory towns by the year of Healy's death in 1900. Healy's immediate successor would be compelled to deal with an increasingly heterogeneous Catholic Church and a growing labor movement in Maine in the early years of the twentieth century.

Bishop William Henry O'Connell's "Dry Run" for Cardinal (1901–1906)

The death of Bishop James Augustine Healy in 1900 brought William O'Connell of Lowell, Massachusetts, to Portland as the third bishop of the diocese. A recent biography referred to O'Connell's brief stay in Portland (1901–6) as a "dry run" for his imminent selection as archbishop, and later cardinal, of Boston.

O'Connell, from the turn of the century through his death in the middle of World War II, would continue to play a critical role as a leader of the more conservative "ultramontane" wing of the Roman Catholic hierarchy that was then led by New York archbishop Michael Corrigan. This tendency, as discussed earlier, was opposed by the more liberal "Americanist" wing led by Cardinal Gibbons of Baltimore and Archbishop John Ireland of Saint Paul. A swing back to this conservative tendency by Pope Leo XIII less than a decade after *Rerum novarum* had already been noted with pleasure by Bishop Healy in 1899, the year before his death, as representing a "very necessary" rejection of liberalism in church affairs.[22]

There were many predictive signs of the nature of this future powerful ecclesiastical figure during Bishop O'Connell's brief tenure in Portland. A friend had earlier warned him that Portland was "a very bleak and cold place with an equally cold and placid population and I fear that you will notice this all the more after your sojourn in Rome."[23] O'Connell's loyalty to Rome and to the papacy (ultramontanism) would be his hallmark as bishop, archbishop, and cardinal. Like his predecessor, James A. Healy, O'Connell continued to exclude from the sacraments parents of Catholic children who did not send their children to parochial schools where these were available.[24]

In an overt way, Bishop O'Connell sought to increase the status of Maine's Catholic population by increasing his own public status. He was determined to take "whatever opportunity comes naturally in my way to mingle among the professional and influential men here."[25] A fascinating example of this cordiality is recorded in the memoirs of Portland's mayor, James Phinney Baxter, on December 26, 1903. Baxter's diary reveals at least one of the cultural differences between Yankees and the Irish, even among the higher classes of each. After Mayor Baxter attended a Christmas dinner at the Bishop's residence, he recollected: "a most elaborate affair and elegantly served. The bishop had four kinds of wine and afterwards coffee and brandy. I ate very little and declined the wines.... I do not approve of so much luxury and especially of intoxicating beverages in a bishop's house. As Dr. Gerrish remarked to me it is hardly in keeping with a representative of the lowly Nazarene. It seems all too strongly of the World, the Flesh, and the Devil."[26]

When President Theodore Roosevelt visited Portland in August of 1902, he specifically asked to meet with O'Connell. They had a private meeting at the home of the recently retired "czar" of the House of Representatives, Portland's own Speaker Thomas Brackett Reed.[27] O'Connell's "association with high society and the political figures of the city and state was carefully considered." It was suggested by William Leo Lucey that Bishop O'Connell would not have been unaware of the Republican strategy of attempting to court Catholic voters away from their Democratic base. Lucey added, however, that "it was indeed something new to see the Catholic bishop, a son of an Irish immigrant, courted by the social leaders of the state. He was quite at home in their parlors and club rooms."[28]

Bishop O'Connell's views on labor were in part shaped by his place of birth, Lowell, Massachusetts, in the industrial Merrimack Valley. "Placing a high value on discipline and order, he was nonetheless close enough to his own roots among the workers that he could not simply dismiss their demands." His fear of secular radicalism, however, could be seen in his later assessment of labor strife in neighboring Lawrence around 1920. In that year O'Connell told an apostolic delegate that Lawrence was "a city of constant strikes and great disorders." He added that although most of the strikers were originally Catholics, "many of them are socialists and members of I.W.W. [Industrial Workers of the World]." For that reason, according to the bishop, the parishes in that area were among "the most difficult in this part of the country."[29]

A clerical appointee sent to study the unrest in Lawrence in 1919 reported that the labor protesters were "illiterate and of an excitable character, easily swayed by their leaders.... [The] leaders among the Italians are bad men, anti-clericals of the worst type [and] irresponsible I.W.W. *Bolsheviki* parasites." In 1921, as cardinal of Boston, O'Connell would issue a pastoral letter, "Religious Ideals in Industrial Relations," in which he characterized the Church's attempt to "avoid extremists and disturbers" and chart a middle course. "To-day [the Church] condemns the cruel arrogance of wealth and power; to-morrow, with voice no less authoritative, she condemns mob law and mob violence."[30]

Back in Portland years earlier, O'Connell's concern for the laboring classes was expressed in more muted but tangible terms. "Nor did he forget the workingmen and the dock laborers in Portland. The Working Men's Club built at great expense gave them one of the finest social clubs in the state."[31] The Workingmen's Club, the structure of which still exists at 17–19 Commercial Street overlooking the east end of the harbor, was completed in 1904 at an estimated cost of twenty thousand dollars. This money was raised throughout the city by Bishop O'Connell for the stated purpose of providing the "men of muscle, brawn, and industry" with an alcohol-free place to rest and recreate during breaks from shifts on the railroads or the docks.[32] The elevation of O'Connell to bishop and later cardinal of Boston paved the way for the episcopacy of Louis S. Walsh.

Hierarchical Intervention: Bishop Louis Sebastian Walsh (1906–1924)

The role of the Catholic hierarchy in America was often both antiradical and antiunion during the Red Scare that followed World War I. Locally, Bishop Louis S. Walsh, in particular, would prove to be of great significance to Portland's maritime laborers, especially during a highly contentious strike in 1921. Bishop Walsh would eventually become one of the harshest critics of his predecessor, Cardinal O'Connell, within the Catholic hierarchy. This was especially true because of a significant scandal involving the cardinal and his nephew and dealing with the two most combustible elements of any scandal, sex and money.[33]

Walsh would serve as Portland's fourth bishop from 1906 to 1924, nearly eighteen years. These were, of course, critical years for the labor movement nationally with lengthy and bitter strikes inevitably following the business slowdown in the aftermath of the boom years of World War I. While differing with O'Connell on issues of personal morality and responsibility, Bishop Walsh apparently fell in line with the trend in the Catholic hierarchy in the early twentieth century that identified traditional unions as a proper tool for lifting the laborer from poverty without imperiling the workers' souls through the dangers of secular socialism. The Catholic hierarchy would work diligently to provide the trade union movement with "a more coherent anti-Socialist ideology." Both at the parish level and within lay organizations, the Catholic worker in these years often heard "resounding denunciations of socialism."[34]

In 1909 a labor-activist priest from Ohio attended an AFL convention in Toronto for the purpose of enrolling the "class-conscious children of our Holy Mother Church" in the labor movement, which he believed to be the "classic battleground of socialism in this country."[35] The early twentieth century was a period of nearly constant agitation on the question of the relationship between labor, socialism, and religion. In Ireland, for example, the greatest labor leader of this period, James Connolly, was often engaged in debates over this very question both in Belfast and in Dublin.[36] In Maine the issue of anti-Catholicism was engaged in the pages of *The Issue*, published by the Socialist Party in Portland. A controversial sectarian book advertisement appeared there in 1913: "POPE or CHRIST—We defy any Priest or Catholic to disprove the facts given in this book, in which we prove the Roman Catholic Church to be Un-Christian. Every page an eye-opener."[37] Two weeks later another equally provocative excerpt appeared in the same source in response to the question of the relationship between Catholicism and socialism: "Roman.—No, a Catholic cannot be a Socialist, according to high officials of the Catholic Church. We know several who claim to be both Catholic and Socialist, but who would believe evidence as weak as that against Cardinals and Popes? In regard to your second question, 'Can a Catholic be a Christian,' we recommend that you apply to Ringling Bros., circus managers. If there is one who is both Catholic and Christian, they probably have him on exhibition."[38]

In 1915 Bishop Walsh opposed a Maine legislative bill to create a recreational board in Portland. The Catholic hierarchy in this period was often quite suspicious of state-run programs, innocuous by modern standards, that interfered with what they identified as the realm of the individual, family, or Church. Walsh referred to the bill as "an Incubator of Socialism."[39] It appears that his opposition came from his concern over the unfettered growth of state power and its threat to the sanctity and autonomy of the patriarchal family. Although Walsh did support several significant pieces of social legislation in Maine between 1909 and 1915, "Walsh was for the old order of life and was 'always found in the ranks of those who are ever fearful' of proposed political changes."[40]

Two years earlier, on October 12, 1913, Bishop Walsh had appeared at a civic celebration at the Portland municipal auditorium where, in the company of Mayor Oakley C. Curtis and Gov. W. T. Haines, he spoke of the role of the Church in modern society as "the great conservative force around which the friends of law and order may always rally and count upon her constant assistance whenever in danger from social and moral upheavals."[41]

By 1920 union membership was at its peak in the United States. In Portland the PLSBS membership had reached its all-time apex of 1,366 members in 1919, immediately following the end of the war. Members still referred to their union as the PLSBS although it was officially now also the ILA Local 861. In the years from 1917 to 1920 union membership in the United States had doubled, and stood at 5 million in 1920. It should be remembered that this was also the period of a devastating nationwide influenza epidemic, the influence of which was strongly felt in Maine.[42]

World War I had served to bring many new laborers into the workforce, but the war had also changed the nature of American trade unionism, essentially increasing the alienation between labor moderates and militants. "The second decade of the twentieth century was the decisive period in the battle for the 8-hour day, which American workers had been waging since the 1860s." In 1910 only 8 percent of Americans worked forty-eight hours or less per week, while by 1919 the number was at 48.6 percent. This movement had started before 1917 at which point it was accelerated by the National War Labor Board's "basic 8-hour day." This period during which the concept of the eight-hour day and collective bargaining became entrenched in union thinking also represented the victory of the AFL and Samuel Gompers' moderate brand of "pure and simple unionism."[43]

This was certainly representative of Portland's longshoremen as well, who, since 1914, had come under the moderating influence and collective security of the ILA. As the war came to an end late in 1918, the Portland longshoremen were faced with several significant challenges. The economically pacifying effect of the war, with its attendant increase in union membership, volume of work, job security, and patriotism, was now over. What would replace it?

Nationally, these years immediately following World War I marked a period of change and confusion for labor. Organized labor desired to cement its gains made during the war years, such as the eight-hour day and other perceived positive collective bargaining provisions of the National

War Labor Board. Management was also anxious to reassert its rights. The postwar era commenced with a bitter steel strike in Pittsburgh in 1919. A brief recession that began in 1920 tended to depress both wages and jobs just as returning war veterans were searching for civilian employment and a return to "normalcy."

Nationally, organized labor declined throughout the decade of the 1920s from a high of more than 5 million members in 1920 to less than 3.5 million by 1929. Simultaneously, the number of organized workers as a percentage of all nonagricultural employees was nearly halved in this decade, dropping from 19.4 percent in 1920 to only 10.2 percent in 1930.[44]

In Maine, as in the nation as a whole, employers attempted to undermine the gains that labor had made during the war years by ideologically linking these gains with Bolshevism, therefore opposing labor's gains and demands on "patriotic" grounds. Gov. Carl Milliken in an address to the Maine legislature in 1919 implied that the end of the war had not solved all problems. Milliken warned that "the crisis has by no means passed with the overthrow of military despotism. The menace of mob rule and Bolshevism still threatens."[45] In this environment of conflict, labor strikes inevitably increased in the early years of the 1920s.

Bishop Walsh and the Longshore Strike of 1921

Longshore contracts were being renegotiated all along the Atlantic Coast with major concessions demanded in both wages and working conditions. Between May and June 1921, strikes involving more than 125,000 sailors and longshoremen on the Atlantic, Pacific, and Gulf coasts briefly shut down most American ports before succumbing to significant pressure by shipping agents and the U.S. Shipping Board, acting in concert. Scab labor was used extensively to break the strikes, and many significant work rules were lost in this period.[46]

Late in the year 1921, the PLSBS, closely following this national pattern, struck for higher wages. This represented the first strike since the local's ILA affiliation in 1914, and it occurred at a time when work was still plentiful along Portland's docks.

In 1921 Terrence V. O'Connor ended his term as ILA president. Two of the leading figures in the international union, both of whom were destined to become future International presidents after O'Connor, Anthony J. Chlopek and Joseph P. Ryan, were each mentioned in the union minutes of 1921. The ILA has had only eight International presidents since its formation in 1892: Daniel J. Keefe (1892–1909); Terrence V. O'Connor (1909–21); Anthony J. Chlopek (1921–27); Joseph P. Ryan (1927–53); William V. Bradley (1953–63); Thomas W. Gleason (1963–87); John Bowers (1987–2007); and Richard P. Hughes Jr. (2007–present).[47]

Joseph Ryan was first mentioned in the union records in April of 1921: "Moved and seconded the Secretary communicate with Brother President Ryan and tell him this local will back him up in his new propositions in regards holding as a body." Later that year the current and future ILA leaders were mentioned together when on December 23, 1921, Local 861's committee on working conditions was directed to send telegrams to ILA presidents Chlopek of Buffalo and Ryan of New York.[48]

Although wages at first appeared to be the major point of contention between management and the longshoremen, it soon became apparent that local work rules and conditions were equally at risk. The sling load fell primarily under local jurisdiction, as an issue of local work rules rather than under the control of the international union. An interesting twist, therefore, was recorded at the meeting of March 3, 1921, when financial secretary John Caselden reported a telephone conversation with ILA president O'Connor, who suggested that the local put more railroad ties into each sling load.

The clear suggestion here was that by 1921 the Portland longshoremen were out of step with other ILA locals. Caselden visited a Captain Sproul who considered nine ties weighing one thousand pounds "to be a fair load."[49] This was but an opening skirmish in what would prove to be a long and bitterly fought battle. The issue of limiting the size and weight of the sling load was a classic contest between labor and capital. The former was primarily concerned with its own safety and controlling the pace of its work, and the latter was primarily concerned with worker efficiency, that is, the productivity of each worker per hour and, ultimately, profits. The resolution of this issue was inconsistent over the years with each side constantly pushing the merits of its position. In the final analysis, the issue would be largely resolved by the constantly changing maritime technology, the parameters of which neither side could ever exactly predict.

In October of 1921, Portland's longshoremen followed the lead of other ILA Atlantic Coast locals in accepting significant reductions in wages for handling general cargo. Regular wages dropped from their wartime high of 90 cents to 65 cents per hour, and overtime fell from $1.20 to $1.00. At a special meeting held on December 1, 1921, the members were told that the companies that specifically shipped grain were determined not to pay more than 85 cents ($1.30 overtime) for labor per hour during that shipping season. The prevailing wage for handling grain in Portland was $1.00 ($1.50 overtime).[50]

The membership at this meeting was called upon to decide between holding fast to the earlier rate or going to arbitration. By a vote of 157 to 75, they decided to stand firm.[51] The low count, considering a total membership of more than 1,000, could be partially explained by the overtime labor that was prevalent in these busy years. Many of the members could have been working at the time that this special meeting was called, coming as it did in the middle of December, the busy season for shipping grain from Portland. However, this followed a pattern of rather low turnouts at union meetings, which suggests a history of inadequate participation by the union's general membership.

William Dempsey, the ILA Atlantic Coast district secretary, was at the next special meeting the following day at the request of the local steamship officials. The local press headlined this issue as "Local Steamship Business Hangs in Balance," and characterized it as a question of "whether the port of Portland is to have the busy season promised, or the Grand Trunk docks are to remain idle." The shipping agents claimed that the "wages offered here are the maximum wages paid for like work anywhere on the Atlantic coast."[52]

Management's rationale for cutting longshore wages and curtailing local work rules specific to Portland at this time was simple. They argued that due to the major concessions won by shipping agents in most other American ports earlier that year, a parallel cut in Portland was necessary to maintain their competitiveness.

William Dempsey spoke of "the trouble this Local was up against." He mentioned grain handling techniques in other ports, and "concluded by saying to the members of this Local to use good judgment."[53] Pressure placed on Local 861 included the threat by an agent of the White Star–Dominion Line to send Canadian grain by rail to Halifax for shipment aboard their steamship the *Megantic* instead of via the Grand Trunk to Portland. This threat would soon become a reality as Canadian policy after the war increasingly involved the development of Canadian ports for the shipping of Canadian goods. This policy would shortly result in major capital investments largely in Saint John, New Brunswick, and Halifax, Nova Scotia.[54] It had probably not occurred earlier because of cost, the ease of an already existing and shorter rail route to Portland, and Portland's ice-free status throughout most winters.

In another thinly veiled threat, the White Star–Dominion Line agent further stated that while no more steamships of his line would be sent to Portland, "no attempt would be made at present to have the work performed by strike breakers." This disclaimer sounded even more unconvincing, especially "at present," in the context of the widely reported use of strike breakers in many other ports between May and June of that same year.[55]

The counsel of the ILA would often be moderate. "[ILA] union leaders like [first ILA president Daniel J.] Keefe not only opposed sympathetic strikes but also advocated arbitration of all disputes."[56] If by using "good judgment" Dempsey meant accepting the agents' offer of eighty-five cents per hour, Local 861 showed good judgment by a vote of 400 to 191, which also signified a very good turnout at the meeting. Once again the ILA, both at the international and the district level, had demonstrated its influence over the PLSBS. Brother William Dempsey continued in this episode to demonstrate an extremely close working relationship and a very high level of acceptance by the society.[57]

Nevertheless, this concession on the part of the PLSBS was not sufficient to bring the steamship companies into accord with the union. At a special meeting held on December 18, 1921, it appeared that union work rules and the length of the contract were now the major sticking points, not simply wages. At this meeting the membership voted to stand firm on their demands this time. At the next regular meeting on December 20, 1921, the labor committee was empowered to sign the old agreement, but an amendment was made threatening the complete withholding of work unless this agreement was signed.

The steamship officials were so notified and gear was removed from the docks. It appeared as though a strike was inevitable, and indeed the PLSBS voted to strike as of December 21, 1921. A citizen's committee was formed, led by the newly elected Republican mayor-elect Carroll S. Chaplin. The problem, clearly stated, was that "while the question of wages was settled several weeks ago, the matter of working conditions was left over for latter consideration." A longshore official stated that "the steamer people were trying to change working conditions which have existed here for a long term of years." One specific point of contention mentioned was the shorter duration of the contract, as proposed by the shipping agents, six months as opposed to one year. The Grand Trunk was reportedly ready to ship grain out of New London, Connecticut.[58]

After some initial resistance, a committee on working conditions was given permission on December 23, 1921 to meet with the local citizens' committee and the current mayor, Charles B. Clarke, "to try and straighten out the troubles on the waterfront." Meanwhile it was reported that ten steamships had been diverted from Portland and that two partially laden vessels had sailed. Local newspapers reported that "already a large economic loss has resulted from the longshoremen's actions." The subcommittee of the citizen's committee appointed to meet directly with the longshoremen included Mayor-elect Carroll S. Chaplin; Henry F. Merrill, chairman of the State Pier commission; ex-mayor Charles B. Clarke; local Irish building magnate John J. Cunningham; and the Rt. Rev. Louis S. Walsh, Bishop of Portland.[59]

The Portland longshoremen voted to keep the union hall open "until this trouble is over." Telegrams were sent to ILA president Anthony Chlopek of Buffalo and to Joseph Ryan of New York, who together would direct the association for the next thirty years: Chlopek, 1921–27, and Ryan, 1927–53.[60]

Relations had apparently soured between the PLSBS and the local chamber of commerce by this time, which caused concern about the impartiality of the citizens' committee. At this meeting, the citizens' committee stated that they had no connections whatsoever with the chamber of commerce. This disclaimer was seen as necessary in light of the views of longshore business agent John Caselden, who "expressed at the outset a great deal of bitterness for the local Chamber of Commerce and declared that he would not meet the citizen's subcommittee in discussion unless assured that they had no connection with the Chamber of Commerce."[61]

Newspaper accounts reported some of the remaining sticking points when it listed previously unmentioned specific local work rules, such as meal hours, the shifting of gangs from one hatch to another, the length of the contract, and that the sling load was "to be left to [the] discretion of the steamship officials and stevedores." Steamship officials, apparently unaware of potentially undercutting their own fiscal arguments, optimistically cited 1918–19 as "a normal season" and stated that businesses and laborers in Portland would stand to lose Grand Trunk expenditures locally of more than $3 million for supplies and $875,000 in wages.[62]

There was no attempt to pretend that the Grand Trunk operation in Portland had been anything but profitable, but now, in this postwar economy, management was concerned about their future ability to successfully compete for exports within a diminished maritime market. There had been a dramatic decline of one-half in the volume of grain shipped out of Portland between 1919 (more than 1 million tons) and 1920 (slightly more than five hundred thousand tons). The amount of grain shipped from Portland would level off at the five-hundred-thousand-ton figure until 1923, after which it would decline steadily until it nearly disappeared altogether by 1934.[63]

One longshore leader, James McGrath, referred to the "selfish stevedores." He conveniently ignored the strikes of 1911 and 1913 to make a point when he stated that "the forty-one years for which the longshoremen had got along without a strike were some evidence that they were fair in their contentions."[64] Members of the subcommittee addressed the longshoremen directly.

Henry Merrill, chairman of the State Pier Commission, praised them for their efficient work alongshore but threatened an end to the Maine State Pier building project unless the strike was soon settled. Bishop Walsh warned that some sacrifice was necessary to ensure permanent prosperity, and that they must consider their families and the future. Mayor Chaplin cautioned that something must be done to prevent Portland from becoming a "fishing hamlet."[65] The society praised the citizen's subcommittee and then adjourned until after Christmas.

When the society reconvened at a special meeting on December 26, 1921, it was clear that one prominent Portland citizen had intervened to break the deadlock in the strike and attempt to make progress for Mayor Clarke and his citizens' committee. At this meeting the recommendations of the citizens' committee on working conditions were accepted, and two members were sent to Boston to see if the two boats that left Portland were being unloaded there. On that morning the members of Local 861 were addressed by one of the citizen's committee members, Bishop Louis S. Walsh. The union records reported: "[Walsh] addressed the members as a citizen of Portland. He said [that] we should try and have the good will of the public, and we ought to pull together and realize that we have an obligation to undertake by helping our homes and families, and [should] try [to] keep away from strikes."[66] The newspaper reiterated this essentially conservative plea by these workers' episcopal leader when it further reported that Bishop Walsh "urged the men to give heed to the duties which they owe their families, as well as the city where they gain their livelihood."[67]

The union membership was still largely Irish in these years and overwhelmingly Catholic.[68] By the 1920s, "greenhorns," those first-generation immigrants who were directly from Ireland, were slowly being replaced by "narrow backs," second- and later-generation Irish American laborers. There was no evidence that the PLSBS would follow Bishop Walsh, or indeed any church leader, unquestioningly on issues of labor and work rules in Portland, or specifically on the question of what appeared to be a damaging strike continuing from December 21 to the end of the year 1921. Rather, it seems the longshoremen realistically accepted the inevitability of having to make certain concessions—in addition to those already made regarding wages—to their employers, the shipping companies, and their agents. This was apparent given the national business climate and particularly the major concessions recently made by longshoremen in most other American ports.

Bishop Walsh had carefully followed the labor unrest on the Portland waterfront, and before the strike commenced, he wrote in his diary on December 3, 1921, "Longshoremen, on a referendum, voted to go to work on scale of wages offered." Then, eighteen days later, reversing the initial optimism, on December 21, 1921, Walsh wrote in his diary: "Sudden strike and lockout of Longshoremen on question of rules and regulations—was invited to conference with Mayor, which was postponed to tomorrow Sent for Brown and Green, both said it was very serious and threatening."[69]

Brown and Green probably represented two longshoremen who had the confidence of the bishop. For the next week, Walsh's diary was concerned mainly with the strike and his role in helping to settle this impasse. On December 23 he referred to a meeting of the citizen's committee as "long—arduous—oratorical and at times acrimonious." Walsh heard discussion "that disclosed many serious facts and conditions, showing both parties to be responsible for the break." He surmised that "the whole situation was very critical."[70]

On Christmas Eve 1921, the committee met in the aldermen's chambers from 10 A.M. to 3:45 P.M. "without recess." The meeting was "long, interesting, at times noisy and dangerous, threats of leaving, etc.—but patience saved the situation," and a proposal was made and accepted to cover all the important points. On the day after Christmas 1921, Bishop Walsh's diary again dealt with the longshoremen's strike:

Bright day—Three leaders of Longshoremen called at my request and I urged calm patient action at their meeting—They wished me to go to the meeting and I promised to go, if the body so requested—A committee was sent for me—I went and spoke for about one-half hour, on all the important phases of the strike and explained what the proposal of the Citizens Committee was and in what spirit it was made, assuring them that it was protective to all parties in the dispute—and that the Committee did wish and hope for its acceptance—They voted soon after and unanimously accepted the proposal, as per enclosed copy—It was really a great point gained by them and for them.[71]

The longshoremen voted to accept the compromise package of the citizens' committee, and they sent it next to a steamship official in Montreal, most likely representing the most crucial shipping company involved in this particular impasse.[72] Bishop Walsh's intervention was seen as crucial.

Management had labor over a barrel and was aware of its relative strength in these negotiations. A critical snag in these final negotiations emerged concerning the possibility that the compromise may have "contravened some of the regulations of the United States Shipping Board."[73] Bishop Walsh's diary again sheds valuable light on this episode, suggesting that local work rules may have been the problem: "Meeting was long and interesting, including two members of U. S. Shipping Board and there seemed very little hope of settlement, as the Steamship Companies at Montreal would not yield on any important point . . . and the Shipping Board men declared it was 'stand pat' for their part of a practically uniform agreement for all ports—thus cutting out any preferential conditions for Portland."[74]

On December 28, 1921, an all-day conference was held at City Hall. The bishop, at least in his private writing, appeared to view management's position as intransigent: "Shipping men—Shipping Board and Stevedores [met] with Committee and the first position of all three was to hold tight, no surrender, we cannot and we will not." After a while some movement did occur, because, in Walsh's opinion, "none of the three parties dared to assume responsibility for failure." The bishop, at a subsequent moment of impasse, suggested that "the public would be told the truth of failure and its responsibility." After wringing some concessions from management, the committee next dealt with the longshoremen, who, in the bishop's own words, "went up into the air, but came down again," referring to the longshoremen's high emotion. At 8:00 P.M., ILA district secretary William Dempsey returned to City Hall with the longshoremen "who again went up into the air, but soon came down with proper explanations."[75]

The longshore delegation next proceeded to the union hall where they asked for acceptance on behalf of the PLSBS. It was 11:30 P.M. before the report of the arbitration board reached the union hall. The agreement was signed, the strike was over, and the members voted to return to work at 1 P.M. the following afternoon.[76] The bishop captured the moment on December 28, 1921, with gratitude to God: "[The longshoremen] signed up—then the other three parties signed up and there was a general good will and cheerful exchange of congratulations and hopes just about midnight—It was a great and interesting fight and a real triumph for the Citizens Committee and for Portland's Civic and Commercial Interests—*Deo Gratias*."[77]

While the agreement may have represented a civic and commercial success, the results would have to be considered a loss for the PLSBS, but a predictable one in light of similar concessions all along the Atlantic Coast. "An early outcome of the conference was [giving] authority to the contracting stevedores and steamship men to regulate the size of the sling load." Of the five specific articles dealt with under arbitration, the union lost most if not all of its demands. The major losses included, in addition to the significant loss of the limited sling load, time and a half instead of double time for working the meal hour, a shorter contract duration to coincide with other Atlantic ports, restrictions on going from hatch to hatch and passing lines, and a call for the prosecution of any member found in the act of "broaching" or pilfering.[78]

On this latter issue, many longshoremen recalled that small amounts of pilfering occurred, such as opening and eating a can of fruit on occasion. Phil O'Donnell recalled one exception in the case of bonded alcohol where there would sometimes be customs guards or inspectors present when this product was being off-loaded. Once, allegedly, a dockworker feigned an injury requiring a stretcher so that bottles of whiskey could be pilfered under cover, so to speak. Larry Welch embellished the story of the transshipment of Scotch whisky to Canada claiming, "There was handsprings and uppercuts [and] by the afternoon they'd be all drunk, fighting." When armed police arrived on the docks, the longshoremen were incensed and "knocked off" the ship, refusing to work any further, reportedly stating, "We ain't slave labor."[79]

The sling-load weight would now be increased, an issue of safety and working conditions; restrictions on going from one hatch to another would limit the income that a longshoreman could expect to receive for loading a specific ship; and on the question of pilfering, the call for prosecution appears to have taken a step away from the union's self-regulation of its own workforce and introduced the threatening possibility of outside legal remedies employed by the shipping companies themselves. Despite these clear losses, at least to the autonomy of the longshore union in Portland, there was reportedly relief and "general rejoicing in the city on the outcome of the strike."[80]

The local newspaper's headline read "Dock Strike Ends." The work of unloading the four ships that had been delayed in Portland began almost immediately, as of 1 A.M. on Wednesday, December 28, 1921. It was also reported that no longer would a stoppage of the construction work then in progress on the Maine State Pier be "seriously considered." Portland was reported to be "the last Atlantic port at which the longshoremen have reached an agreement. [The] last port previous to Portland to sign up was Boston."[81] Those signing for the union included John Caselden, Stephen J. Mulkerrin, Michael Gorham, Bartley Connolly, and James A. McGrath. The signatories for the steamship lines and stevedores included J. M. McDougall (Robert Reford Company); Robert M. Smith (Cunard, Anchor-Donaldson, Thompson, and other lines); M. H. Gault (White Star–Dominion line); Fred C. Gignoux (Howard and Isles, North Atlantic, Western Steamship Company); Clinton T. Sweat (Portland Shipping Ceiling Company); and a representative from W. H. Dugan and Sons.[82]

The rejoicing was short-lived, however, and with the coming of the new shipping season in the fall of 1922, the wage question was open once again. The contract year usually started at the beginning of November. This year, however, the agreement was much easier to obtain, although some excitement was generated by the visit to Portland of the new ILA president Anthony J. Chlopek on October 27, 1922, at the invitation of Local 861. Chlopek clearly was in Portland to strengthen the hand of labor moderates.

The ILA was under attack, particularly along the Pacific Coast, by more militant elements of maritime labor, and Chlopek's concern for the unity of his organization was foremost in his thoughts. The PLSBS was aware that other ports had not ratified the 1922–23 wage agreement, and the ILA leader was called upon to answer questions concerning that. President Chlopek explained that most ports were signing on the basis of last year's agreements. In his address, ILA president Chlopek mentioned

> the trouble with some locals by having troublemakers or fanatics amongst the members . . . about the different locals on the West Coast and the trouble caused there by members of their own local boring from within, San Francisco, Seattle, Columbia River. . . . Frisco locals had $2600 . . . reduced to nothing by a small bunch of radicals boring from within. [He] told us about how Portland, Oregon is on [the] account of the I.W.W.'s [Industrial Workers of the World] and that he has sent out appeals to all sister locals for aid to help Portland, Oregon to help win the Big Battle they are up against.[83]

The "Big Battle" was clearly an internecine labor struggle for control of the Pacific ports between the ILA and the IWW. In his reference to the IWW as "boring from within," President Chlopek was clearly following the AFL lead concerning "pure and simple" unionism. This was often referred to as "pork chop" unionism due to its primary concern for wages rather than the more militant labor style of the IWW or later Harry Bridges' Pacific coast longshore union, the International Longshoremen's and Warehousemen's Union (ILWU). Wobbly (IWW) and later Communist organizers were expelled routinely from AFL-affiliated unions, and independent or partisan political action was discouraged. "Any union lacking the mark of legitimacy was branded as a dual and outlaw organization, an enemy to be given no quarter or sympathy."[84] This would also be the case within the ILA in general in the 1920s and within the PLSBS specifically.

Candidates supported by the international office regularly defeated left-wing, radical, or independent candidates for office. Heavy-handed tactics by the ILA were generally not employed in Portland because this local was considered too small to be worth the trouble, and, with some notable exceptions, the PLSBS generally stayed loyal to the ILA through most of these years.[85]

President Chlopek concluded by explaining that the international headquarters could pay no strike benefits because of the low per capita taxes, or dues, charged to members. Ironically, he used this same opportunity to reveal to the PLSBS plans to present a new automobile to former president T. V. O'Connor. On October 31, 1922, the Portland local voted to sign the new wage agreement. The international office and ILA president Chlopek were apparently well served by his trip to Portland.

The Portland longshoremen were, since 1914, part of an international organization that since the early 1920s encompassed most dockworkers in America. Causes of labor concern were publicized and discussed in Portland. These Irish dockworkers were maturing along with their society under the umbrella of the ILA, the AFL, and local central labor organizations such as the Maine State Federation of Labor (MSFL) and the Portland Central Labor Union (CLU). Before affiliation with the ILA, the PLSBS had not been as active with labor federations within the city and state, but now the labor concept of solidarity was stressed.

By 1923, however, the union was walking a tightrope. On the one hand it had made significant gains in new membership between 1915 and 1919, but on the other hand the next few years after 1919 hinted at instability, even though total membership had remained very high. Nationally, this was also a period of labor concessions and rollbacks of the gains made before and during the war, and of instability across the board for many American workers.[86]

Ironically, the 1915–19 boom in membership occurred along with a dramatic decline in total tonnage handled through Portland, from an all-time high of more than 3,700,000 short tons in 1916 to a low of fewer than 2,500,000 short tons in 1920. A 1935 state of Maine report graphically illustrated a 50 percent decrease in the two types of crucial commodities handled in Portland at this time. Coal declined from an all-time high of more than 2,000,000 short tons in 1913 to a low of just over 1,000,000 short tons in 1919, and miscellaneous commodities likewise dropped by half from 900,000 tons in 1915 to about 450,000 tons in 1919.[87]

Portland's Canadian connection via the Grand Trunk Railway had been a blessing for seventy years (1853–1923), but it would now come back to haunt the Portland waterfront and its longshoremen. At long last, after well over a half century of relying on one commodity, Portland's precipitous loss of Canadian grain shipments now undermined the city's maritime economy and left the maritime labor force of Portland vulnerable by the mid-1920s. Earlier warnings had not been taken seriously, and city officials had failed to initiate effective countermeasures in a timely fashion to protect Portland's shipping interests and its longshore workers. There was widespread knowledge in Portland of the vast modernization schemes then nearing completion in the Canadian ports of Saint John and Halifax.[88]

Would Portland be able to compete with these modern Canadian ports to the north, or with the larger and technologically more efficient American ports to the south? One retired longshoreman who worked in the 1920s reflected back on this period. In Roy Caleb's opinion, "if you had the right politicians then I'd say they could have got more work than they got here." He obviously thought that the Canadian government was doing more to promote their ports than were officials in Maine. "The Canadian government passed a law that anything going out of Canada had to be shipped out of a Canadian port. Automatically, that would kill the port of Portland."[89]

Another retired longshoreman had a slightly more analytical approach to this problem. Larry Welch remembered the suddenness of the loss of work in Portland. "Lost it all at once! One bang there. One winter they had it, one winter they didn't." Looking for a reason to explain why this occurred, Welch mentioned both the lack of an industrial hinterland around Portland and the competition from the larger port of Boston, "with much more political clout and the railroads all coming in." He saved his sharpest criticism, however, for the Portland business community. In analyzing why Portland had not developed its own port infrastructure earlier to compete with Canada, Welch answered, "That would be socialist, and [local business leaders] wouldn't stand it. They weren't politically conscious enough."[90]

To those who could see the economic writing on the wall, the future of Portland's Irish longshoremen after 1923 appeared precarious. Local historian Joel Eastman wrote of an attempt by the Portland City Council to create a local port authority, together with South Portland, to search for a replacement for the lost Canadian commerce. Despite some short-term successes, the authority failed to stem the decline of locally handled maritime commerce. The port authority was eventually disbanded in 1939, just as World War II was commencing in Europe. The war would serve to increase work on Portland's docks, at least temporarily. Some leaders of the port authority placed blame for the decline of Portland's maritime trade on competition from overland trucking and "the high wages of unionized longshoremen."[91]

Economically, the early 1920s were trying times for laborers in Portland and nationally as well. This was doubly true for ethnic workers, especially along social and cultural fronts. The newly elected Republican president, Warren G. Harding, spoke of recently arrived immigrants and promised "such a policy relating to those who come among us as will guarantee not only assimilability of alien born but the adoption by all who come of American standards, economic and otherwise, and full consecration to American practices and ideals."[92] The cultural implications were crystal clear: there would be little room for "hyphenated Americans" in the 1920s.

The years 1921 and 1924 would bring about two major pieces of highly restrictive immigration law. This would coincide with the dramatic rebirth of the Ku Klux Klan and its surprising spread northward to such states as Indiana, Pennsylvania, and even Maine.[93] The rebirth of the Klan, especially in the north, created a rare opportunity for solidarity between two otherwise dissimilar Klan targets, blacks and Irish Catholics. One prominent leader of the National Association for the Advancement of Colored People (NAACP), Robert Bagnall, counseled Portland's blacks in October 1922 to fight the Klan with a "steady" rather than "spasmodic" approach, and to join with other local allies whenever possible. Bagnall argued prophetically: "We would advise that you arrange conferences with the leading Jews and Roman Catholics, also Labor Leaders, as the Klan is against all of these, as well as against the Negro, and that you get them to enter actively into the fight. You can obtain very easily the cooperation of the Jewish women clubs and the Knights of Columbus for the Roman Catholic Church."[94]

This counsel toward mutual interracial cooperation was all the more significant in light of the horrible killing of a New Bedford, Massachusetts, black sailor, James Walker, along the Portland waterfront in May of the previous year. Walker and other black crewmen aboard the schooner *Mary F. Barnett* had allegedly violated a boycott of vessels that was then under way locally due to a waterfront conflict with ship owners in Portland in the spring of 1921. On May 20, 1921, a gang of fifteen whites beat several black sailors. "Walker received the worst treatment. His assailants fractured his skull and threw him in the harbor where he drowned. Searchers had to employ grappling hooks to retrieve his body."[95]

Racial relationships along the waterfront in Portland had been strained since the replacement of black laborers with Irish from the mid-nineteenth century onward. Retired longshoreman Larry Welch recalls the early 1920s as a time when "local blacks never applied [for longshore membership] anyways, they knew better. There wasn't any of them around [the waterfront] anyways."[96] James Walker had been attacked and killed apparently because of a perceived violation of unwritten labor and racial codes.

Race relations, especially on Portland's Munjoy Hill, were not uniformly tense, however. There were several examples of cooperation across the color line in the early to mid-twentieth century, perhaps prompted in part by the

22. KKK parade in Portland on Cumberland Avenue, c. 1923. Seven thousand successfully rallied to change Portland's form of municipal government from an elected mayor to a city manager.

working class residents' mutual struggle against the Klan. Munjoy Hill had long housed a small but prominent black neighborhood. It was also home to both of Portland's major black churches, the Abyssinian Meeting House, which closed in 1917, and the Green Memorial AME Zion Church located on the corner of Sheridan and Monument streets. Green Memorial opened its doors in 1914 and is still very active today.[97] Beverly Dodge, a black former resident of Munjoy Hill, later favorably recalled, "It was a wonderful neighborhood, although we probably didn't realize it at the time. But looking back, it was quite nice. Both my mother and father worked, so the neighbors used to watch us. And I used to say we had Irish grandparents because you had to behave no matter what. . . . In the summer-time the neighbors used to take me to the beach every day. The Eastern Promenade. We were a very close neighborhood."[98]

The Klan in Maine in the 1920s had several targets, as Robert Bagnall of the NAACP had counseled, and among these were immigrants in general and Catholic immigrants specifically. "No doubt much of the bitterness voiced against Bishop Walsh was sired by the Ku Klux Klan, which was riding under full sail during the last five years of his life. This voice was raised, not against Walsh, but against the Catholic Church."⁹⁹

The Portland longshoremen were overwhelmingly Catholic in these years and, therefore, a potential Klan target. Roy Caleb remembered the KKK headquarters with its "big white building [and] big tents out on Forest Avenue." Tom Mulkern voiced the opinion of many Catholics in Portland when he recalled that "Governor [Ralph Owen] Brewster was a leader of the Klan, he was in the Klan." Mulkern recalled the name of the local Klan leader, F. Eugene Farnsworth, and repeated a story he had heard at this time. Supposedly the KKK leader had told a young bellhop at the Eastland Hotel, "I'm making money off that racket." Ultimately, with true Irish bravado, Mulkern dismissively claimed that "the Irish didn't worry about them at all."¹⁰⁰

The Klan in Portland had political clout, however, and supported a significant and successful charter change in the city government in 1923. That change replaced the nine wards, board of aldermen, common council, and elected mayor, a system that had been in effect since 1832, with a city manager and a council elected at large. This was clearly an attempt to preempt the increasing political influence of the Irish and other ethnic minorities within the city's predominantly Democratic neighborhoods and wards. A

23. KKK headquarters (Klavern) in Portland. The Witham Estate, c. 1920. Courtesy of State Representative Herb Adams.

prominent Jewish lawyer claimed, "If this plan goes through, every man of Irish descent may as well pack up his trunk and leave the city as far as representation on the city government is concerned."[101]

Fighting the increasing influence of the KKK in Maine, with its prominent local headquarters in Portland, "contributed to the break in [Bishop] Walsh's health" and quite possibly hastened his death in 1924. In his journal, Walsh stated that 1923 had been "perhaps the hardest, most trying year of my life."[102] Bishop Louis S. Walsh's flock in Maine, including most members of the PLSBS, was in an ambivalent position in the early twentieth century. America had been good to them, but it was not a Utopia. James O'Toole has written about these immigrant families as carrying a form of "mental baggage" from their place of birth. "With one foot in each world, they were to some degree marginalized in both: no longer pure expressions of their old national identity, nor yet fully adapted to their new one."[103]

In 1923 the city of Portland, as with the nation as a whole, was in a state of transition. The 1920s marked the period in which America gradually changed from a largely rural society to an increasingly urban one. This decade was marked by many conflicting developments that denoted the difficulty of such a change from old to new, from tradition to innovation, and from the known to the unknown. Concerning its maritime future, Portland had finally acted upon the long-discussed and long-delayed proposal for a modern, publicly funded waterfront facility for handling dry cargo.

The Maine State Pier, adjacent to the Grand Trunk wharves, was by then nearing completion. But in 1923 the bottom fell out of Portland's deepwater export market and there were other signs of potential trouble ahead for the labor force that had sustained Portland's maritime prominence over at least the past seventy years.

6

Longshore Culture and the Decline of the Port of Portland in the Mid- to Late Twentieth Century

The post–World War I period marked a vital turning point in the history of Portland's Irish longshore union, indeed for the maritime future of the city as a whole. The membership of the Portland Longshoremen's Benevolent Society (PLSBS) hovered for a few years at nearly 1,300, after reaching an all-time peak of 1,366 in 1919. A bitter strike late in 1921 had left a legacy of mistrust along Portland's docks, and in 1922 the union was counseled by ILA president Anthony J. Chlopek to accept the status quo rather than ask for a wage increase. The year 1923 marked the completion of construction of the Maine State Pier, Portland's first publicly owned and financed waterfront facility, but, ironically, that very same year also signaled the beginning of a half-century of decline in cargo handling in this port.

Several factors converged in the first half of the twentieth century to spell disaster for Portland's longshore industry. This chapter will analyze several key developments in these years:

- The decline and then the absolute disappearance of Canadian grain as an export commodity from Portland's wharves
- Continuing high levels of immigration up to the year 1924, which was opposed by the Portland longshoremen and the AFL in general
- The increasing prerogative of management to weaken protective measures and working conditions within the industry, such as the limited sling load
- The lack of militant, effective leadership at the national level, as symbolized by the increasingly corrupt administration of ILA president Joseph P. Ryan and his running battle with the Pacific Coast longshoremen led by Harry Bridges

- The Great Depression of the 1930s with its impact on shipping
- The brief resurgence of the union during World War II, followed by the postwar era (1946–1954) that was so detrimental to organized labor with a conservative, Republican-controlled Congress that passed Taft-Hartley and other antilabor legislation
- The antiracketeering atmosphere surrounding organized labor
- The Red Scare of the McCarthy era that tainted many unions as communist-inspired or controlled
- The changing modes of technology within the transportation and energy industries, which substituted container cargo, oil tankers, airplanes, and trucks for the traditional modes of maritime cargo shipping

All of these factors were interrelated, at least in terms of chronology, and served together to weaken and eventually all but eliminate the economic viability of bulk shipping to and from smaller Atlantic Coast ports, such as Portland. This chapter will briefly discuss each of these factors and others in an attempt to understand why Portland declined and then failed as a major American cargo port between 1923 and the end of the twentieth century. The chapter begins, however, with a brief look at the culture of maritime labor in Portland through the eyes of the last group of surviving longshoremen, several of whom had vivid memories stretching back to the maritime heydays of the 1920s.

Longshore Culture in the Early Twentieth Century

High membership levels and public pier construction in Portland in the early 1920s should have indicated a seemingly optimistic picture for maritime activity. Events were under way in Canada, however, that would seriously affect Portland's economic future.[1] Phil O'Donnell's earliest memories of longshore activity in Portland in the 1920s were ebullient. When asked how many worked on the waterfront, O'Donnell replied, "There would be 1,200, sure. It would look like Holy Name Sunday up at the Saint Dominic's! O, jeepers, the place would be packed."[2]

The Saint Dominic's west end parish began roughly at Gorham's Corner where several streets converged, including such modern major thoroughfares as Fore, Danforth, and York streets. One longshoreman, Tom Mulkern, fondly remembered the working-class nature of the place and the ease

24. Composite of retired longshoremen (top left, clockwise): Larry Welch, Phil O'Donnell, Tom Mulkern, Roy Caleb. From photo collection of the author.

of life in its close-knit neighborhoods. This included corner grocery stores with affordable produce and many small businesses that catered to the local citizens. He gleefully exclaimed, "You could buy a smoked shoulder for half nothing!"[3]

The longshoremen who worked in Portland, whether from Gorham's Corner in the west or Munjoy Hill in the east, all faced similar challenges. One problem was the casual nature of the work. In other words, it was not steady labor, especially in the summer months when Canadian grain was

25. Composite of retired longshoremen (top left, clockwise): Pat Malone, Steve Concannon, Jack Humeniuk (active), Pat O'Malley. From photo collection of the author.

shipped out through the St. Lawrence River rather than through the port of Portland. "The only handicap about longshore work was it wasn't steady." One even equated it to an addiction. "Some of them that had been a few years in longshore, they wouldn't take a steady job." Another longshoreman agreed stating, "Once you got down there, you wouldn't go anywhere else." Perhaps for that reason, several dockworkers shared the conviction that "no longshoreman ever wanted his kids to go down there in the later years.

They'd get independent and wouldn't want to work anywhere else."[4] These and other similar sentiments expressed by Portland's Irish longshoremen over the years tend to reinforce the thesis that most waterfront laborers saw this occupation as merely a starting point for their family's economic security, but that they wished for more for their children—dreams lived by the second generation.

Although it was strenuous labor that forced these workers out into the worst of weather, almost all of the older waterfront laborers recalled their time alongshore with the fondest of memories. Roy Caleb noted the camaraderie of maritime work concluding, "It was a good job—you were working with men you could mix with. I'd rather work with the old timers than with a lot of the kids that are down there today." Comparing their lot with the Boston longshoremen, Tom Mulkern opined, "There wasn't that much crookedness around." He gave credit to the founders and early members of the union when he added, "We always had better [working] conditions than they had in Boston 'cause we made them. We sat around the table and we made those conditions."[5]

As the longshore work continued in Portland, there were at least four or five locals under the aegis of the International Longshoremen's Association (ILA). These included the Irish longshoremen (local 861), the Italian freight handlers (local 912), the checkers (local 1130), the coopers, and even a separate local for the Eastern Steamship Line.

Maritime commerce equilibrium required that ships coming into Portland should have been loaded with imports as much as possible, and the ships leaving the port should be filled with exports. In other words, imports were as necessary as exports for the shipping companies to achieve the desired level of profit. The single greatest export commodity out of the port of Portland up to the early 1920s was Canadian grain, especially during the winter months. This single commodity, largely shipped to English ports, put Portland on the maritime map. Its increasing loss after 1923 would likewise create a hole in the maritime mix that was never adequately filled.

In addition to grain, the other major export commodities were paper products from the many paper and pulp mills in Maine, New Hampshire, and the surrounding hinterland. These would have included paper towels, toilet paper, napkins, and fine finished paper. Much other agricultural produce from Maine would be exported, and seafood was a featured item.

Larry Welch remembered that the Burnham and Morrill Company, now famous for its baked beans, "did a big business" shipping out various other

26. Composite: Larry Welch as a young seaman (June 4, 1920) and his identification card while working for the Fred Gignoux Company. From photo collection of the author.

products including canned corn, succotash, beans, canned lobster ("What the longshoremen didn't steal—very little of that got out"), crabmeat, and a creamed fish like haddock that Welch fondly deemed to be "delicious." In addition to these, Portland also exported flour, boxed meat, canned lard, and "all kinds of oatmeal for Scotland."[6]

The major imported commodities, other than the passengers who would sometimes come into Portland when the major immigration stations of Boston and New York were overwhelmed, primarily included materials needed by Maine's paper industry. The largest single item coming into Portland over these years was coal—both for commercial and domestic use. Coal was a major heat source for many of Portland's homes well into the late twentieth century. Coal was also used to power many paper mills and to create the steam needed for railroad locomotives, such as those running between Montreal and Portland, laden with grain.

The domestic coal was largely destined for either the A. R. Wright Company or Randall & McAllister. The domestic supply largely came from the huge coal wharves at Hampton Roads (Norfolk), Virginia. Foreign coal was brought in by the English steamers and was doubly useful as ballast for the dangerous trips across the North Atlantic. The major companies handling this foreign coal included the Pocahontas Coal Company and the Maine Central Railroad. Some of the biggest consumers of this commercial coal, in addition to the railroads, included the S. D. Warren paper mill in West-

27. Loading flour for export. Courtesy of ILA Local 861.

28. Unloading Scottish bonded whisky at Grand Trunk Wharf (1920).

brook, the Great Northern paper mill in Millinocket, and the Eastland and Congress Square hotels in Portland, owned by the Rines family.[7]

China clay was a crucial ingredient necessary to put a gloss on paper. It was first shipped from Fowey, in Cornwall, England, but in later years a domestic supply from Georgia largely replaced this foreign source. This variety was known locally as Georgia clay. Many longshoremen remember shoveling this product with a distinct lack of fondness. Larry Welch remembered it as "terrible hard work," and he was happy to see the end of "my skulldraggin' days shoveling that God-damned stuff." Tom Mulkern remembered it as "hard work" but added that it was steady work, with as many as five gangs working at one time. Phil O'Donnell confirmed the others' opinions stating that china clay "was bad stuff, awfully slippery when it was wet. The men would be all gray."[8]

Another important paper-related import was sulfur, largely from Texas, which the longshoremen tried heroically to keep out of their eyes. One stated that it was usually all right until you returned to your warm house where your eyes would begin to water profusely. Baled pulp was also imported in huge quantities into the port to be further refined and turned into paper products in the nearby mills. Every two weeks the "West Coast boat" would arrive with its varied cargo of lumber, canned goods, Hawaiian pineapples, peaches, prunes, and other dried fruits. This was an example of domestic brown-water shipping. Ironically, the main ingredient needed for the B&M baked beans was California pea beans, shipped through the Panama Canal to Portland where they would be processed and then returned to the West Coast as the magically transformed and famous New England baked beans.

Canadian Port Development after 1923

The vibrant maritime culture of Portland's waterfront was of course dependent upon a steady and adequate supply of goods to ship from this port. The Grand Trunk Railroad (GTR), which connected the Portland docks with Montreal, had come under the ownership of the nationalized Canadian National Railroad (CNR) on January 20, 1923. Together with the completion of significant improvements in waterfront facilities at Halifax, Nova Scotia, and especially at Saint John, New Brunswick, these changes would result in a crucial policy shift by the Canadian government.[9]

After 1923 a significant portion of Canadian grain, formerly shipped through Portland, "Montreal's winter port," would now be loaded on steamships at the significantly more distant Canadian ports of Halifax or Saint John. Although it would have been more economical to continue to ship seasonally through the existing rail lines to the much nearer port, Portland, rather than through the Maritimes, Canadian nationalism would prevail over purely economic considerations, and Portland would suffer consequently.[10] This changing Canadian shipping policy, however, was not the only dark cloud on the horizon for Portland's Irish longshoremen in the early years of the 1920s.

Work was steady, membership in the longshore union was at near-record levels, and construction was nearing completion on the $1.5 million Maine State Pier, the only publicly funded cargo facility in Portland. Despite these positive realities, there was also cause for alarm. Early in 1923 the Maine Legislature had been requested to add $165,000 for further renovations to the western side of this pier, implying that even at that late date the state was seeking to complete these badly needed infrastructure improvements as cheaply as possible.[11]

The growth of Portland as a cargo port had, since 1853, become nearly totally entwined with the seasonal export of Canadian grain and other pro-

29. Maine State Pier, opened 1923. Courtesy of ILA Local 861.

duce to Europe, but changes then under way within the Canadian government and private industry would soon lead to a rapid decline and eventual total elimination of this erstwhile mutually profitable maritime connection. All of Portland's eggs had been placed in one basket, and between 1923 and 1934 the bottom literally fell out. The ties between Montreal and Portland had been purely economic ties, with the lines of commerce following their easiest, shortest, and most profitable route.

In the early years of the twentieth century Canadian, British, and American entrepreneurs had maintained that "the Grand Trunk Railway, a British controlled private company, was not about to be swayed by nationalistic pleas."[12] The Grand Trunk came under increasing political pressure during the first two decades of the twentieth century, however, and once the GTR was placed under Canadian government control as part of the CNR, it would become more and more vulnerable to Canadian nationalistic pressure. Saint John and Halifax had paid almost exclusive attention to the relatively smaller port of Portland while ignoring the larger and potentially more injurious competition from larger American ports such as Boston and New York.

Allan Jeffrey Wright offered the following thesis as a possible explanation for this focus on Maine's largest port: Portland was closer to Canada and therefore more noticeable; a huge percentage of Portland's total exports (well over 90 percent) consisted of Canadian produce; Canada was practicing the "art of the possible," they could control Portland's railroad outlets; and, finally, Portland often made the proud, almost boastful, assertion that it was "Canada's Winter Port."[13]

The Maritime ports were successful in eliminating the Portland competition. Between 1923 and 1934 Canadian exports through Portland virtually evaporated. The "method of friendly approach," which was a low-key campaign by Maine officials to promote the purely economic argument for its continuation, ultimately failed. After 1934, "mounting a strong campaign quite similar to the earlier Maritime rights campaign in Canada, the Portland residents attempted to rejuvenate their port." The 1935 Brann Study, commissioned by Maine's Democratic governor Louis Brann, is seen as a central element in this rejuvenation campaign. Portlanders "never seemed to fully understand the political side of the argument," and while acknowledging that nationalism and Maritime sectionalism were factors, they continued to believe "that economics would ultimately prevail."[14]

Economics would prove to be an unequal combatant in this political struggle, and Portland was the battlefield upon which most of the casualties occurred. Canadian trade through the larger American ports was unaffected, and the Maritime ports did not immediately become the major Canadian transshipment centers to rival Boston or New York, as was intended. The campaign that brought economic hardship to Portland had only a minor effect on the Canadian winter trade, with less than projected initial improvements for Halifax and Saint John.

Despite these changes in the economic relationship between Portland and the Canadian ports, it was necessary to carry on the business of the longshore union even with diminished work and membership. Changing ethnic factors in these years, particularly the nativist push to restrict immigration, also affected the Portland longshoremen and their jobs on Portland's waterfront. Ironically, in this battle it was management, symbolized by the National Association of Manufacturers (NAM), that promoted unrestricted immigration. Second- and now third- and fourth-generation Irish Americans in AFL-affiliated unions such as the PLSBS largely favored restrictions on the flow of unskilled, potentially nonunion labor into this country. These ethnic Americans were reacting simply out of a concern for protecting their own jobs. Thus they helped to promote the closing of the gates to any "new" immigrants chiefly from southern and eastern Europe and largely of Catholic or Jewish religious affiliation. The very act of immigration, by which nearly all of their families had entered America and secured jobs, had now become a threat to their increasingly precarious occupational security.

The high levels of immigration from Ireland during the early 1920s never again approached the massive influx of the 1880s. This was partly because immigration as a whole was so drastically reduced by two highly restrictive immigration laws, the Dillingham Act (1921) and the Reed-Johnson Act (1924). Although many American industries had become dependent upon a steady stream of "new immigrants" for cheap labor, they would now have to find unskilled laborers among African Americans migrating from the South as well as other young, newly arrived urban dwellers, largely from rural America.

In an article titled "Industry Seeks Foreign Labor," NAM stated that "there is a shortage of common labor . . . and that there is little hope of correcting this situation under the present law." NAM urged the abolition of the literacy test for immigrants although "retention of the mental, moral and political tests [was suggested]. Retention of the literacy test for granting citizenship, however, is favored."[15] Describing contrary legislative initiatives, in the words of historian Irving Bernstein, "Congress was more concerned with safeguarding American 'racial' purity than with the needs of industry."[16]

With the passage of time, these facts simply meant that there would be fewer Irish-born longshoremen along Portland's waterfront and in the city as a whole as the twentieth century progressed. Therefore, Portland's maritime workforce from the 1920s onward consisted of more second- and subsequent-generation Irish American longshoremen whose ties to Ireland were often much less direct, and eventually also more non-Irish workers.

Of those Portland longshoremen at the turn of the twentieth century who had been born outside of the United States, fully 80 percent had immigrated in the more recent years since 1880. Of the longshoremen with Irish ancestry, 46 percent were themselves Irish-born and another 24 percent were born in America with at least one Irish parent. This accounted for a minimum of 70 percent of all longshoremen working in Portland in 1900.

But this Irish ethnic concentration was now weakening as the twentieth century progressed.[17]

The first specific reference to ethnicity in this period was found in the minutes of November 20, 1923, which referred to a communication from Harbor Commissioner Mr. Henry Merrill, "praising the longshoremen for services rendered on [the Maine] State Pier the week the emigrants arrived here." This was a reference to the arrival in Portland of four transatlantic passenger liners in a two-day period, November 1–2, 1923, at a time when New York and Boston were overwhelmed with the processing of new immigrants.

During these days, referred to as the "Port's busiest 48-hour period," a total of 4,363 passengers landed here. Most of the passengers disembarked and were immediately taken by rail to New York City.[18] The liners involved were, in order of arrival, the SS *Seydlitz* of the North German Lloyd Line; the SS *Tuscania* of the Cunard-Anchor Line; and the SS *George Washington* and the SS *President Polk*, both of the United States Line.

The *George Washington* was the largest ship ever to enter Portland harbor up to that time, and on board were prominent passengers such as Sen. Robert M. La Follette Sr. LaFollette was returning from a three-month fact-finding tour of Europe just prior to his candidacy for president of the United States on the Progressive Party ticket in the election of 1924, then exactly one year away. Also on board was the French ambassador to the United States, Jules Jusserand. This was reported to be the first time an ambassador had ever landed in Portland. After a brief period of quarantine at House Island in Portland harbor, each of these steamers proceeded to the Maine State Pier where their passengers disembarked. For House Island, this year 1923 marked a remarkable coming full circle historically from its early colonial use as a fisheries staging ground exactly three hundred years earlier by Capt. Christopher Leavitt around 1623.

Immigration officials were on hand to inspect those who entered America from many countries. There were twenty-eight nationalities listed among the third-class passengers aboard the *George Washington* alone. Immigration regulations under the Dillingham Act (1921) were then in operation, and as such the quota restrictions placed upon each country of origin were considered. Those immigrants from Russia, of undisclosed religion but presumably Russian Jews, were detained in Portland until it could be determined from Washington, D.C., whether the Russian quota had yet been exceeded. Regular service between Portland and Europe would be maintained that winter by five steamship lines including Cunard, Anchor-Donaldson, Thompson, Rogers and Webb, and White-Star Dominion.[19]

The longshoremen's union meeting of April 8, 1924, referred to a communication from the AFL on the immigration question. The AFL, of course, took a stand quite opposite that of NAM on the issue of unrestricted immigration. The business community favored cheap labor while the trade unions favored immigration restrictions to control the labor pool, thus encouraging wage increases.

It was voted on September 30, 1924, "that a man must have his first papers of citizenship at least six months before becoming a member of this Society." This demonstrated that even an ethnically based union felt the pressure from a decline in the demand for maritime labor in this port. Ethnic ties with Ireland were becoming more tenuous for two major reasons. First, the percentage of first-generation longshoremen in the PLSBS was declining due largely to attrition, and second, there were simply fewer immigrants arriving in Portland and elsewhere because of the passage of restrictive national legislation in 1921 and 1924.

Immigration restriction, however, cut both ways. There was still an evident identification with the ancestral homeland. As an example of continuing Irish nationalist sentiment within the PLSBS, on October 11, 1927, forms were filled out for the Irish Free State bonds. These bonds had obviously been purchased earlier by the society to support the newly created twenty-six-county national entity then officially named Saorstát Éireann, popularly known as Southern Ireland.[20]

According to Irving Bernstein, "the average annual number of immigrants entering the United States fell from 1,034,940 in prewar years (1910–1914) to 304,182 in 1925–1929, a drop of 70.6 per cent." On February 4, 1930, the society discussed "a man becoming a member of this Society without being a citizen." Newly arriving immigrants were even fewer in numbers by 1930, by then fully six years since the passage of the highly restrictive Johnson-Reed Act of 1924.[21] Economic factors also affected the work of Portland's longshoremen, and a recession had settled onto Portland's maritime industries in these years long before the Great Depression of the 1930s.

The handwriting was on the wall for the longshoremen of Portland and, indeed, the maritime labor force of many of the smaller and even larger Atlantic Coast ports. Although Portland managed to hold onto the limited sling load in one form or another until the 1940s, one could see that most unions in other ports were capitulating or modernizing, and so too Portland's time would come. Perhaps it was the diminishing portion of East Coast shipping out of Portland that allowed it to maintain its relatively favorable work rules for so long. Disputes alongshore in the 1920s were most often prompted by concern over the maintenance of these union work rules, particularly the limited sling load and the use of nonunion labor.

This local versus national jurisdictional division of functions could partly explain the concern over conditions and safety, as opposed to a purely economic consideration of wages and benefits alone. But this could also have been a reflection of national economic trends. "During the prosperity of the twenties wages, money and real [wages], moved gently upward. Unlike the two preceding periods of good times, the turn of the century and the first war, there was no sharp rise. In fact, wages in the era 1923–29 were characteristically stable, reflecting the surplus of labor and weak unions."[22] Defense of union work rules was a crucial concern for Portland's longshoremen in the depressed years of the 1920s and 1930s, but for the international union, the ILA, events then occurring three thousand miles further west were seemingly of much greater significance.

Joseph Ryan was clearly the dominant figure in the ILA in the twentieth century.[23] He would shape the style and substance of this union in a way that had not been done since its inception under Daniel J. Keefe. Ryan had succeeded Anthony Chlopek as ILA president in 1927, and he quickly became a recognized figure among the Portland longshoremen, addressing a local meeting as early as May 28, 1928, on the issue of nonunion labor used at the Rolling Mills docks along the South Portland waterfront. "Brother Ryan stated that work was scarce all over the country. [He] pointed out the benefits gained from internationally formed bodies. [He] said [that] all ports on the American North Atlantic had a uniform wage. Said this condition did not exist in the South. Told how we got our raise. Brother Ryan thanked Local 861 for their support."[24]

Joe Ryan would be a somewhat frequent visitor to Portland in these years, and he attended PLSBS meetings at least three times in the next three years.[25] The issues of nonunion labor along Portland's docks and the limited sling load continued to be of paramount importance locally in the Depression years. While the ILA negotiated uniform wage rates along the Atlantic and Gulf coasts, local unions were somewhat free to negotiate their own unique work rules. Retired longshoreman Larry Welch recalled that

30. Joseph Ryan, president of ILA (1927–1953). University of California Press/ public domain.

the longshore wages in the 1920s were better than most manual labor jobs in Portland. He believed that this union was the only closed shop in Maine, outside of the bricklayers. Regarding working conditions, specifically the limited sling load, Welch stated, "Compared to New York and Boston, those places, we had the best working conditions of any local in the whole ILA, anywhere. And that's what killed us, they claim. We had the limited sling load and other ports had unlimited sling loads."[26] These work rules, it seems, could be a double-edged sword.

ILA president Joseph Ryan and the issue of the limited sling load also became prominent factors in a bitter longshore strike between October 1 and December 5, 1931, in Boston, the ILA-affiliated major port nearest to Portland. Boston's local longshore work rules, especially concerning the limited sling load, extra pay for working during meal hours, minimum pay rates for being called out on Sundays or holidays, and other issues, had all been in dispute over the past several years in negotiated agreements with the steamship agents and their local stevedores.

The limited sling load and other work rules in Boston were threatened by proposed changes by the steamship officials and, ironically, even changes proposed and agreed to by President Ryan himself. "In fact, it represents a deterioration in both working conditions and wages from the viewpoint of Boston longshoremen, who had conditions superior in many respects to those in New York and other Atlantic ports." Boston longshoremen repudiated Ryan and supported local leaders, and they voted unanimously on October 31, 1931, to reject Ryan's proposed compromise.[27]

The 1931 strike, however, was lost by the Boston longshoremen who were forced to return to work largely under employers' terms. At least they had succeeded in preventing a permanent employer-run alternative union, the Boston Dock Workers Federation, from gaining a hold on the waterfront. The Boston longshoremen had maintained remarkable discipline and "solidarity with not a single man deserting ranks during the strike." According to one analyst, "what was really at stake was the meaning of a fair or reasonable pace of work." Finally, contrary to President Ryan's optimistic assessment, the long-term legacy was to create an "antagonistic spirit" along the Boston waterfront that "made good labor relations even more difficult to achieve in the following years."[28]

Longshore wages and local working conditions were clearly negatively impacted by the Depression-era decline in shipping.[29] This fact was demonstrated graphically at a special meeting held in Portland on October 14, 1932, with ILA president Joseph P. Ryan again in attendance. Ryan spoke at length about conditions in New York, but he concluded, "It was up to each port to make their own port conditions." Ryan, most likely with the previous year's failed Boston longshore strike in mind, noted that the local steamship companies "were determined they would get what they wanted," and he pragmatically suggested that Local 861 should simply attempt to have the last year's agreement renewed. Ryan further stated that the steamship companies were "all set to have [the] unlimited sling in Portland after this agreement." The 1932 negotiations resulted in a holding pattern, at best, for Portland's maritime laborers.

As of late 1934, however, little progress had been reported in the effort "to organize Burr's Rolling Mills wharf." At that time it was moved that the wage conference committee "stand by [its] original demands." Portland was one of the last ports to have a limited sling load in effect, given its abandonment in the failed strike in Boston late in 1931.[30]

The conservative nature of Joseph Ryan and the ILA during his tenure was best demonstrated during the battle over jurisdiction with the Pacific Coast longshoremen in the mid-1930s. This struggle shaped the nature of the separate dockworkers unions on the Atlantic and Pacific Coasts for years to come, and had a demonstrable impact on Portland.

Harry Bridges and the West Coast Model

On May 9, 1934, a historic labor struggle, which has since been commonly referred to as "The Big Strike," began on the Pacific Coast. It would last for eighty-three days, until July 31, and it led to the formal rupture between the East Coast ILA longshoremen under Joe Ryan and the more militant West Coast longshoremen under Harry Bridges. These events marked the rise of Harry Bridges as the leader of the rank and file Pacific Coast longshoremen, and eventually president of the ILA breakaway union on the West Coast, the International Longshoremen's and Warehousemen's Union (ILWU).[31]

A preliminary longshore strike had tied up the port of San Francisco since May 9, 1934, but it soon boiled over with the arrival of two thousand National Guardsmen ordered in by California governor Frank Merriam to safeguard state-owned property. One month later on June 12 a message to the East Coast longshoremen from ILA Local 38-76 of Everett, Washington, regarding the strike on the Pacific Coast was read to the PLSBS. The Big Strike was about to take a violent turn when, on July 3, 1934, Local 861 sent letters to President Ryan and the president of the Pacific Coast district of the ILA "in regards to working of [a] steamer due here from [the] Pacific coast for discharge."[32]

Three days later the deaths of a San Francisco striking longshoreman, Howard Sperry, and a strike sympathizer, Nicholas Counderakis, and the serious injuries to sixty-nine others, thirty by bullet wounds, were all graphically reported in the local newspapers. "Fighting reminiscent of World War battles raged on the San Francisco waterfront today as strike pickets fought hand-to-hand over an area a mile square with police mid the roar of pistols and riot guns and the blinding fumes from tear gas bombs."[33]

Coming as it did just two years prior to the formation of the Congress of Industrial Organizations (CIO), this strike was an ideological weather-

31. Harry Bridges, president of ILWU (1937–1977). University of California Press/public domain.

vane, and "Harry Bridges found himself at the head of the largest and most powerful maritime strike in American history." The eighty-three-day strike "transformed American maritime labor."³⁴ On October 16, 1934, the PLSBS received yet another letter from Local 38-76 of Everett, Washington.

The year 1935 began with the reported decision by the PLSBS membership to "give $100.00 to [the] I.L.A. of Portland, Oregon, local 38-78, for [the] I.L.A. defense committee for strikers on [the] West Coast, and [that it] be sent by air mail."³⁵ On November 3, 1936, two communications were received from the West Coast, one from San Francisco Local 38-79 and the other from the Pacific Coast District.

The division between the ILA and the ILWU Pacific Coast longshoremen has often been portrayed in terms of a personality struggle between the respective leaders of these unions, Joseph P. Ryan and Harry Bridges.³⁶ Frances Perkins, President Franklin D. Roosevelt's secretary of labor, remembered Bridges as a "small, thin, haggard man in a much-worn overcoat." This was greatly in contrast with Joe Ryan of the ILA who was frequently referred to as "dapper." In reality, it was much more of an ideological split, paralleling the split in American labor at the time between high-skilled craft and low-skilled industrial workers. When the CIO split in 1936 with the AFL over this class and ideological divide, Bridges logically took his West Coast ILWU with the more militant CIO.[37]

In the PLSBS record books there was but one specific reference to Harry Bridges, and this left little doubt as to with whom the Local 861 leadership would side late in the year 1936, after the national labor split. It was "moved and seconded—This local go on record as endorsing [President] Ryan's actions in disposing of Harry Bridges, organizer, and accept communication he sent regarding same."[38]

Along the docks of Duluth, Minnesota, in this same period there was a creative solution to this ideological split within the labor movement: "The conflict was particularly intense along the waterfront where immigrant radicals had long enjoyed significant support.... With the formation of the CIO as a separate organization, the question of whether to remain with the AFL or go over to the CIO became an issue.... With charges of raiding coming from both directions, ultimately the AFL got the Coal Dock Workers and the CIO got the Ore Dock Workers."[39]

The PLSBS played it safe by backing the conciliatory, moderate, "pork chop," Ryan-led ILA/AFL union leadership rather than the more militant brand of Harry Bridges and the ILWU/CIO. In a revealing and commonly heard phrase in the 1930s and beyond, even up to the 1950s, workers and stevedores alike would often be asked, "Who would you prefer to deal with, an honest Communist or a crooked patriot?"[40]

Ryan's ILA, however, became more clearly identified with racketeering, especially in his home port of New York, and Joe Ryan himself was eventually forced to resign under a cloud of suspicion late in 1953. In this period the ILA was asked to withdraw from the AFL because these allegations of corruption were hurting the image of organized labor as a whole.[41] Most of the local longshoremen claimed to be unaware of any significant racketeering on the Portland waterfront. Most interviewees offered a simple rationale for this lack of graft locally. Many were of a similar fashion to that given by Larry Welch, who responded convincingly that "[Portland] was a small port. I suppose the rackets didn't bother with them, you know. See?"[42]

Ironically, while Joe Ryan constantly denounced Harry Bridges as a radical communist, it was the former who was forced to resign in disgrace while the latter continued to serve the ILWU, which was often cited as a model of union militancy, democracy, and efficiency, for another three decades into the 1980s.[43] Perhaps one of the clearest indications of the respect gained by the Pacific Coast longshoremen and their leader, Harry Bridges, is the sheer volume of scholarly research done on this group compared to the relative academic amnesia concerning both Ryan and the ILA.[44]

Several of the old-time longshoremen interviewed in the early 1980s had greatly differing degrees of knowledge or memory about the Ryan–Bridges, or East Coast–West Coast, or ILA–ILWU split in these years. Steve Concannon did not mention Bridges but felt that a union was essential in the early 1920s, especially given the labor conditions in Maine where union workers "were a small minority." He spoke of other jobs he had held locally as being almost like sweatshop conditions, and he credited the ILA with linking Portland with the more influential ports of Boston and New York in what he referred to as "one big union." He credited the organization of the ILA in New York with giving Portland better conditions without having to go out on strike. Phil O'Donnell could not quite remember Bridges' name, asking, "What was that fellers name?" Roy Caleb seemed a bit more familiar with these issues stating, "[Bridges] was a good organizer [and] he had his own mind." When pressed on his opinion of Bridges, Caleb added, "All you can do is surmise, but I don't think Bridges was a Communist . . . but anybody that isn't satisfied with conditions today is [viewed as] a Communist. If you don't go along with the Big Brass and them that have, you know, then you're a troublemaker." Tom Mulkern, when asked directly, added, "They say Harry Bridges was a pretty good man for the men."[45]

One notable exception to the rule locally was PLSBS member Lawrence F. Welch of Munjoy Hill who played an active, albeit clandestine, role in promoting Harry Bridges on the East Coast. In a 1982 interview, Welch claimed that if seen at any meeting promoting Bridges, a member would have been charged with "dual unionism" and expelled from the ILA. He added, "In the end, all Ryan was was a front man for the Mafia." Welch's rationale for supporting Harry Bridges was simple: "We'll all be stronger that way [with a federation], both coasts together." Larry Welch even ran once for union president, but his candidacy was strongly opposed by the national ILA officers and their local supporters in Portland, including the local union leadership. In referring to the Big Strike in San Francisco in

1934, Welch reasoned, "That was one of my ideas in running for president—that you'd go along with the West Coast. One federation, like, [and] you'd get the hiring hall."⁴⁶

Welch's positive view of Harry Bridges was even shared, surprisingly perhaps, by some maritime employers. In the late 1940s there appeared in the *New York Sun* a series of articles dealing with organized crime along the waterfront, especially the Ryan-controlled East Coast ILA. In the midst of this exposé there appeared a sort of grudging endorsement of Bridges by management. "West Coast operators found Bridges an honorable man to bargain with, and ties between waterfront labor and organized crime were far less an issue on the West Coast than along the Atlantic Seaboard."⁴⁷

The struggle between East and West coast maritime unions was part of a larger national labor struggle. "The greatest fault line was the age-old animosity between sailors and longshoremen." In 1936 when Bridges' ILWU left the AFL, Harry Lundeberg's Sailors' Union of the Pacific (SUP) rejoined this same organization. The 1936 split between the AFL and CIO would not be healed until their eventual merger in 1955, but the fault lines still exist.⁴⁸

The membership of the PLSBS had dropped steadily since 1923 when it stood at close to 1,300. By the start of the Depression, membership was already below 1,000 and steadily dropping. In the decade of the 1930s, membership was nearly halved again, declining from 970 in 1930 to only 537 by 1941, the year America entered World War II.

The Depression years were lean times for Portland's longshoremen and for maritime labor in America in general. Low points for total PLSBS membership were reached in 1936 (617 members) and 1941 (537 members) before the war orders kicked in and drove membership back up to 745 by 1946. Both of these highs were anemic when compared with the post–World War I high of 1,366 achieved in 1919.

Also problematic during the Depression years was an antilabor stance of both the U.S. and the Maine supreme courts, along with many local governments. "In 1936, the Maine Supreme Court ruled against union members picketing an open-shop theater in Portland." During the next year, when workers attempted several "sit down" strikes, the Portland City Council authorized the police to "use every legal means to prevent [the occupation of] stores and factories."⁴⁹

Franklin Delano Roosevelt's New Deal was starting to have a positive effect on the labor situation both nationally and locally. The Works Progress

Administration (WPA) became operational in 1935 and by December 1938 had peaked in Maine with 10,986 men and women employed. In Portland, cultural and public works projects employed many, as did projects such as the building of staff residences and dormitories at the U.S. Maritime Commission Hospital at Martin's Point, a significant extension of the municipal airport, and a dramatic modernization and expansion of the Portland Water District's fresh water supply to Portland and environs from nearby Sebago Lake. "The so-called 'Second New Deal' emphasized unions as a way to increase wages and improve working conditions, and unions in Portland needed assistance."[50]

There was plentiful work in Portland during these war years, but for Portland's longshoremen, World War II was not nearly as rewarding as had been the earlier wartime expansion. Other factors largely beyond the control of local maritime concerns were at work. This period would essentially only serve to temporarily slow down the inexorable decline in maritime-related commerce out of Portland that had commenced a generation earlier, around 1919–23.

One of the greatest local sources of employment was the South Portland Shipbuilding Corporation, an amalgamation of the Bath Iron Works and the Todd Shipyard of Philadelphia. The corporation ran three shifts around the clock and distinguished itself by constructing an amazing 274 Liberty ships, the so-called ugly ducklings that supplied our allies and forces during the war, and thirty additional ocean-class freighters. A major part of the work force was female, the famous "Rosie the Riveter." In Maine, in 1943 alone, some 22,463 women "were placed in war-related work, accounting for thirty-six percent of all the nonagricultural job placements."[51]

One of the last of these Liberty ships to survive is the *Jeremiah O'Brien*, named after an Irish-born hero of the Revolutionary War from Washington County, Maine. This ship, to the delight of thousands of survivors of the war and veterans of the shipyard, visited Portland in 1994. It was on its way back to its home base in San Francisco from helping to celebrate the fiftieth anniversary of the D-day invasion of Normandy. The other remaining Liberty ship, the *John W. Brown*, also visited Portland in August 2007 and was likewise very warmly received by large and enthusiastic crowds.[52]

Along Portland's waterfront dry goods were replaced by petroleum as the major commodity handled. Unfortunately for Portland's longshoremen, oil was not a labor-intensive material to handle. A small nonunion crew operating large flexible suction pipes did most of the work. The proportion of petroleum handled locally compared to other commodities had been increasing since World War I, and as early as 1924 it actually surpassed grain as the second most important single commodity, after coal.[53] With the completion of a major oil pipeline between Portland and Montreal in 1941 only weeks prior to the bombing of Pearl Harbor, Portland eventually became, at least as measured by total volume, a major oil port. This was reflected in the continued loss of longshore jobs.

The Portland pipeline was designed in part to allow tankers from South America or the Caribbean to avoid German U-boats operating in the North Atlantic. It has remained a major supplier of petroleum to eastern Canada in the seven decades since its opening. By the turn of the twenty-first century the Portland Pipeline made Portland "the largest port in New England by volume of tonnage handled, much of this volume being accounted for by shipments of oil bound for Canada."[54]

The ever-increasing domestic and worldwide demand for oil has continued unabated since World War II. Portland was linked to Montreal through this oil pipeline, just as these same two cities had been previously economically linked by the Grand Trunk Railroad, a grain pipeline, if you will, between 1853 and 1923. The demand for foreign petroleum had major national implications for maritime trade. Continental supplies were never sufficient to meet the domestic demand, even after the discovery of oil in Alaska. "Petroleum and petroleum products accounted for 38.9 percent of American waterborne foreign commerce in 1988 and 51 percent in 2000, even though world trade in oil leveled off late in the twentieth century."[55]

World War II and the increased shipping out of Portland that it stimulated served only to temporarily postpone the steady drop in union membership. In the war years and shortly thereafter, between 1941 and 1949, PLSBS membership fluctuated between 500 and 750 members. Although the union continued to give its support to President Ryan, there were voices of dissent heard in Portland.

The sling load continued to be a pressing concern throughout the World War II period. At their meeting of October 3, 1945, the longshoremen discussed this matter specifically in relation to the Jarka Corporation (stevedore), and the handling of bales of wool. At this same meeting there was a disagreement between district vice president John Silke and Brother Bartley Conley over allegations by the former against the latter of jumping ship and of opposition to taking veterans into the society. This conflict, which at first seemed to be merely personal, soon deepened at subsequent meetings and served to expose the larger ideological conflicts between the local and the international headquarters, at least as represented by these two members. On October 17, 1945, the charge of jumping ship was dismissed, but Conley countered by accusing Silke "of being one of Joe Ryan's gunmen."

These charges and countercharges led to the calling of a special meeting on October 19, 1945, at which time several items of interest emerged. Primarily, the case revolved around the accusation made by Conley that ILA president Joseph P. Ryan was a "dictator." Conley stated that he preferred to give his support to William E. Warren of the National Maritime Union (NMU) and "the rank and file longshoremen of his organization." The majority of local longshoremen present at this meeting, however, voted "that this organization back Joseph Ryan to the limit."[56] This special meeting served to illustrate some of the turmoil just below the surface between the local and the international headquarters, and it further characterized the leadership of the PLSBS as supportive of the conservative ILA agenda in the post–World War II period.

In this period, Bartley Conley was representative of a small militant rank-and-file group within the PLSBS that desired to remain independent of control by Ryan's ILA. In the 1920s and 1930s this group had been represented by such workers as Bartley Conley, James McGrath, and Lawrence Welch. However, they never succeeded in gaining power or anything near majority support. Welch, in explaining his reasons for contesting for the union presidency in the 1930s, referred to himself and his associates as members of the "rank and file," colorfully and provocatively adding, "those who read a little."[57]

In interviews in the early 1980s, Welch spoke of what he viewed as abuses by President Joseph Ryan. He also gave his opinion about changes on the Portland waterfront since 1923 such as a steady decline in the volume of work and a gradual erosion of the Irish monopoly on the workforce with the emergence of younger Italian members of the society. The ILA was responsible for eroding the protection of the limited sling load, he thought. "I just wanted to get Ryan and that outfit out. . . . One of my ideas for running [for Local 861 President was] to go along with the West Coast in one federation and get the hiring hall."[58] An excellent analysis of the different style of employing longshoremen on the Atlantic and Pacific coasts, and of how this crucial difference really defined the two unions involved, may be found in a seminal 1955 study by Charles P. Larrowe, *Shape-Up and Hiring Hall*, based on his Yale University dissertation.

32. Exporting potatoes (Jimmy Barter). Courtesy of ILA Local 861.

On August 20, 1947, the society heard the report of a committee recently returned from an ILA wage conference at which there was reported to be "quite a lengthy discussion over the size of the sling loads." The fact that the unlimited sling load, demanded by the shipping companies, had already been conceded by Local 861 could be witnessed in the following albeit somewhat contradictory proposal from a 1948 special meeting: "Article 59–Clause E: The unrestricted sling load to consist of one ton to be handled by a minimum of nineteen men and a foreman."[59] On August 17, 1949, Brother William Gorrivan "explained the start of the unlimited sling locally." It appears that the Portland longshoremen accepted the inevitability of the loss of the limited sling load in the years just before World War II, but they attempted to lessen the blow by ensuring a minimum number of workers per gang under these new conditions.

This was still the case as late as August 6, 1954, when a motion was made that asked for "nineteen men on unlimited sling of lumber." This motion, made during a deep-water negotiation with the Jarka Corporation, showed little change from the earlier reported position taken in 1948.

Antilabor Legislation and Anticommunism

The immediate postwar years between 1946 and 1949 marked the start of an era of unbridled attacks nationally upon the gains that labor had made during the Progressive and New Deal periods. As part of the American labor movement, the PLSBS was involved in these struggles and played a role in dampening the antiunion fervor then sweeping America. The society actively fought against the wave of antiunion legislation that emerged in this period. In 1946 President Truman vetoed the restrictive Case bill (HR 5262) titled "Labor Disputes Act, 1946," which would have mandated a mediation board. The most significant piece of legislation relative to labor in this era was, of course, the Taft-Hartley Act. This occupied the attention of the union throughout much of 1947.

The Taft-Hartley Act (Labor-Management Relations Act of 1947) revised the Wagner Act (National Labor Relations Act of 1935). It succeeded in being passed where the Case bill of the previous year had failed. It was a conservative reaction to the growing strength of labor unions since the mid-1930s and resulted in part from charges of communism and corruption within major unions. The closed (exclusively union) shop was outlawed along with jurisdictional strikes, secondary boycotts, political expenditures, and excessive dues. "Cooling off" procedures were established as well as requirements that unions file reports on their funds and organizational procedures. Under section 14(b) of the act, several states passed "right to work" laws.

Taft-Hartley affected all workers in America, but it "cast a particularly revealing light on the dilemma of maritime labor."[60] It represented a deteriorating position for organized labor within the American political system, a decline that would continue throughout the last half of the twentieth century and into the twenty-first century, at least in terms of union membership. Even President Harry Truman, whose veto of Taft-Hartley was over-ridden by what he famously called the "Do Nothing Congress," had perhaps inadvertently contributed to the antilabor mood in America by his earlier confrontation with the United Mine Workers during their 1946 strike. Truman's earlier "ambivalence toward labor may well have contributed to the climate in which the act nonetheless became law."[61]

The next year the attention of the union shifted back to the state of Maine where two related pieces of antilabor legislation were scheduled to be voted upon in statewide referenda on September 13, 1948. The Barlow bill on the referendum read as follows: "Shall a bill entitled, 'An Act to Protect the Right to Work and to Prohibit Secondary Boycotts, Sympathetic Strikes and Jurisdictional Strikes,' become law?"[62]

On April 7, 1948, society delegates to a meeting of the prolabor Maine Protective League at Waterville reported that "it will be necessary to spend a large amount of money for radio advertising and pamphlets and newspaper space to defeat [the Barlow] bill, and every working man will have to get his friends and relatives to vote on Election day."[63]

In Maine in this period these two pieces of antilabor legislation, the Barlow bill and the Tabb bill, essentially attempted to outlaw the closed shop by which a union could stipulate union membership as a requirement for being hired. Under the closed shop, therefore, a job site would consist entirely of union members. The Tabb bill, for example, innocuously read as follows on the referendum: "Shall a bill entitled 'An Act Protecting the Right of Members and Non-members of Labor Organizations to the Opportunity to Work' become law?"[64]

Maine's electorate, despite a virtual sweep of statewide offices by the Republican Party, handily defeated both of these bills through referenda. Organized labor had proven itself an effective political machine in Maine. Republican senator Margaret Chase Smith, by contrast, was returned to office with 75 percent of the vote. The vote in favor of the Barlow bill was 39,329; those favoring the Tabb bill numbered 12,528; but "No to Both," favored by Maine's labor organizations, polled 83,189.[65] Maine labor historian Charles A. Scontras in his *Labor in Maine* provides an extensive analysis of these antilabor bills and the organized effort to defeat them.[66]

The anticommunist, antiradical hysteria, often referred to as McCarthyism, also marked this postwar period.[67] The ILA, under President Joseph P. Ryan, fully subscribed to the principles of this movement, both for foreign and domestic reasons. Ryan's Pacific Coast rival, ILWU president Harry Bridges, was under scrutiny throughout this period and was eventually charged several times with harboring communist sympathies. In fact it would be the successful Bridges' defense in his case before the U.S. Supreme Court that prohibited the assumption of "guilt by association."

A request for financial aid was made on May 19, 1948, on behalf of the Free Trade Union Committee for Human Rights. This effort to promote the growth of noncommunist trade unions in Europe after World War II was strongly backed by President Ryan. Ryan was as concerned with the growth of radical labor organizations in Europe as he obviously was with their potential growth domestically, both along the Pacific Coast and in his own backyard along the Atlantic Coast.

Although this was just prior to the emergence of Sen. Joseph McCarthy, anticommunism had long been a political tendency within both the Democratic and the Republican parties. By June 15, 1949, its nascent influence was noticed within the Portland shipping industry when the society noted that "a communication has been received from the NLRB [National Labor Relations Board] stating that some of our officers have not yet signed the non-communist affidavits as required by law." By September 21, 1949, one member of the society's executive board had still not signed the noncommunist affidavit and the union was so notified by the regional office of the National Labor Relations Board.[68]

Anticommunism continued to influence the PLSBS well into the 1950s. At the meeting of February 13, 1957, the society was informed that their bargaining committee had been refused a meeting in Boston with representatives of the A. R. Wright Coal Company because "they had not signed non-communist affidavits."[69]

International vice president John "Red" Moran, so named presumably for his hair color rather than his political inclinations, told the society while visiting Portland in 1959 "that any man that had belonged or subscribed to any communistic order in the last five years could not belong to or hold office in any local."[70] The impact of McCarthyism did not die with the censure of its namesake by the Senate in 1954, which was courageously aided in no small measure by the "Declaration of Conscience" of Maine's own senator, Margaret Chase Smith, among others. This warning in 1959 showed the impact of the recently passed Landrum-Griffin Act (1959) that strengthened the Taft-Hartley Act by increasing governmental surveillance of trade unions. The provision in this act that forbade communists from holding union offices was not declared unconstitutional until 1965.

Containerization: The Longshoreman's Coffin?

In the years since 1950 the decline of the Portland longshore industry continued apace.[71] Antilabor legislation probably played a role in its demise, but more important was the revolution in the entire cargo-handling industry in America, and worldwide, by changing technology.[72] The introduction of containerization, specifically, tended to make smaller ports like Portland, Maine, less commercially viable. In essence, the main purpose of such smaller regional ports evolved to serve merely as "feeder ports" to larger commercial centers such as New York, Boston, Montreal, and Halifax.[73]

The idea of feeder ports serving a "hub-and-spoke" system similar to that used today by major airlines had long been applied to coal and other domestic bulk commodities. In the United States, coastal or short-sea trade, often referred to as brown-water trade, had long been more voluminous than transoceanic trade, and it would remain so for most of the nineteenth and twentieth centuries.[74] Along the waterfront, containers greatly increased the efficiency and volume by which goods could be handled. Simultaneously, containers decreased the need for physical labor, replacing dockworkers with constantly evolving machinery and innovative technology. Containers were sometimes referred to by skeptical maritime workers as the "longshoreman's coffin."[75]

The proefficiency argument to the unionized maritime laborers had been used by management in one form or another to support all technological innovations in both American and foreign ports. One example optimistically stated: "The trade unions of the world are very reluctant to accept our new metal rectangle because they think it will reduce the number of jobs and lead to smaller work gangs. They would be wiser to look ahead to the day when, because of retraining and education, the containerization concept will increase trade by making it easier, which will in turn create more jobs; in fact, it will lead to the formation of new careers in our society."[76] Statistical evidence exists to substantiate this longshore fear of its own maritime redundancy and decline. In 1969 longshore laborers on all coasts numbered some 68,700. Just three decades later, by 1999, that number was cut by two-thirds to a mere 23,562.[77]

Malcolm McLean, owner of the McLean Trucking Company, searched for ways to expedite transport of commodities from trucks to ships, and vice versa, in order to increase productivity and, therefore, profits. Addi-

33. Entering Portland harbor under the gaze of a nineteenth-century cannon in Fort Allen Park on Munjoy Hill. Courtesy of ILA Local 861.

tionally, shippers hoped to control what they saw as an "unholy trinity" of longshore labor—loss, damage, and pilferage. McLean and others had experimented with similar ideas since World War II, but McLean finally brought these ideas to fruition in 1956 with the launch of his ship *Ideal X* with a load of containers on a run between New York City and Houston. McLean's container-based shipping company soon became known as Sea-Land. Eventually, it merged with the Maersk Group in 1998 and was known as Maersk Sealand between 1999 and 2006 when it dropped the latter part of the name.[78]

The foundational idea of containerization was not unique to McLean, or to the mid-twentieth century, for that matter. Dutch merchants in the seventeenth century had perfected the *fluit*, or "fly boat," an unattractive but highly functional means of transporting large quantities of relatively low-value bulk cargo. Compared to the Maine-built sleek clipper ships of the nineteenth century, the *fluit*, though not as beautiful, was much larger and more functional, and therefore more profitable. Also sometimes referred to as the *flyte*, these early vessels have been described as "large, simply rigged, inexpensively built ships with a tonnage-per-man ratio far superior to that of competitors. They were the most efficient bulk carriers of their day." Another maritime historian described their axiomatic function as "measure little and stow much."[79] The 1960s development of global containerization by McLean and others appears to have been a modern adaptation of this same maxim.

Another major innovation brought about by Malcolm McLean was the successful standardization of this new shipping mode, both within the United States and internationally. This was not an easy task given local traditions and the international preference outside of the United States for the metric system of weights and measures.

Eventually, McLean's American standard measurement for the container became universally accepted at 8' by 8.5' by 20', and this became known as the twenty-foot equivalent unit, or TEU. This TEU standard was designed to be compatible with trucking needs and regulations, and it therefore helped to smooth the path toward acceptance of this potentially competitive form of long-distance transport by the trucking interests. One argument used by McLean was that efficiency was good for all components of the transport industry. The intermodal transport system was, by McLean's reasoning, good for each of the separate parts as well as good for the whole.

By the late 1950s, prior to containerization, it was estimated that 60 to 75 percent of the cost of transporting break-bulk cargo was incurred alongshore. Eventually container ships would be designed to carry containers nine deep in the hold and up to five deep on deck. Domestically, new and more efficient container ports were developed in places such as Port Elizabeth, New Jersey, adjacent to New York City. In Europe, Rotterdam soon became the world's largest container port of its day. On the Pacific Coast, several such ports were developed to handle the fast-growing trade with Asia and the Far East, especially during the Vietnam War.[80]

Portland, after World War II, despite the enormous increase in the handling of petroleum, had not made the maritime adjustments in technology that would be necessary to compete with the larger American, Canadian, or European ports.[81] Changes in the transport industry were not serving Portland well by the mid-twentieth century. The shift to air transport and the increasing use of long-haul trucking along the nation's heavily subsidized interstate highway system were both making deep cuts into the maritime shipping domain, especially outside of containerization. Increasing American trade with Asia and the Far East, rather than with Europe, also benefited the Pacific Coast ILWU longshoremen relatively more than their Atlantic Coast ILA fellow dockworkers. Rapidly growing maritime facilities at Long Beach, California, and elsewhere on the Pacific coast demonstrated this increasing transpacific trade.

Membership in the PLSBS stood at 537 in 1941, rose to 579 by 1949, dropped to 231 in 1958, and then leveled off to around 100 by 1970. An all-time low was reached in 1975 when the society numbered only 87 members. Although there was a mini-boom in work and membership in the late 1970s, the numbers continued to decline by the year 1980. A move to decasualize, or make longshore labor more permanent in Portland in this period, together with a proposal to provide a guaranteed annual income, failed due to the overall lack of maritime work locally and the low number of full-time longshore wage earners.[82] Portland's former geographical advantage as the closest North Atlantic American port to Europe had, by the 1980s, turned into a distinct economic and demographic disadvantage.

Containerized shipping, primarily serving only the largest Atlantic Coast ports directly, was now the cutting-edge technology. Portland was not equipped to handle this innovation, and apparently did not have a sufficient hinterland to support a major investment to compete with Boston or the Canadian ports of Saint John or Halifax.

Portland's declining longshore maritime presence was not unique, however. Even in ports with modern container facilities the number of dock workers needed to handle the ever more efficient technologies declined. In New York, as an example, longshore workers numbered around 31,000 in the mid-1950s, but that number was reduced by almost 90 percent by 1998.[83]

Of course, the longshore unions on both coasts had to respond in a way that best represented their members' immediate as well as long-term needs. Often these long- and short-term needs appeared to be in conflict. In essence, the longshore unions were eventually convinced that change was inevitable and that managing change was their only realistic option. Therefore, the longshoremen over time, albeit skeptically and reluctantly, bought into Malcolm McLean's argument that they could trade more jobs for better jobs. They were promised the jobs that would remain, and that they would be better paid and more secure.

To further ensure labor's cooperation, the shipping companies allowed a certain amount of redundancy to occur for the first few years. In other words, employers agreed to keep on more longshore laborers than were actually required to operate the new machinery efficiently. This was criticized by some in management as "featherbedding," and to them it seemed to undermine their drive to maximize profit. However, this "overstaffing" did serve to make the difficult technological transition less contentious between labor and management. Along the Pacific Coast ports alone, it was estimated that labor costs were reduced by one billion dollars in the 1960s.[84]

With all of these developments occurring, the prediction of Portland's veteran newspaper writer and resident philosopher, Bill Caldwell, in the early 1980s appears to have been well founded. Unless special efforts were quickly made, he warned, young Portlanders would soon be returning home from school with a question on their minds, "Daddy, what's a longshoreman?"[85]

The Late-Twentieth-Century Roller Coaster along the Waterfront

The last twenty years of the twentieth century were a roller coaster ride for Portland's maritime interests and its longshore laborers. Potentially positive developments were quickly followed by significant disappointments. In a 2008 interview with the longtime local ILA business agent Jack Humeniuk, this period was analyzed.[86]

With the expansion of the Bath Irons Works (BIW) onto the Portland waterfront in the early 1980s at the site of the Maine State Pier, the dream of the Portland longshoremen to retrieve at least a portion of their lost work appeared to have all but vanished. According to Phil O'Donnell, "They're out. They haven't got any docks! The Maine State Pier is the last dock they had. [Longshore work in Portland] is dead certainly now—there's no place to put it, no place to put the ship." Tom Mulkern agreed but reflected upon Maine's failure to generate enough business to maintain regular cargo service. "I don't see any future for the ILA here. They're not manufacturing anything here."[87]

An anticipated referendum for a modern container cargo terminal at the Maine State Pier was changed almost overnight in order to subsidize a newly proposed BIW ship repair facility. This would help to facilitate the building of President Ronald Reagan and Secretary of the Navy John F. Lehman's proposed modern six-hundred-ship Navy. Clearly, the influence of the Bath Iron Works and its parent company, then Congoleum Corporation and later General Dynamics, was stronger than those arguing on behalf of developing Portland's maritime transport capacity. BIW represented the largest single employer in the state of Maine, with between five thousand and six thousand employees, as compared with only about one hundred active longshoremen in Portland. In December 1981, the last vessel at the Maine State Pier was handled by the PLSBS, which was ironically then marking exactly one hundred years as a maritime labor presence here. The anniversary was not a sweet one for Portland's longshoremen.

What would be the future of the port of Portland? Some suggested that the harbor was dead as far as cargo was concerned. One large commercial firm, however, the Merrill Transportation Company, evaluated Portland's waterfront as being worthy of its own private capital investment. In the early 1980s when state revenues were diverted from a proposed public cargo handling facility in Portland to fund the BIW ship repair facility, Merrill filled the vacuum with its own nonunion bulk cargo facility at the western edge of the inner harbor along West Commercial Street. Originally developed to handle lumber for the preexisting Merrill Transport Company, the expanded maritime facility also brought in large quantities of coal to power the S. D. Warren (later known as South African Pulp and Paper Industries, SAPPI) paper mill in nearby Westbrook, Maine. With the death of founder P. E. Merrill in 1982, the ownership and directorship of the company passed to his son, P. D. Merrill.

According to spokesperson Mike Kane in a telephone interview, by 1987 the Merrill facility handled some 282,561 metric tons of cargo (311,467 short tons), which marked a significant increase over the previous year. The leading commodities imported were coal and salt, with newsprint and scrap metal as the only sizeable exports. These figures, however, paled in comparison with Portland's past as a cargo port, when as late as 1934 more than one million short tons of coal alone were handled by longshoremen along the waterfront. Any proposal for a separate container facility on the Portland waterfront was viewed by Merrill as a government-subsidized competition with his privately owned, nonunion pier and transport facility.

This period between 1981 and 1986 marked the low point for the ILA in Portland, with absolutely no work available and no pier from which to work. The Portland longshoremen by the mid-1980s knew that they must organize politically if union labor in maritime transport was to be restored to the Portland waterfront. This they did. In 1984 Gov. Joseph Brennan, himself the son of a PLSBS charter member, supported a proposal for a $5 million bond referendum for a new cargo facility in Portland. In the mid-1980s, the PLSBS could count on the support of at least five of the nine

34. *Prince of Fundy* at International Marine Terminal (roll on/roll off capability). Courtesy of ILA Local 861.

City Council members, including Mayor Joseph Casale, who also served as president of ILA Local 861. Portland's director of transportation services, Tom Valleau, was also a strong supporter of this proposal. The referendum passed even though supporters did not have a specific location designated for the pier itself.

Around 1985 this state money helped to rebuild the eastern half of what was then called the Lion Ferry Terminal and is now called the International Marine Terminal. Lion Ferry Service to Yarmouth, Nova Scotia, had been encouraged by local business concerns to locate its American facilities in Portland. Business leader, civic activist, and owner of a waterfront industry Joseph "Chet" Jordan of Jordan's Meats later wrote that raising $1.26 million from 126 local businesses was "the most exciting [fund-raising effort] of all" and that "this was accomplished with John Menario, the then city manager of Portland, in just five days."[88]

The 1985 referendum paid immediate, if only modest, dividends to the longshoremen because they were able to service the lines and stores for the Bermuda Star Cruise Line. Although not significant, at least relative to their earlier volume of work, this maintained a minimal longshore presence along the waterfront of Portland.

The unexpectedly wide margin of victory of a major 1987 Working Waterfront Referendum, which placed a five-year moratorium on all non-marine-related construction along Portland's waterfront, provided the breathing space to make the crucial decisions necessary at that time. One wondered whether Portland could create a maritime transportation alternative to Boston, where the Rouse Company, with its New Quincy Market and Boston Harbor development, had developed a popular tourist mecca.

Other similar models at that time included the Chelsea waterfront in New York City and the Inner Harbor of Baltimore. Each of these larger cities provided chic, fashionable workplaces for real estate, fashion, and commercial business interests, and the pressure was substantial to duplicate that in Portland. Could this development be undertaken without damaging the maritime prospects for fishermen, stevedores, and longshoremen? This question is still very much open to debate today.

Since 1987 the city of Portland has struggled with a set of questions common to other New England coastal metropolitan urban centers—in what direction should they grow, and should their maritime futures be based on industry, commerce, fishing, and transportation, or, alternatively, tourism? For many of the years between the passage of the waterfront referendum in 1987 and the early years of the twenty-first century, that question was partially answered by the dominating presence of a huge dry dock and ship repair facility adjacent to Portland's Maine State Pier. This facility was owned and operated as a subsidiary of BIW, itself a component of General Dynamics Corporation. The pier itself was leased to BIW by the city of Portland for the purpose of providing a marine-related industrial presence on the waterfront.

Toward the end of the century, BIW decided to consolidate and modernize its original and main facilities a few miles down the coast in Bath, and to get out of the ship repair business, thus making the Portland facility redundant. The city happily accepted the lease back, and around the millennium the debate swirled locally as to what would be the greatest and best use for this invaluable oceanfront property, both short and long term. In essence it was the old debate revived once again: retail and/or commercial versus maritime and/or industrial.

A major maritime development occurred on March 21, 1991, with the arrival of the *Yankee Clipper*, of Hapag-Lloyd. This was Portland's first container ship. Running between Portland, Boston, and Halifax, this vessel would help export finished paper (from S. D. Warren), shrimp, and apples, among other commodities. It would bring into the port Jøtul stoves from Norway, simplex wire cable, and yarn for rug manufacture, among other commodities. The Jøtul connection was particularly advantageous and was largely the result of Portland being the place of residence of Eva Horton, the North American distributor for Jøtul. The *Yankee Clipper* would sail weekly, usually on Thursdays. The old issue of trade imbalance was still present, as exports still outpaced imports by nearly two to one.

In 1994 a statewide jobs bond was passed, $4 million of which was for the renovation of the remaining western half of the Lion Ferry Pier, whose name was officially changed to the International Marine Terminal (IMT) at about this same time. Coordinating sailing times was crucial, however, and the *Yankee Clipper* would usually arrive in the early morning and depart by mid-afternoon. During the summer sailing season, this would allow the *Prince of Fundy* to arrive around 7 P.M. and depart at 9 P.M., a very fast turnaround in order to make the run to Yarmouth, Nova Scotia, on schedule. This would even leave time for cruise lines to intermittently use this facility, with longshore labor providing stores and lines, on the days when the *Yankee Clipper* was not due in. This service lasted for three years, between 1991 and 1994. By 1996 Portland was merely a feeder port exporting paper and pulp from South African Paper and Pulp Industries (SAPPI), formerly S. D. Warren, via Halifax, Boston, and Portland.

Together with the continued expansion of the adjacent Old Port District's retail and restaurant sector, Portland's working waterfront was being badly squeezed in the 1980s and 1990s. The decision in 1988 to remove the railroad tracks from the middle of Commercial Street was historic. After many starts and stops, this was only completed in the summer of 2008 and was certainly symbolic of Portland's century-long ideological struggle between an actual working waterfront and the concept of a tourist- and service-based retail mecca.[89] These rails had formerly been part of a highly functional and nearly unique belt-line service that connected all of Portland's wharves with its major rail terminals heading out of the city in all directions. It had represented a genuine competitive advantage for Portland when compared to other maritime ports on the Atlantic Coast.

35. Pat Malone, an Irish speaker from Inverin, County Galway, Ireland, and a veteran of the old IRA still working longshore on December 29, 1969. Courtesy of ILA Local 861.

Well over one hundred years of continuous longshore union labor in Portland, on the wane for over half a century, was now greatly diminished and threatened with outright extinction. When asked for his opinion as to the future role of Portland's waterfront in the early 1980s, one retired longshoreman answered sadly, "A rich man's playground."[90]

Conclusion

The Port of Portland in the Twenty-First Century and Its Maritime Future

Portland, Maine's maritime presence was set by nature. What is done with these natural resources, however, is very human and subject to human motivation, imagination, and choices. Olaf Janzen, in another book in this maritime series, has written, "The key to understanding changing patterns of trade and domination at sea rests with our ability to recognize the significance of what was happening ashore."[1]

Whether one remembers, as did Portland's hometown poet Henry Wadsworth Longfellow, "the black wharves and the slips," or the many ships that were built and outfitted along the Maine coast and crewed by seasoned seamen from Portland and its hinterland, the connection with the sea had defined Portland from the very start. The sea shapes the city in many and profound ways and gives Portland its unique qualities. One comical yet instructive example of this can be found in a local maritime story: "An exasperated mother was chasing her twelve-year-old son in a gale of wind. The mother with her wide spread of skirts was bearing down on him and fast overtaking him when his eight-year-old brother sang out, 'Take her on the wind, Jimmy!' And Miss Colcord [the Maine author] comments, 'Only a longshore boy could have said that.'"[2]

At the midpoint of the nineteenth century, the outlook for Portland as a commercial center was indeed bright. By 1853 Portland was connected by rail to Montreal, a fact that was not overlooked by an Irish traveler to the city, Thomas Mooney, who wrote back to his cousin in Ireland that Portland was "a most important city [which will soon] double its population and wealth."[3]

Portland certainly also had its share of aspirations and dreams. No one better epitomized the wider view of Portland's potential in these years than did John Alfred Poor. By his reckoning, this city should have settled for nothing less than first-class status along with the other leading metropolitan centers of North America and Europe. Its geographical location demanded greatness, and only inertia or lack of vision could deny that status.

Saint John, New Brunswick, however, was more faithful to its maritime-related potential than was Portland, and it eventually succeeded in capturing the bulk of Montreal's winter trade. Neither city, of course, ever matched their larger competitors—Montreal, Halifax, and Boston—in terms of commercial maritime development. At least for a time, "both New England and the Maritimes remained dependent upon the Hub [Boston] for a variety of important functions." Portland may have fared better overall, due largely to its development as a regional service and distribution center for its traditional hinterland. By the start of World War I, Saint John still looked toward the sea for its wealth while Portland was turning inward. Each city was aware of its location "on the rim of the North American economy." Both had been influenced to a degree, as yet largely unrecognized, by the vision and the energy of this Portlander, John Alfred Poor.[4]

It could be argued that the Irish longshoremen of Portland, Maine, gained as much if not more than any other group in this city from the "Montreal connection" that gave at least two or three generations of these maritime laborers guaranteed work in their new home. Between 1853 and 1880 the railway cars of the Grand Trunk brought an ever-increasing volume of Canadian grain to Portland for export during the winter months when Montreal and Quebec were virtually transformed into landlocked cities.

This labor-intensive opportunity arrived in Portland simultaneously with these new and hungry workers, many of whom were refugees from recurring bouts of famine in the west of Ireland. The Irish continued to arrive in waves coincidental with its frequent agricultural disasters, primarily between 1845 and 1850, but again in 1879 and 1881 and beyond.

In 1880 improving conditions dictated that these laborers should protect themselves economically, and, following existing maritime labor models, they established the Portland Longshoremen's Benevolent Society (PLSBS) late that year. They survived in an inhospitable environment. Along with the rest of the country, they prospered after the economic depression of the 1890s, and by the turn of the twentieth century they could boast of nearly nine hundred members.

Following difficulties in the early twentieth century, during which they lost two maritime strikes in 1911 and 1913, the PLSBS opted for the solidarity, collective security, and protection of a nationwide union. They joined the International Longshoremen's Association (ILA) in February 1914. The next six years, during World War I, would represent the union's heyday, and by 1919 its membership peaked at 1,366 making it one of Portland's and Maine's major labor organizations and source of employment.

Between the end of the war and 1923, although membership remained very high, forces largely beyond the union's control were conspiring to bring an end to this prosperity. With the carefully planned development of modern, efficient maritime ports at Saint John and Halifax, which would ship "Canadian goods from Canadian ports," the end was in sight for Portland. With the exception of a brief respite during World War II, the decline of Portland as a major cargo-handling port that had begun in 1923 was both steady and precipitous.

What remains is to provide a summary analysis of the causes for this decline, and to answer questions concerning its perceived inevitability while also assessing the maritime future of this city. The conventional wisdom maintains that Portland was, since the mid-nineteenth century, nearly totally dependent on Canadian export policy. It is often conjectured with a certain degree of facetiousness, but some degree of truth, that if Maine ever seceded from the United States and politically and geographically were joined with Canada, Portland would have become an entrepôt to this southeastern appendage of the Canadian Maritimes. Thus, Portland inevitably would have developed into a world-class port, along the lines of John A. Poor's dream, with a population potentially rivaling that of Boston. This represents Poor's thesis absent the critical factor of American nationalism. In reality though, Portland was firmly, albeit peripherally, a part of the United States.

The antithesis to this conventional wisdom was provided by Professor Emeritus Robert H. Babcock of the University of Maine at Orono. Babcock argued that despite Canadian decisions that elevated national politics over pure economics, Portland itself, in the final analysis, never did enough to promote its own status as a major maritime presence. Its business and political leaders, at the turn of the century and arguably still today, were infatuated with its potential as a tourist, retail, and distribution center for northern New England. Whenever these commercial aspirations conflicted with Portland's development as an industrial or maritime shipping center, the latter dreams were most often jettisoned in favor of the immediacy and lure of the former.

It seems that a synthesis of these two conflicting analyses of Portland's industrial waterfront status is not only possible but also the most realistic method by which to appraise its maritime decline since 1923, especially in terms of cargo handling, and to assess its maritime future. This synthesis would maintain that while Portland was responsible to a large degree for its own maritime decline, it was simultaneously the victim of circumstances somewhat beyond its control. Between 1853 and 1923, Portland's longshore laborers shipped millions of tons of Canadian grain and other commodities through this port. The local economic spin-offs of this business were enormous. At the very least, it allowed many thousands of families to live and prosper in this city while giving the male offspring of these longshoremen the option of following in their fathers' footsteps alongshore, or of branching out into other occupational fields.

A central theme of this book is that the sacrifices of the first-generation Irish longshoremen allowed the second and subsequent generations these occupational options, thus a recurring theme for this book, "the dreams of the first generation are lived by the second." The safety net of this labor niche was used by many longshore children, some only temporarily while many others, not so inclined, chose careers in business or public service. Most important, the option was theirs.

One of the most notable of these second-generation longshore children was Joseph E. Brennan, who has kindly contributed the foreword to this book. His humble beginnings as a longshoreman's son who grew up on Kellogg Street on Portland's then solidly working-class Munjoy Hill demonstrated upward social mobility in its finest sense. Success at Cheverus High School, Boston College, and the University of Maine Law School allowed Brennan to enter Democratic Party politics. He eventually rose to high office such as Maine's attorney general, two terms as governor, and U.S. representative from the first congressional district, which includes Portland. Today, in an appropriate conclusion to his career given his family history, Joe Brennan serves as federal maritime commissioner.

Clearly, no one would argue against the significance of Portland's "Montreal connection." A point of contention, however, arises at the turn of the twentieth century, some fifty years after the first Grand Trunk Railway car had pulled into Portland. At that point, while still profiting from the export of Canadian grain, Portland arguably could and should have looked ahead to its future and attempted more strenuously to diversify its mix of imports and exports.

At that time even the shipping agents were complaining to the Portland Board of Trade about the uneven nature of commodities in and out of this port. Exports far exceeded imports, and "foreign" produce, primarily Canadian grain, composed the vast majority of these maritime exports. Any port that existed primarily on the basis of one product alone, as did Portland, should have recognized the precarious nature of its maritime economy. Warning signs abounded and were readily apparent concerning the danger of putting all of one's eggs in one basket.

Who was at fault? There is always more than enough blame to go around for failure. All groups, at one time or another, acknowledged this potential flaw in Portland's maritime mix, but few did anything of significance to remedy the problem. By the early 1920s, ironically at the very time that the city government was finally convinced to expend public monies to build the Maine State Pier, the battle had essentially already been lost. Saint John and Halifax were becoming ever larger, more modern, and more efficient ports and the Canadian national card was being played in their favor. Portland's city fathers had opted to promote their city as a tourist and retail center, and that is what it has largely become. This provided an uneven return after the 1920s, at least until Portland's remarkable commercial and economic recovery beginning in the late 1960s.

Around the millennium, a consensus eventually developed that the eastern portion of the Portland waterfront should be further developed as a commercial and tourist destination, contiguous to its premier shopping district known as the Old Port, with a state-of-the-art marine passenger facility, now known as Ocean Gateway, which was constructed adjacent to the Maine State Pier. The State Pier, according to this consensus, could itself hopefully also be simultaneously repaired and redeveloped with a strong maritime function.

Two competing private waterfront development plans for the Maine State Pier were emotionally debated throughout most of 2008. By the beginning of 2009, the adjacent Ocean Gateway was built but lacked the crucial megaberth pier. After much highly contentious debate and many public false starts by the Portland City Council and the two competing companies, at the time of this writing neither the Olympia Company (Portland, Maine) nor Ocean Properties (Portsmouth, New Hampshire) is currently under contract for the rebuilding of the Maine State Pier, both having been offered the opportunity to develop but both eventually backing away from any firm commitments. Its future as the premier waterfront property in this maritime city is currently very much in doubt.

This plan for the east end of the harbor would allow the central portion of the waterfront to continue to serve as a fishing-related area, adjacent to the Marine Trade Center (formerly called the Portland Fish Exchange). That trade center anchors the central section of the harbor, along with the Gulf of Maine Ocean Research Facility completed in 2005.[5] The Fish Exchange got off to a strong start, but the constantly decreasing landings of ground fish all along the New England coast since then have placed its viability in question. Related to this is the ruling that disallows local fishermen from selling in Portland any lobster that may have been inadvertently caught, known as bycatch, while dragging for fish. This ruling has apparently, together with other factors, resulted in a significant number of Maine fishermen electing to sell their catches in Gloucester and other Massachusetts ports rather than at Portland's Marine Trade Center.

This plan preserved the western zone of the waterfront, up to the Casco Bay Bridge, for the consolidation of container freight handling at the site of the former Prince of Fundy Cruise Lines, since the mid-1990s known officially as the International Marine Terminal (IMT). "Sixty percent of the value of oceanborne trade now comes and goes from the United States in containers."[6] Locally, a state-funded 1998 study of Maine's "three port" strategy was quite optimistic about Portland: "The feeder container operations would increase from 5,000 to 9,000 TEUs [twenty-foot equivalent units, or containers] per year moving through the port with potential added ship calls by larger vessels."[7]

One graphic symbol of the difficulty of keeping Portland's maritime cargo history alive was the demise of the *Shamrock*, the container vessel that made the Portland to Halifax run in the early twenty-first century. By 2004, however, the *Shamrock* poignantly and helplessly lay dormant within Portland harbor for six months only to eventually be repossessed after bankruptcy. For much of the period between 2004 and 2006 cargo service to and from Portland was intermittent at best. Lack of dependable service is the kiss of death for containerized cargo handling, and Portland in these years could not guarantee regular service.

Beginning in July of 2007 a single container company was serving Portland, the Icelandic firm Eimskip. The following month a local newspaper buoyantly reported that Eimskip would soon be joined by another container firm, Columbia Coastal Transport. This momentarily gave local businesses more options for shipping into and out of Portland, and this might have created a potentially larger presence for longshore workers again in the city. Then-director of Portland's Ports and Transportation Jeffrey Monroe was quoted at this time as saying, "This is a huge milestone for the port." Monroe added that this "validates the city's decision to move passenger operations to the east end of the waterfront, opening up room for containers and freight operations at the former International Ferry Terminal on the west end."[8]

By December 18, 2007, however, Eimskip had suspended service due to poor market conditions. Columbia Coastal, a subcontractor for Hapag-Lloyd, did briefly continue its barge service between New York/New Jersey, Portland, and Boston until forced, by lack of work, to withdraw from this waterfront in late June of 2009. Hapag-Lloyd had provided continuous stevedoring service in Portland for seventeen years beginning in 1991 and ending only in 2008.

It appeared in early 2009 that Portland's longshoremen finally had their own facility through which to develop this city's maritime container cargo transport services. The question that remained to be answered, however, as with the earlier development of the Maine State Pier in 1923, was did this facility come at just the right time or was it once again too little and too late?

Could Portland provide enough oceanborne commerce to justify a container ship or two coming on a regular basis to connect Portland with Boston and New York/New Jersey to the south and Halifax to the east? Specifically, could such a service provide significant and regular employment for Portland's remaining longshoremen and their agents? Nationally, due in large part to the efficiencies brought about by containerization, redundancies in the number of longshoremen working over the last thirty years of the twentieth century, between 1969 and 1999, resulted in a steep decline in their numbers from 68,700 to 23,562.[9]

Over the years the Prince of Fundy Cruise Lines, through vessels that were highly visible such as the *Marine Evangeline*, the *Prince of Fundy*, and the *Scotia Prince*, provided seasonal passenger and freight service between Portland and Yarmouth, Nova Scotia. This service was temporarily discontinued after the 2004 sailing season due to an acrimonious dispute between the operating company and the City of Portland. This important tie with Maritime Canada recommenced, however, nearly without lapse when Bay

Ferries Limited introduced to Portland's waterfront *The Cat* with its ultramodern and speedy catamaran service to Nova Scotia taking less than six hours. This ferry, acquired by Bay Ferries in 1998, has the capacity to board 775 passengers and more than 250 cars, trucks, and trailers.

As of the 2008 sailing season, *The Cat* served both Portland, on weekends, and Bar Harbor, Maine, midweek. In May 2008, the newly opened Ocean Gateway facility became the east end Portland terminal for this service.[10] Hope was expressed, informally at least, that eventually an additional vessel might be purchased, thus allowing the company to run full-time summer service from both ports simultaneously. The rapidly increasing price of fuel in the early months of 2008, however, surely negatively impacted that possibility, as would any future upward oil price fluctuation.

The nonunion Sprague Energy (formerly Merrill) Marine Terminal, further west of the Casco Bay Bridge, currently handles the majority of the bulk cargo in Portland. As of 2008 large quantities of pulp and finished paper from the Westbrook SAPPI Fine Paper mill and the Red Shield Environmental plant in Old Town arrived at the Sprague terminal. These were then placed in containers there for shipment by the ILA longshoremen through the nearly adjacent IMT.

The relocation of the Portland terminal for *The Cat* to the Ocean Gateway facility in the east end of the harbor in May 2008 cleared the way for an expanded and modernized container facility at the IMT. This is the current maritime labor site of the unionized longshoremen of Portland, PLSBS, ILA Local 861, but would there be any work left for them?

The state of Maine Department of Transportation, through its agency the Maine Port Authority, with the strong support of the city municipal government, began the process of taking control of this facility in 2008. This would bring Portland more in line with other maritime centers in America that normally have state or regional rather than municipal control of their major maritime facilities. This entire restructuring process was promptly derailed, at least temporarily, by the bankruptcy of the Red Shield Environmental plant in Old Town. Consequently, Columbia Coastal Transport of Liberty Corner, New Jersey, suspended container cargo service to Portland in late June 2008. The city and longshoremen still hoped to convince the state to run the marine terminal, a plan also supported editorially by Portland's largest daily newspaper.[11]

The PLSBS and the city both hoped to convince the state to consolidate and further modernize this important resource as a crucial lynchpin of its long-stated three-ports strategy for maritime commerce in Maine, with regional port developments at Portland, Searsport, and Eastport.

John Henshaw, executive director of the Maine Port Authority, a "quasi-independent arm of the Maine Department of Transportation," stated, "the city has other appropriate priorities. Handling cargo operations is what the Port Authority was set up to do." Portland was described as "Maine's only cargo container facility," and the number of containers shipped through Portland reportedly increased 84 percent between 2006 and 2007. This same newspaper source quoted ILA business agent Jack Humeniuk as agreeing with this potential transfer of jurisdiction stating, "The real benefit here is to the state of Maine as a whole. It's not all on Portland." The article reiterated that "the transfer to state management is supported by the International Longshoremen's Association Local 861, which represents the employees who load and unload the orange, tractor-trailer-like cargo containers at the terminal."[12]

As of October 2007, the longshoremen finally had the space they needed to operate effectively at the 15.5-acre IMT, which was by then cleared of any passenger liner competition for its limited space. Any new publicly funded improvements needed for the IMT were thought to be relatively inexpensive. Such improvements would have included an additional crane and yard equipment, mainly top-lifters, to help make the longshore labor more efficient and therefore more productive.

For the last five months of 2007 Portland was served by two stevedoring companies with service to both major container ports, Halifax and New York/New Jersey, each with an international reach. Increased maritime shipping volume created a synergy with widely held environmental concerns, such as reducing the carbon footprint and increasing transportation fuel efficiency. This synergy served to enhance public support and possibly to entice greater corporate interest in containerized cargo. This marked a heady time alongshore.

In the summer of 2007 a group of local business leaders with maritime interests in Portland shipping met in New Jersey with representatives of the city of Portland, the state of Maine, and the Portland longshoremen's union. These businesses included the Red Shield pulp mill, SAPPI Fine Papers, and Sprague Energy. All present stated that they were willing to give the new container service to New York/New Jersey a try, but they were also conscious of the omnipresent challenge of attracting more imports into Portland and not merely relying principally on exports, in this case primarily paper and pulp. Following this line of reasoning, local companies such as L. L. Bean and Poland Spring Bottling Company were mentioned as two large Maine-based corporations that might make use of this service for both imports and exports.

Ultimately, Warren Pullen, manager for the pulp business at Central National Gottesman, the then-owner of Red Shield, reflected that the barge business would only survive if increased volume could make the cost more competitive with traditional forms of transport such as overland trucking. Pullen warned, "This thing could end as quickly as it got started."[13]

Two developments since 2007, however, again called the maritime future of the port of Portland into question. The first was the loss of the Eimskip container company with its direct connection to Halifax in December 2007. This again left Portland with only one container service active as of early 2008, a weekly coastal barge that transported containers directly to the Atlantic Coast's largest container facility at New York/New Jersey. Columbia Coastal, even when limited to its earlier biweekly barge service, still carried a greater capacity than the previous service via the *Yankee Clipper*. The latter averaged only 3,000 to 3,500 TEUs per year out of Portland. The Columbia Coastal barge service as of May 2008 was shipping about 12,000 TEUs per year, three to four times the previous total volume.[14] Just one month later, by late June 2008, however, because of the economic difficulties in Maine's paper industries, Columbia Coastal was forced to suspend its services to Portland. This once-bustling waterfront was again left without work for its longshoremen.

Second, due to very tight budget constraints, the city of Portland also in the spring of 2008 announced layoffs of some ninety-eight city workers. Included in these layoffs, to the surprise of many, was Jeffrey Monroe and, indeed, the entire municipal ports and transportation department. These duties reportedly would be parceled out to other surviving city agencies, as well as possibly to the Maine Port Authority, as cited earlier in the case of container cargo.

In Portland up through 2008, the stevedoring functions were run by Ports America. This followed a long association with previous stevedores such as the Jarka Corporation prior to the mid-1950s, the International Terminal Operating Company (ITO) roughly from 1955 to 1999, followed by P&O Ports, which morphed into Dubai Ports and AIG, before being renamed Ports America. This current stevedoring contractor is recognized by the ILA and services major and minor ports all along the Atlantic and Gulf Coasts.

The question as to the survival of Portland's working waterfront as of 2008 remained very much open. It centered on whether the city's business and political leadership would take full advantage of new opportunities, or, as has happened so often in the past, delay decisions or squander the natural advantages of Portland's deep-water harbor for more immediate, superficial, or temporary gains.

Even maritime-related investment is no guarantee of desired results. The first edition of *The Bollard* (June 2008) featured an article by Colin Woodard titled "Chump Change" that was highly critical of the cruise ship industry and Portland's financial expectations from it. Woodard claimed that Portland had based its projected revenues from cruise ships on faulty data, using North American port averages and figures from Bar Harbor, Maine, rather than the more appropriate, and lower, figures from Canadian Maritime ports such as Halifax and Saint John. Woodard coupled this with the fact that most passengers upon disembarking in Portland would likely head immediately to better-known local tourist destinations, such as Kennebunkport, Freeport, or the White Mountains of New Hampshire, thus spending their money elsewhere. Because meals are included aboard ship, there is even less incentive to pay twice by frequenting local restaurants and eateries.

Data was reportedly never properly collected for Portland itself, so these projections were just that. The president of a local ship chandlery company claimed, "People have been lying to the people of Portland all along about this. Nobody wants to be honest." An added problem discussed by Woodard was the incomplete nature of Ocean Gateway, which at least up to 2009, lacked a "megaberth" needed to handle ships exceeding eight hundred feet in length, which are quite common nowadays.[15]

In two equally troubling addenda to the featured article, Woodard discussed in "Know Your Boats" the dubious environmental and labor records of several of the cruise ships that frequent the Portland waterfront. He cited a highly critical 2005 book on the cruise ship industry by Kristoffer A. Garin, *Devils on the Deep Blue Sea*.

In a further addendum, "Well Contained," of direct interest to maritime transport, Woodard briefly addressed the failure of the city of Portland to carry out the previously mentioned state of Maine ten-year growth plan for the port, originally published in 1998. As the major commodities making use of containers for export from Portland were from the pulp and paper industry, "which is rapidly divesting itself of land and facilities," the future, according to Woodard at least, would be very much in question. It seems that concentration on one major commodity, as was the status quo with grain in 1923, is still one of Portland's great maritime weaknesses. Even Maine Port Authority executive director John Henshaw, representing the state agency that was actively considering taking control of the IMT from the city, stated that "cargo volumes have remained quite modest [and] net growth, for the foreseeable future, will be small."[16] Obviously, the loss of the Red Shield exports in mid-2008 had an immediate and deleterious effect on the port and on this process, but larger issues were still unaddressed.

A warning was given by Jeffrey Monroe, before he was made redundant, that tourist and private real estate interests often compete with the public development of the city's finite and unique waterfront space, often to the detriment of the latter. In a tongue-in-cheek historical reference to the late-eighteenth-century British shelling of colonial Falmouth, Monroe was quoted as saying, "More damage is done today by people with non-maritime interests in the waterfront than could ever be done by enemy gunfire."[17]

In the opinion of ILA business agent Jack Humeniuk, the future of the port of Portland today hangs in the balance. He acknowledged both Woodard and Henshaw's concerns adding, "If nothing changes, we may go out of business." Somewhat more optimistically Humeniuk added that the maritime business of Portland could either be "on the verge of elimination or scoring big." This pragmatic yet guarded assessment seems to be in line with that of other key waterfront players. The Portland longshoremen, of course, and other local maritime constituents would prefer to realize the latter option of "scoring big."

The longshoremen, the city of Portland, and the state of Maine all have a vested interest in Portland's maritime success, unlike merely dispassionate journalists. In order to ensure the maritime future of a working waterfront in Portland, Jack Humeniuk mentioned several current needs:

1. Public political education—the city is changing quickly and many of Portland's long-term residents who were once quite familiar with the city's working waterfront have either died or moved away from the city's peninsula.

2. Some limited public investment is still needed to increase efficiency and volume handled.

3. Stress that the statewide and regional benefits of port development are not limited to Portland. Follow the state's "three port strategy" of maritime development.

4. Overcome myopia concerning incompatibility of marine industrial development with commercial, retail, and tourism.

5. Diversify the port—don't put all your eggs in one basket. One segment may be economically up, e.g., cargo, while another is down, e.g., fishing or retail.

6. Educate the public that marine transport decreases the carbon footprint. In many cases containerization is a "green" alternative for heavy volume marine transport.

7. Teach the lesson that once maritime-related usage of this port is lost, it may well be gone forever. The 1987 Working Waterfront referendum acknowledged that point by specifically targeting a ban on future residential condominium development along Portland harbor's deep water piers, east and south of Commercial Street.[18]

Since these concerns were expressed by longshore business agent Jack Humeniuk in May of 2008, two significant and positive developments have occurred alongshore in Portland. In late March 2009 the former Red Shield company of Old Town, which had since been reorganized as Old Town Fuel and Fiber, recommenced container shipments out of Portland. As a direct result of this change, on June 1, 2009, the Maine Port Authority formally took control of the IMT from the city of Portland.

These two long-awaited developments have given a new sense of optimism to Portland's longshore union as it is about to celebrate 130 years of nearly uninterrupted service on this city's waterfront. Presently negotiations are under way that may result in Portland becoming a home port for major cruise lines, especially in the North Atlantic. Of even greater significance is the possible recommencement of container service to Halifax. While these are reasons for optimism, history has taught the Portland longshoremen to temper this emotion with pragmatic realism and patience.

The ILA-affiliated dockworkers in the PLSBS in 2009 are the direct descendants of a long and sustained union workforce along the Portland, Maine waterfront. They number far fewer than their earlier counterparts, but their presence is an unmistakable link with a cohesive, ethnically based, working-class group of predominantly Irish longshoremen who have labored on these docks at least since the mid-nineteenth century and formally since 1880. Their presence today, although greatly diminished, is a direct link with Portland's rich labor and social history. Local historian and director of the University of Southern Maine's New England Studies Program Joseph A. Conforti claims that despite large-scale migration off the peninsula, especially in the years since World War II, "nevertheless, even with such twentieth-century suburban growth, at its core Portland remains a nineteenth-century maritime city whose identity has become fixed on the Old Port."[19]

One is left to wonder, however, as to the direction and health of Portland's current and future maritime presence. By late in the year 2009, the city had a hopeful yet still precarious single-container cargo service, but it still lacked a plan for the redevelopment of its Maine State Pier. Still to be determined is whether Portland will ever achieve what its voters unequivocally demanded by a two-to-one margin in a 1987 waterfront referendum led by State representative Larry Connolly and Portland West's director Jim Oliver, among others. Can Portland protect its working waterfront, or will the concern of former longshoreman Larry Welch prove prescient as Portland's precious and unique maritime and waterfront resources become simply "a rich man's playground?"

Appendix A

Portland Town

Words and Music by Steve Romanoff

Chorus:
    I see the light not far away,
    And I hear music all around,
    I'm gettin' close to Portland Town,
    So, Mother, won't you make my bed,
    I see the light of Portland Head,
    I see the light, I'm comin' 'round,
    I'm comin' home to Portland Town.

    Some years ago, out on my own,
    I set a course for parts unknown,
    Leavin' behind both friend and foe,
    Needin' to find what I've come to know,
    As I watched the islands fade away,
    And bid farewell to Casco Bay,
    Though it's been years and years since then,
    My heart has brought me home again.

    Of all the places I could go,
    She's still the fairest port I know,
    She works the sea and tills the farms,
    And holds her children in her arms,
    No place could know a prouder past,
    Here comes the future full at last,

Here comes that beacon 'cross the sky,
And when I hold my head up high . . .

Copyright 1979 Steve Romanoff and Outer Green Records/Schooner Fare
304 Foreside Road
Falmouth, Maine 04105 USA

Appendix B

Day of the Clipper

Words and Music by Steve Romanoff

You can see the squares of canvas dancing over the horizon,
You can hear the chanty wailing to the heaving of the men,
You can feel the seas up to your knees and you know the sea is risin'
And you know the clipper's day has come again.
To the men on high the bos'n's cry commands a killing strain,
'Til every mother's son begins to pray.
With a hearty shout she comes about and she heads into the rain,
And the ship has never seen a better day.

Chorus:

Sailing ships and sailing men will sail the open water,
Where the only thing that matters is the wind inside the main.
So all you loving mothers keep your eyes upon your daughters;
For the sails will mend their tatters and the masts will rise again.

Wooden beams and human dreams are all that make her go;
And the magic of the wind upon her sails.
We'd rather fight the weather than the fishes down below;
God help us if the rigging ever fails.
As the timber creaks the captain speaks above the vessel's groans
'Til every soul on board can hear the call.
It's nothing but the singing of the ship inside her bones,
And this is when she likes it best of all.

Where the current goes the clipper's nose is plowing fields of green.
Where fortune takes the crews we wish them well.

Where men could be when lost at sea is somewhere in between
The regions of a heaven and a hell.
Well they're sailing eastern harbors and the California shore;
If you set your mind to see them then you can.
As you count each mast go sailing past you, prouder than before,
Then you'll know the clipper's day has come again.

Copyright 1979 Steve Romanoff and Outer Green Records/Schooner Fare
304 Foreside Road
Falmouth, Maine 04105 USA

Appendix C

PLSBS Retirement List as of January 1983

Name	Date of Birth
James Brown	November 24, 1905
Royal Caleb	October 12, 1905
Frank Carlista	April 7, 1910
Samuel Casale	August 26, 1915
Bartley Connolly Jr.	October 3, 1911
John F. Connolly	July 6, 1896
Joseph L. Corkery	June 13, 1910
Philip Coughlin	June 19, 1905
Philip A. Curran	May 28, 1912
John Derrig	April 18, 1912
Fiore DiPietrantonio	June 2, 1912
Felix P. Dyro	May 18, 1909
Richard Elliott	September 1929
Patrick H. Feeney	March 14, 1914
Joseph Ferrante	November 23, 1911
John J. Flanagan	May 7, 1902
Mark Foley Jr.	November 14, 1915
Philip Foley	April 9, 1890
Patrick E. Geary	March 22, 1912
John P. Gorham	March 18, 1918
Michael Greely	August 15, 1892
John J. Joyce (Jackie)	March 25, 1925
John J. Joyce (Mickey)	April 17, 1921
Martin Joyce	August 2, 1919
Michael J. Joyce	July 29, 1911
Walter J. Joyce	December 18, 1915

Charles R. Kane	March 3, 1910
Martin E. Lee	May 2, 1908
Joseph A. Lydon	December 27, 1911
William H. Malia	May 3, 1907
Vincent Manchester	December 1929
Edward Manning	February 1921
Bartley McDonough	February 12, 1914
Peter J. Mealy	June 22, 1915
Thomas Mulkern	October 7, 1905
James Myatt	April 1, 1910
Patrick Myatt	May 6, 1908
Frank J. Naples	July 26, 1910
James O'Brien	September 9, 1916
Michael O'Brien	September 22, 1914
Patrick O'Brien	August 31, 1912
Philip J. O'Donnell	May 25, 1905
Philip T. O'Donnell	October 3, 1910
John M. O'Malley Jr.	July 22, 1915
Patrick O'Malley	February 14, 1901
Joseph Palmacci	March 16, 1899
Joe Phillipo	November 1, 1912
Patrick J. Walsh	December 27, 1897
Thomas Walsh	1921

Appendix D

Oral Histories

Author's Taped Interviews with Longshoremen

Caleb, Royal	February 5, 1982
Concannon, Stephen	February 3, 1982, and December 15, 1985
Costelloe, Séamus	December 15, 1985
Humeniuk, Jack	January 31 and February 1, 1983, and May 19, 2008
Malone, Patrick	February 20, 1984
Mulkern, Thomas C.	January 22, 1982
O'Donnell, Philip	January 13, 1982
O'Malley, Patrick	February 20, 1984
O'Toole, Patrick	December 14, 1984
Welch, Lawrence F.	January 6, 1982, January 31, 1983, and February 3, 1983

Videotapes for University of Southern Maine Television

Stephen Concannon and Philip and Nan Conley Foley, December 8, 1987
Patrick O'Malley and Lawrence Welch, December 19, 1987

Appendix E

Longshore Nicknames

Geary, Charles	Albie Booth
Geary, John J.	Alger
Green, Patrick H.	American Legion
Joyce, Patrick	Anderson
Emerson, Andrew	Andy
O'Donnell	Arab
Green, Patrick	Average Man
Joyce, John	Bád ni nyarn
Hopkins, James	Baker
Lydon, John	Baldy
Lydon, Patrick	Baldy
Joyce, John	Ball of Yarn
Palmacci, Joseph	Balloons
Kenny, William	Bananas
Salvador, John	Baron
Curran, Bartley	Bartla Tadhg
Conley, James W.	Baxter
Joyce, Martin	Beano
Mulkern, John	Beast
Murray	Becker
Murray	Beefer
Quinn, James	Bible-back
Maloney, John	Biddie
Mulkern	Big Auto
McDonough, Dan	Big Dan
Mulkern, Michael J.	Big Ira
Foley, Mark	Big Marcus

Coyne, Michael E.	Big Mike
Feeney, Michael	Big Mike
Joyce, Martin	Big Rufus
Gorham, John P.	Billie Sunday
O'Toole, Martin	Bing
Coyne, Peter	Black
Reilly, John	Black Jack
McDonough, Michael	Black Mike
Connolly, Thomas	Black Tom
Lee, John P.	Blackie
McDonough, Michael	Blessed Virgin
McDonough	Bold American
Conley, William	Boloney
Barry, Edward	Bonehead
Flanagan, John	Bones
McKay	Bonjie
Deetjin	Bonky
Conley, John	Boobie
King, Francis	Booty
Butler	Boozy
Cochran, William	Boozy
McHugh, Thomas	Bowery Boy
Conley, Martin	Brandy
Welch, Lawrence	Breathnach
Gorham, Michael	Bridget
Corkery, Lester	Broken Dishes
Graffam, Percy	Bruno
Principi, Vincent	Bubble Eyes
O'Donnell, John	Bubbles
Napolitano, Barbato	Buggo
King, John	Bull
Lee, Martin E.	Bull
Jenkins, Ralph	Bullet Eye
McDonough	Bungy
Duffy, Martin	Butch
Lee, Edward	Buttons
Welch	Buttons
Welch	Cabbagehead

Longshore Nicknames 205

Welch, James	Calibhfuinse
Coyne, Peter	Center
Bellino	Cha-cha
Corradini, Charles	Charlie New York
—	Charlie the Indian
Coyne, John	Chicago
Mulkern, Stephen	Chicamauga
Bellino	Chi-chi
Maloney, Charles	Chick Chick
Renaud, Charles	Chick Chick
Foley	China
Coyne, Peter	Chink
Brogan, William	Chuck
Gorrivan, William	Church Mouse
—	Cinnamon Bear
McDonough, Thomas	City Hall
Foley, Joseph	Clay
—	Clegger Dubh
McDonough, Joseph	Climax
McDonough, Martin J.	Cockaneeney (Cac an éinín)
Micucci, Mark	Cocoa
Foley, Philip	Co-father (Go fáda)
Conley, Michael	Cois Fharraige
Stearns, Paul	Cold Cuts
Conley, Coleman	Colm
Coyne or Green	Corned Beef
Malia	Criqui
Foley, Patrick	Cubeen
Lee, John P.	Curley
—	Cuxey
Gordon	CWT—Hundred Weight
DiPhillipo, Joseph	DaFlip
Flaherty, Stephen	Dago
McDonough, Thomas	Dancing Master
Black, Thomas	Danger
Coyne, Jeremiah	Darby
—	Deacon
O'Connell, William	Deke

Davin, John	Devil Dog
Coyne, Patrick	Diapers
Coughlin, Richard	Dick the Rat
Wallace	Dido
Welch, Lawrence	Dinish
Green	Dinty
—	Diver
O'Donnell, Thomas	Doc
Hubner, Harry	Dog
Myatt, James	Dondy
Cummings	Donkey
—	Doody Daddy
Coyne, Jeremiah	Doughty
Kane, Daniel	Doughty
Myatt, James	Doughty
Connolly, Thomas	Dry Dollar
Nastovich, Joseph	Dry Goods
Joyce, Thomas F.	Dude
Curran	Duke
Garbarino, Louis	Duke
Ward, Robert	Dummy
Gorrivan, William P.	Dustpan Willie
Reardon	Dutch
Joyce	Dutchy
DiPietrantonio, Fiore	Dynamite
Lee, Martin E.	Eddie
Moran, John E.	Eggo
Feeney, Coleman	Eli
Shaw, Thomas	Eric the Red
Conroy, James	Federal
Humeniuk, Jack	Ferret
Joyce, Festus	Festy
Burke, John	Fiddler
Myatt	Fink
DiPietrantonio, Fiore	Firecracker
Casale, Joseph	Fish Hooks
Welch	Fluther
Lee, Coleman F.	Francis

Talbot, Francis	Fritz
—	Frosty
Mulkern, Stephen	Frozo
Gorham, Festus	Gaffer
Flaherty, Coleman	Gazelle
Gorrivan, George	George Pep
Flaherty	Gerpel
Conroy, John	Giant
Moran, Joseph	G.I. Joe
Reardon, Edward	Gimpy
Loring, George	Ginner
Foley, Philip	Go Fáda
Joyce, Martin	Goon
Beatty, Patrick	Goose Neck
Griffen, John	Gorgeous George
Shaw, James	Grace
Walsh, Patrick	Grape Juice
Joyce, Walter	Grassi
Asali, William	Greeley
Mulkern	Greenhorn Geimhridh
Flynn	Gummy
—	Gunboat
O'Donnell	Gurrier
DiSimon, Christopher	Gusty
Gorham, Patrick J.	Gutty
McDonough	Hail Mary
Ferrante, Joseph	Half-a-day
—	Half-a-man
Jordan, Arthur	Hanky Pank
Joyce, Thomas	Harmonic
O'Donnell, John	Harp
Thornton, John	Harp
Nee	Haugerman
Glenn, John	Haystack
Morgan	Herring
Lyden, Thomas	Hickory
—	High Tide
McDonough, Thomas	Hinky

Foley	Hock-a-mock
Talbot, John	Holly
Jennings	Holy Name Gang
Delaney, John	Hub
Kenney, Edward	Huck
Coyne, Patrick	Humpy
Griffin, Michael	Icy
Mulkern, Michael J.	Ira
Warsaw, Harry	Irish Jew
O'Donnell, Philip T., Jr.	Iron Colt
O'Donnell, Philip T.	Iron Horse
Greeley, Michael	Iron Mike
McDonald, John	Jack
—	Jackass Feathers
Talbot, John	Jackeen (Jackín)
Joyce, John J.	Jackie
Foley, John T.	Jackson
Greenwood	Jake
Renaud, Charles	Jap
Pettis, Jeremiah	Jerry the Louse
Walsh, James J.	Jesse
Brown, James	Jimmy
Mulkern, James	Jimmy Shit
Nee	Jitter
DiPhillipo, Joseph	Joe Flip
Coyne, Joseph	Joe Mhike
Flaherty, John	John #2
Brennan, John	Johnny
Doyle, James	Joker
Brogan, John D.	Jonno
—	Kaisar
Donohue	Kid
Rice, James	Kid
—	Kitchen
Casey	Lackey
Connolly, Coleman	Lamb
Jordan, Raymond	Lanky
Green, Coleman	Larkin

Moran, Lawrence	Larry
Anthony, James	Leaky Roof
Griffen, John	Lefty
Joyce, Michael J./John	Lindy
Kane, Michael	Little Mike
Connolly, John F.	Long John
King, John F.	Long John
Conley, Michael	Long Mike
Walsh, Patrick	Long Pat
Conley, Michael	Longboat
Foley, Martin	Louseback
Mulkern, Michael	Lovely Mike
Stearns, Paul	Mad Dog
Robinson, Edward	Maggie
Conley, Michael	Mandy
Gorham, Marcus	Marcuisín
Concannon, Stephen	Marcus's Greenhorn
Gould, Mark	Marcus the Gould
McDonough, Mark	Markie the Housis
Connolly, Matthew	Matty
O'Grourke, Martin	Maucheen (Máirtín)
Greenwall, Max	Maxie
Foley, Martin A.	Mert
Kane, Michael	Michilín
Joyce, John J.	Mickey
Joyce, Michael J.	Mickey
Quarry, Michael	Mickey from Lynn
Quarry, Michael	Mickey from Newton Upper Falls
Quarry, Michael	Mickey Go Fetch 'Em
Mulkern, Thomas C.	Midnight
Feeney, Michael	Mike Joe
Lynch, Harold	Minnie
Caulfield	Mohungo
Gorham, Edward	Mohungo
Curran, Martin	Monceine
Concannon, Stephen	Monk
Ryan	Monk
Morey	Monsignor

Conley, James	Monty Blue
Connolly, John	Moose
Joyce, Michael	Moose
Lydon, Michael	Moose
Lee, Coleman F.	Morgan
Lee, George B.	Morgan
Lee, John P.	Morgan
Coughlin, William	Mouser
Carlista, Francis	Mousey
Foley, Philip	Moustache
Lee	Mucka
Yankowski, Edward	Mud Man
Joyce, Michael	Muggsy
Mulkern, James E.	Mulligan
Collins, Daniel	Nevada Dan
Curran, Philip A.	New York Boat
—	Nickles
Napolitano, James	Nigger Jim
Gorrivan, Joseph	Nigger Joe
Conley, William	Noisy
Myatt, James	Noisy One
—	No-nose
Carlista, Emmanuel	Nutty
O'Malley, John	Omie
Mulkern, Patrick A.	Otto
O'Brien, Patrick	Packy
Joyce, Patrick	Paddy na gCnoc
Herbert, Thomas	Papa
Silke, John B.	Paper Legs
Flaherty, Michael	Parnell
Griffin, Peter	Pather (Peadar)
O'Malley, John	Paver
Green, Patrick	Pavin' Blocks
Walsh, Patrick	Peak's Island
Kenney, William J.	Peanuts
Woods, Edmund	Pecker
Russell, Edward	Peekaboo
Curran, John	Penard

Gorrivan, Thomas	Pepper
Foley, Philip	Phil the Short Way
Foley, Philip	Phillipín
O'Donnell, Philip J.	Philly
O'Donnell, Philip J.	Philly Fitz
Phillipo Joseph	Pink Eye
Folan, Thomas J.	Polack
Folan, Paul	Polikeen
Coyne, Martin	Pollock
Lomax, Joseph	Pollock
Powell, Timothy	Pooduck
—	Poor Frank
Jennings, Michael	Pork Chops
Conley, Michael J.	Pratick
Gorham, Michael J.	President
Joyce, Thomas	Psycho
Bellino	Pubby
Coyne, John J.	Ragtime
—	Rat eye
Connolly, John R.	Red John
Foley, Mark	Red Marcus
Mulkerrin, Patrick	Red Pat
Green	Ride-the-goat
Garbarino, James	Rip
Green, Patrick	Robert Emmet
Lee	Robie
Conley, Coleman	Rocco
Manchester, Vincent	Rock-in-you-shoe
Riley, Andrew	Rory
Lee, Thomas	Rosey
Lee, Thomas J.	Rosie
Connolly, Patrick	Rube
Joyce, Martin	Rufus
Ridge, Thomas S.	Rusty
Catarina, John	Rymo
Mulkern	Sally
Conley, Matthew	Sarge
Murray	Sarge

Coyne	Sceadog (Scaird)
Thornton	Scoope
Connolly, John A./Joseph	Scotch
Connolly, Patrick	Scotch
—	Screech Owl
O'Malley, John	Seán
Foley, Philip	Seán Charles
Brennan, John	Seán John
Reagan	See-you-later
Gorham, Michael J.	Senator
Rumo, Samuel	Senator Cleghorn
Brown, James	Sergeant
Foley, Martin	Shaga
Geary, Patrick	Shaggy Dog
Trott	Shaky
Donahue, Patrick	Sharky
—	Sharpie
Mulkern, Patrick	Sharpshooter
Kelley, Peter	Shipwreck
Duffy, Thomas	Shorty
Gorham, Festus	Sinai
Joyce, Walter	Sir Walter
Vanier, Oscar	Ski
Cartonio, Neil	Skintail
Foley, Thomas E.	Slavo
Cooper, William	Slick
—	Slippery Jack
Green, Patrick	Smilin' Pat
Eltman, John	Smokey
Foley, Thomas E.	Smootho
Silverman, Sam	Snake
Mulkern	Soldier
Conley, James	Soup
Silke, John B.	Soup Bone
Conroy, James	South Portland
Welch, Patrick	Spareribs
Connolly, Michael	Sparideog
O'Donnell, John J.	Speck

Naples	Spider
Clancy, Harold	Spike
Flaherty	Spike
Lapomarda, Francis	Spinach
Jennings, Michael	Spit
Gorham	Spit Shine
—	Splinter
Foley, Michael	State
Foley, Martin	State of Maine Forever
Flaherty, Stephen	Steeple Jack
Manchester, Vincent	Step-and-a-half
Foley, Patrick J.	Stepper
O'Toole, Thomas	Stew
Quinn, James	Stick 'Em
Flaherty, Patrick	Stinky Pat
Welch, Stephen	Stíofáin ni Calibhfuinse
Green, John	Stocks and Bonds
Joyce	Stubby
LaRose, Francis Stuart	Stubby
Mulkern, Timothy	Sucky Duke
King, Joseph	Tad
Curran, Thomas	Taimín George
Brown, Theodore	Teddy
Connolly, Bartley, Jr.	Teddy
Gorham, Michael	Texas Mike
McDonough, Martin	Thunderbolt
Ridge, Patrick	Tobaccy
O'Toole, Patrick	Tom Tailor
Mulkern, John	Tomatoes
Mulkern, Thomas J.	Tonna
Andrews, Anthony	Tony
Cartonio, Anthony	Tony-the-yap
Phillipo, Joseph	Town Crier
Walsh, Thomas	Tucker
Beatty, Patrick	Turkey Neck
Mulkern, Michael	Turkey Neck
Wallace	Twigg
Brogan, John D.	Uncle Jonno

—	Unkie
O'Donnell, John	Wagon Wheels
Gorham, John S.	Weasal
Conley, Michael	Wharf 4
Germaine, Rocco	Whip
Loring, Mark	Whip
McDonough, Martin J.	White Hope
O'Malley, Pat	White Hope
Curran, Philip	White Line
Foley, Mark	White Marcus
Burke, William	Wilder
Fox, William, Sr.	Willie
Foley, Mark	Wilson
Gorham, John	Windy
Gorham, Patrick	Windy Pat
Joyce, Thomas M.	Worm
Bellino	Ya-ya

Appendix F

Membership Levels of the Portland Longshoremen's Benevolent Society

See charts on following pages.

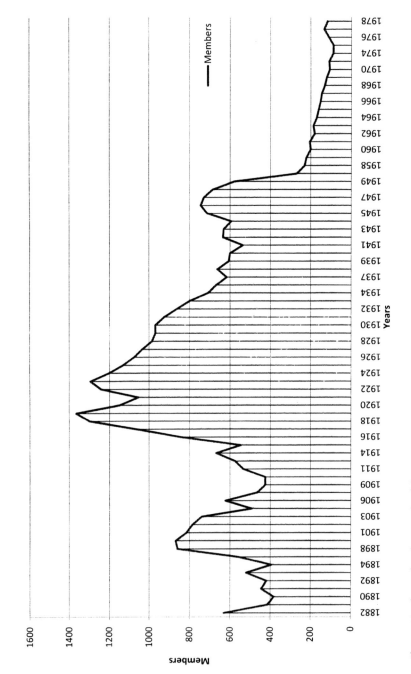

Chart 1. Total Membership Levels of the PLSBS (1882–1978). *Note:* Data is unavailable for 1880, 1881, 1883–88, 1895, 1897, 1900, 1904, 1907, 1913, 1936, 1950–54, 1956–57, and 1972–73.

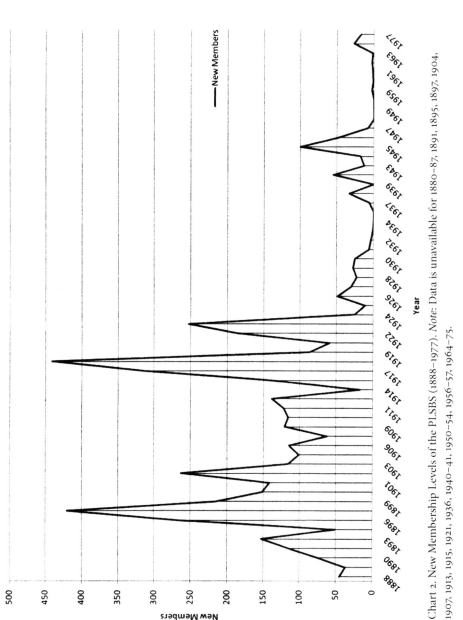

Chart 2. New Membership Levels of the PLSBS (1888–1977). *Note:* Data is unavailable for 1880–87, 1891, 1895, 1897, 1904, 1907, 1913, 1915, 1921, 1936, 1940–41, 1950–54, 1956–57, 1964–75.

Notes

Chapter 1. "Delightfully Situated on a Healthy Hill"

1. Rowe, *Maritime History of Maine*, 24; Baker, "Formerly Machegonne," 5 (see entire essay). Duncan, *Coastal Maine*, chs. 1–4, gives an extensive history of the early European exploration of the New World with emphasis on the French and English expeditions to the coast of Maine. For early reference to English expansion to Ireland and the Americas (1480–1650) see Andrews, Canny, and Hair, *The Westward Enterprise*; and Canny, *Kingdom and Colony*.

2. Duncan, *Coastal Maine*, 113.

3. Foulke, "Odysseus's Oar," 200.

4. Elwell, *Portland and Vicinity*, 9. The early history of Falmouth and Maine can be found in the following: Banks, ed., *A History of Maine*; Clark, *Maine, Maine During the Colonial Period*, and *Eastern Frontier*; Goold, *Portland in the Past*; Hatch, *Maine*; Neal, *Portland Illustrated*; Outwin, "Thriving and Elegant, Flourishing and Populous," and "Thriving and Elegant Town;" Sullivan, *History of the District of Maine*; Williamson, *The History of the State of Maine*; Willis, *History of Portland*; and the Writers' Project of the WPA, *Portland City Guide*.

5. Nash, *Urban Crucible*, 3.

6. Fernández-Armesto, quoted in Daniel Finamore, ed., *Maritime History as World History*, 2; and Janzen, "A World-Embracing Sea," 102–114.

7. Neal, *Portland Illustrated*, 5; see also Eckstorm, *Indian Place Names*. See Baker, "Formerly Machegonne," 1–19.

8. Jennings, *Invasion of America*. The first chapter of this book surveys the similarities between the British treatment of both Native Americans and of the Gaelic Irish in the early seventeenth century.

9. Elwell, *Portland and Vicinity*, 10. See also Churchill, "Too Great the Challenge."

10. Roland, Bolster, and Keyssar, *Way of the Ship*, 10.

11. Wallace, "The Scotch-Irish of Provincial Maine," 41–42, deals with early European relationships with Native Americans in Maine. See also Conforti, *Creating Portland*, xiii.

12. Willis, *History of Portland*, 325. For more information on this group, see Wallace, "The Scotch-Irish of Provincial Maine," 41–59.

13. Elwell, *Portland and Vicinity*, 11. An invaluable source of information on the eighteenth-century history of Falmouth is the extensive diary collection of Parson (the Reverend Thomas) Smith covering the period from 1725 to 1788, during which time he ministered to the congregation of the First Parish Church. These are available at the Portland Room of the Portland Public Library and at the Maine Historical Society Library. Elwell and other local historians have used Smith extensively, as in this paraphrasing.

14. For a brief but informative synopsis of the growth of early commerce in Falmouth before the Revolution, see Outwin, "Thriving and Elegant Town," 27–33. For a national look at these and subsequent years, see Taylor, *Liberty Men and Great Proprietors*.

15. Willis, *History of Portland*, 452.

16. Rowe, *Maritime History of Maine*, 54.

17. Willis, *History of Portland*, 453.

18. Barry, "A Concise History," 30–31.

19. Willis, *History of Portland*, 460.

20. Hatch, *Maine*, 29.

21. Paine, *Down East*, 41.

22. Ibid., 43–46.

23. Duncan, *Coastal Maine*, 212–13. See all of chapter 15, "The Battle of Machias and the Burning of Falmouth," including notes, 219–21. For an early and solid discussion of several "myths" concerning this episode, see Churchill, "Historiography of the *Margaretta* Affair."

24. Hatch, *Maine*, 28; Clark, *Maine*, 63–66; and Yerxa, "Burning of Falmouth, 1775," 141–42. A more current assessment of this episode may be found in Leamon, "Falmouth, the American Revolution," 44–71.

25. Yerxa, "The Burning of Falmouth, 1775," 149; see also Sherman, *Life of Captain Jeremiah O'Brien*.

26. Duncan, *Coastal Maine*, 218.

27. Yerxa, "The Burning of Falmouth, 1775," 145.

28. Barry, "A Concise History," 34.

29. Willis, *History of Portland*, 581.

30. Ibid., 579–80. See also Writers' Project of the WPA, *Portland City Guide*, 36–37.

31. Outwin, "Thriving and Elegant Town," 33.

32. Sources on post-Colonial Maine history may be found in Banks, *Maine during the Federal and Jeffersonian Period*. The story of Portland's first century is recorded in Hull, ed., *Centennial Celebration 1786–1886*. Burial records, a much overlooked historical resource, are available in Jordan, *Burial Records of the Eastern Cemetery*,

1717–1962, and *Burial Records of the Western Cemetery, 1811–1980*. See also Jordan, *History of Cape Elizabeth, Maine*.

33. Rowe, *Maritime History of Maine*, 67.
34. Willis, *History of Portland*, 562.
35. Albion, "Introduction," v and vi. Albion was a 1914 graduate of Portland High School (the very same class as America's most prolific filmmaker, John Ford).
36. Willis, *History of Portland*, 562.
37. Ibid., 560–61; and Greater Portland Landmarks, *Portland*, 33. Ship tonnage: 1789, 5,000; 1798, 11,173; 1807, 39,009; 1812, 35,512; 1862, 133,162. Customs duties: 1790, $8,109; 1801, $204,333; 1806, $342,909; 1808, $41,369.
38. Bunting, *Portrait of a Port*, 9.
39. Barry and Holverson, *Revolutionary McLellans*.
40. Winston Churchill, quoted in Duncan, *Coastal Maine*, 255.
41. Ibid., 255–56. See also ch. 17 "Neutral Trade, French Spoliations, Barbary Pirates," 250–53, which deals with the Portland-born future Naval commodore Edward Preble; and ch. 18 "Embargo and the War of 1812."
42. Williamson, *History of the State of Maine*, 603–4. A wonderful children's novel concerning the local consequences of the impressment of American sailors and the fantastic worldwide adventures of a Portland boy from Munjoy Hill during the Embargo period may be found in Hazel Wilson's *Tall Ships*. Students of Miss Josephine Rand at Munjoy Hill's Emerson School at the time of the book's publication were thrilled to hear this larger-than-life story of global travel and the heroic actions of one of their own.
43. Elwell, *Portland and Vicinity*, 15.
44. Greater Portland Landmarks, *Portland*, 33.
45. Paine, *Down East*, 59.
46. *Portland Press*, August 5, 1872. This fascinating tribute to a local hero was signed "W.G." probably referring to William Goold. It is full of details regarding the social and racial history of Portland in the nineteenth century.
47. Barry, "A Concise History," 35.
48. Duncan, *Coastal Maine*, 283.
49. Moulton, *Captain Moody and His Observatory*. See also Paine, *Down East*, 57–58. The Portland Observatory was completely rebuilt between 1994 and 1999 at a cost of $1.2 million. Today it is administered by Greater Portland Landmarks, Inc. It is located at 138 Congress Street and is open daily between Memorial Day and Columbus Day. In 2006 it was officially declared a National Historic Landmark.
50. Duncan, *Coastal Maine*, 267; Hatch, *Maine*, 73–74; Paine, *Down East*, 61–62; and Levinsky, *A Short History of Portland*, 54–56.
51. Longfellow, *Henry Wadsworth Longfellow Poems* (Secaucus, N.J.: Longriver Press, 1976), 193–95.
52. For literature on Maine's separation from Massachusetts and statehood, see Banks, *Maine Becomes a State*. See also Hatch, *Maine*, chs. 6 and 7.

53. Hatch, *Maine*, 726.
54. Paine, *Down East*, 108.
55. Royall, *The Black Book*, as cited in Barry, "Concise History," 24.
56. Hatch, *Maine*, 721.
57. Barry, "Concise History," 35–36.
58. Quoted in ibid., 36–37.
59. Writers' Project of the WPA, *Portland City Guide*, 41.
60. Rowe, *Maritime History of Maine*, 68–69.
61. "The United States Attack on Kuala Batu," http://www.sabrizain.org/malaya/potomac.htm, accessed December 3, 2007. For additional information on this, see Rutter, *The Pirate Wind*; and Long, "'Martial Thunder.'"
62. Mooney, *Nine Years in America*, 126–27. Thanks for this reference go to retired University of Southern Maine history professor Allan R. Whitmore.
63. Duncan, *Coastal Maine*, 281.
64. Morison, *Maritime History of Massachusetts, 1783–1869*; Morris, *Our Maritime Heritage*; and Johnson, "Boston and the Maritimes."
65. Duncan, *Coastal Maine*, 308–9.
66. Ibid., 313. See also Albion, Baker, and Labaree, *New England and the Sea*, 179.
67. Albion, Baker, and Labaree, *New England and the Sea*, 179.
68. Duncan, *Coastal Maine*, 451.
69. For a discussion of the rivalry between Portland and Boston at this time, see Kirkland, *Men, Cities, and Transportation*, 193–222.
70. Neal, *Portland Illustrated*, 96.
71. Poor, ed., *First International Railway*, 26.
72. Clark, *Maine*, 99. See also Barry, "Vignetted History," 13; Pillsbury, "History of the Atlantic and St. Lawrence Railroad Company"; Sheehy, "John Alfred Poor"; Sherman, "Bangor and Aroostook Railroad"; and Jordan, *Historical Synopsis*.
73. Paine, *Down East*, 110. See also Brindle, *Brunel*; and Andrew and Melanie Kelly, eds., *Brunel*.
74. Holt, *Grand Trunk in New England*, 77–81.
75. Currie, *Grand Trunk Railway of Canada*.
76. *Daily Eastern Argus*, July 18, 1853, 2.
77. Ibid., July 19, 1853, 2.
78. Paine, *Down East*, 110–11.
79. Ibid., 104. Portland Trails, Inc., a very active nonprofit group, is currently pursuing several re-creations of the walkways that would have originally paralleled these commercial routes.
80. Conforti, *Creating Portland*, xxiv.
81. Quoted in Clark, *Maine*, 94–95. See also Wood, *History of Lumbering in Maine*; O'Leary, *Maine Sea Fisheries*; and Smith, *A History of Lumbering in Maine*.

Chapter 2. Black Fades to Green on the Waterfront

1. A version of this chapter appeared in Connolly, "Black Fades to Green."
2. Greater Portland Landmarks, *Portland*, 78. For a synopsis of the business growth of Portland see Barry, "A Vignetted History." See also Writers' Project of the WPA, *Maine*.
3. Willis, *History of Portland*, 732–33; also see Albion, Baker, and Labaree, *New England and the Sea*, 176–79.
4. Scontras, *Collective Efforts among Maine Workers*, 147–48.
5. Quoted in Greater Portland Landmarks, *Portland*, 75. For a special report on the Great Fire of 1866 listing all buildings destroyed along with their valuation, see the Portland City Directory, 1869, 319–28.
6. Greater Portland Landmarks, *Portland*, 78.
7. Bunting, *Portrait of a Port*, 11.
8. Stakeman, "Slavery in Colonial Maine," 77. See also Clark, *Maine*, 116. For a comparison with the black experience in other antebellum states, see Litwack, *North of Slavery*.
9. This building, now a National Historic Monument, is currently under major reconstruction as of early 2009. Progress may be followed at the following website: http://www.nps.gov/history/nr/feature/afam/2007/abyssinian.htm.
10. Willis, *History of Portland*, 680.
11. Nash, "Forging Freedom," 43–45. For additional literature on this topic, see also Greene, *Negro in Colonial New England*; Horton and Horton, *Black Bostonians*; Jacobs, "Study of the Boston Negro"; Jordan, *White over Black*; and Litwack, *North of Slavery*.
12. For much of the following information on Portland's black population I am indebted to William David Barry of the Maine Historical Society. Together with Randolph Dominic, Barry published a historical novel whose main character was an African American Portlander. See Dominic and Barry, *Pyrrhus Venture*. The most comprehensive study of Maine's black population may be found in Price and Talbot, *Maine's Visible Black History*. Also of significance are Lee, "'What They Lack in Numbers'"; and Lee, *Black Bangor*.
13. Shettleworth and Barry, *Mr. Goodhue Remembers Portland*, 12.
14. *Portland Transcript*, January 22, 1895, cited in ibid., 6. See also Rubin, *Negro in the Longshore Industry*.
15. Rowe, *Maritime History of Maine*, 117.
16. Rowe, *Maritime History of Maine*, 116–18.
17. Writers' Project of the WPA, *Portland City Guide*, 43, 67. Regarding the Cuba molasses trade, see University of Florida, George A. Smathers Libraries website, John R. Nemmers, "A Guide to the Business Letters Describing the Financial Market in Cuba" http://web.uflib.ufl.edu/spec/manuscript/guides/cubamarket.htm.
18. Albion, Baker, and Labaree, *New England and the Sea*, 122–23.

19. Frank L. Byrne, *Prophet of Prohibition*, 22. See also Greater Portland Landmarks, *Portland*, 44.

20. Goold article in *Portland Press*, April 13, 1872.

21. Rowe, *Maritime History of Maine*, 113. See the entire chapter titled "The West India Trade."

22. John Neal, *Yankee*, July 2, 1828, 215.

23. Horton and Horton, *Black Bostonians*, 2–5. The reference to "Nigger Hill" is taken from the Writers' Project of the WPA, *Portland City Guide*, 274.

24. Horton and Horton, *Black Bostonians*, 4.

25. U.S. Census Office, *Twelfth Census*, vol. I, Population (Part I), 619.

26. Gary B. Nash, "Forging Freedom," 10–11.

27. See James O. and Lois E. Horton, *Black Bostonians*, 4. See also Donald M. Jacobs, "A Study of the Boston Negro"; Peter R. Knights, *Plain People of Boston, 1830–1860*; and Ira Berlin, *Slaves Without Masters*.

28. Elijah Kellogg, *A Strong Arm and a Mother's Blessing*, 148–55 and 195.

29. Gary B. Nash, "Forging Freedom," 6 and 10.

30. Steven J. Ross, *Workers on the Edge*, 195.

31. In the case of Boston see Donald M. Jacobs, "A Study of the Boston Negro"; and James O. and Lois E. Horton, *Black Bostonians*. For New York see *Anti-Negro Riots in the North, 1863*; Adrian Cook, *The Armies of the Streets*; Joel Headley, *The Great Riots of New York*; and *New York Committee of Merchants for the Relief of Colored People Suffering from the Late Riots, 1863 Report*.

32. Prior to 1859, the Town Hall was in Monument Square (then called Market Square). Fire claimed both "new" City Halls, 1859–1866 and 1868–1908. This reference would be to the building destroyed by the Great Fire of 1866. The current City Hall was rebuilt in 1912.

33. Charles A. Scontras, *Time-Line*, 12.

34. Maureen Elgersman Lee, "Locating Black Portland," 223–224.

35. Daniel Rosenberg, *New Orleans Dockworkers*, 16–17.

36. The Bylaws and Records of the PLSBS are housed in a major collection, including over ninety volumes of Minutes and Financial Reports, at the Maine Historical Society in Portland, Maine. See *PLSBS Records*, Volume 1, Bylaws, Section 15, 8.

37. *PLSBS Record of Proceedings of Special Committees 1883–1884*, November 27, 1883, 11.

38. Rosenberg, *New Orleans Dockworkers*, 39.

39. *Portland Transcript*, week ending March 20, 1880; and ibid., January 22, 1895.

40. Portland City Directory, 1837, 1841, and 1844 lists Siggs as living on "Mountjoy." Jordan, *Eastern Cemetery*, shows his death date as June 8, 1858, at the age of seventy-seven years, and that he is buried with his wife, Mary, and daughter Mar-

garet, all listed as "Black." For the Neal Dow parody citing John Siggs, see Mundy, *Hard Times, Hard Men*, 179.

41. Pilcher, *Portland Longshoremen*, 68–69.

42. Ibid., 12–13.

43. Fowler, *Boston Looks Seaward*, 218.

44. Montgomery, *Fall of the House of Labor*, 94.

45. Peter Cole, *Wobblies on the Waterfront*, 19.

46. Ignatiev, *How the Irish Became White*; Roediger, *Wages of Whiteness*, and *Towards the Abolition of Whiteness*; Barrett and Roediger, "Inbetween Peoples"; Rosenberg, *New Orleans Dockworkers*; Wilson, *Declining Significance of Race*; Jacobson, *Whiteness of a Different Color*; and Knobel, *Paddy and the Republic*.

47. *Daily Eastern Argus*, November 15, 1864, 2. This editorial was supplied to me by William B. Jordan Jr., of Portland, Maine, who has published extensively on Portland during the Civil War period, including *Red Diamond Regiment* and *Civil War Journals of John Mead Gould*.

48. Roediger, *Wages of Whiteness*, 155–56.

49. This broadsheet was kindly given to me by William B. Jordan Jr., local historian of Portland.

50. Roediger, *Wages of Whiteness*, 148–50.

51. Ignatiev, *How the Irish Became White*, 120.

52. Cole, *Wobblies on the Waterfront*, 53.

53. Barrett and Roediger, "Inbetween Peoples," 6.

54. *The Christian Mirror* (Portland, Maine), February 1, 1849. Again, I am indebted to William B. Jordan Jr. for this source.

55. Knobel, *Paddy and the Republic*, 71.

56. Quoted in ibid., 72–73.

57. Jacobson, *Whiteness of a Different Color*, 48–49.

58. Ibid., 41.

59. Conforti, *Creating Portland*, xxi–xxii.

60. Dow, *Reminiscences of Neal Dow*; Byrne, *Prophet of Prohibition*; and Miner, "Neal Dow and His Life Work."

61. Kellogg, *A Strong Arm*, 198. See also the reference to Portland's "Negro stevedores" in Rowe, *Maritime History of Maine*, 113. For an updated review of race relations along Portland's waterfront in the early twentieth century, see reports of the infamous case of the murder of James Walker in Lee, "'What They Lack in Numbers,'" 234–36.

62. Rowe, *Maritime History of Maine*, 113.

63. An excellent reference to Ireland and Irish emigration to America in the nineteenth century is Miller, *Emigrants and Exiles*. See also Gallagher, *Paddy's Lament*; Kinealy, *The Great Famine*; Mokyr, *Why Ireland Starved*; Potter, *To the Golden Door*; and Woodham-Smith, *The Great Hunger*.

64. For a discussion of the "two-boater," see Kohl, *Irish Green and Union Blue*. I am indebted to William B. Jordan Jr. for this reference. See also Myers, *Over to Bangor*.

65. Willis, *History of Portland*, 774. See also Handlin, *Boston's Immigrants*; L. Loveitt, "Social History of Portland, Maine from 1820–1840"; and R. Loveitt, "Social History of Portland, Maine from 1840–1860."

66. *Compendium of the Tenth Census of the United States (1880)*, Part I, 455; and *Twelfth Census of the United States (1900)*, vol. I, Population (Part I), 800–3.

67. Gibbs, *Passenger Liners of the Western Ocean*.

68. *Portland Daily Press*, February 26, 1864, 2.

69. Ibid., July 4, 1864, 3.

70. Ibid., November 22, 1866, 1. Reference supplied by William David Barry of the Maine Historical Society. The McGlinchys appear often and colorfully in the pages of the local newspapers as well as in Mundy, *Hard Times, Hard Men*, especially James in chapter 5, "The Cratur," an Irish word for alcohol.

71. Larrowe, *Shape-Up and Hiring Hall*, 7. See especially reference to the Alongshoremen's United Benefit Society (1853) and the Longshoremen's Union Protective Association (1866). See also Connolly, "Irish Longshoremen of Portland, Maine," 62–64.

72. *Portland Daily Press*, May 2, 1864, 3; and ibid., May 7, 1864, 2. These references and those immediately following were kindly shared by William B. Jordan Jr. Professor Jordan kept an informal log from this period with excerpts from the *Portland Transcript*, the *Portland Advertiser*, and the *Portland Daily Press*, the latter which published a "Marine Journal" beginning in the early nineteenth century. Also see Jordan's *Index to Portland Newspapers*.

73. Francis M. McLaughlin, "The Boston Longshoremen's Strike of 1931," footnote 4.

74. *Portland Daily Press*, May 10, 1864, 2; and ibid., July 9, 1864, 3.

75. Scontras, *Time-Line*, 10.

76. Scontras, *Collective Efforts among Maine Workers*, 173; also Scontras, *Time-Line*, 10.

77. *Portland Daily Press*, March 1, 1865, 3.

78. Ibid., September 20, 1866, 1; and ibid., November 22, 1866, 1. My thanks go to Matthew Jude Barker of Portland for these references.

79. PLSBS *Records and Minutes*, Minutes Book 1880–83. See December 18, 1881, 96; December 20, 1881, 97; December 27, 1881, 99; and January 10, 1882, 103. For an analysis of Irish nationalist organizations with local Portland chapters, see Barker, "The Irish Community." For an analysis of the continued links between the PLSBS and Irish nationalism into the twentieth century, see Michael C. Connolly, "Nationalism among Early Twentieth Century Irish Longshoremen." Another useful resource for this subject is Barker's website on the Maine Irish Heritage Trail, which may be accessed at http://www.maineirishheritagetrail.org/.

80. Neal, *Portland Illustrated*, 8–9.
81. Whitmore, "'A Guard of Faithful Sentinels.'"
82. Willis, *History of Portland*, 776.
83. PLSBS, *Records and Minutes*, Records vol. 1, By-laws. Also see Connolly, "Irish Longshoremen of Portland, Maine," especially 64–77, on the founding of the PLSBS and statistics on membership levels in appendices C, D, and E.
84. See by Scontras: *Two Decades of Organized Labor; Organized Labor and Labor Politics; Socialist Alternative; Collective Efforts among Maine Workers;* and *Time-Line*.

Chapter 3. A Mixed Blessing

1. Clark, *Maine*, 96–97. A thrilling account of Portland's successful competition with Boston to become Canada's winter port in February 1845 may be found in Writers' Project of the WPA, *Maine: A Guide "Down East,"* 180.
2. Writers' Project of the WPA, *Maine: A Guide "Down East,"* 169.
3. McCarron, "Facing the Atlantic," 61–95. Edward and Fidelma McCarron have a manuscript in press that deals extensively with Inistioge, County Kilkenny, and the surrounding region of southeastern Ireland and its mercantile connections with mid-coast Maine. For earlier contacts with Ireland and patterns of British commercial contact with both Ireland and the United States, see Andrews, Canny, and Hair, *Westward Enterprise*.
4. Paine, *Down East*, 75–76.
5. *Eastern Argus*, January 1, 1900, 4. The *Eastern Argus* was a significant source of local as well as national and international news. It was one of the oldest papers operating in Portland in this period. Begun in the early nineteenth century as a Jeffersonian paper, it had remained true to the Democratic Party but was not in any way a labor paper. See Writers' Project of the WPA, *Portland City Guide*, 169–76.
6. *Eastern Argus*, January 1, 1900, 2.
7. Scontras, *Organized Labor in Maine* (1985), 12.
8. Rowe, *Maritime History of Maine*, 315–16.
9. Smith, *Confederates Downeast*.
10. A good account of this escapade is given in Duncan, *Coastal Maine*, 332–38, within a larger chapter titled "The Civil War." See also Paine, *Down East*, 73–74. An account of the life of Caleb Cushing may be found in Belohlavek, *Broken Glass*.
11. Paine, *Down East*, 52, 111–13.
12. *Eastern Argus*, January 1, 1900, 4. See also Duncan, *Coastal Maine*, 321; and Albion, Baker, and Labaree, *New England and the Sea*, 204.
13. Roland, Bolster, and Keyssar, *Way of the Ship*, 197.
14. Ibid., 211–15, 223.
15. Higham, *Strangers in the Land*, 107.

16. U.S. Census Office, *Twelfth Census of the United States (1900)*, Population, vol. I, 868. Of the 50,145 residents, 27,303 (54.4 percent) had native parentage while 22,842 (45.6 percent) had foreign parentage.

17. Willis, *History of Portland*, 776.

18. Higham, *Strangers in the Land*, 12–13.

19. *Portland Board of Trade Journal* XII, no. 9 (January 1900): 262 and 266.

20. *Portland Board of Trade Journal* XII, no. 10 (February 1900): 294; ibid., XII, no. 11 (March 1900): 332–33; and ibid., XII, no. 12 (April 1900): 363–34.

21. Higham, *Strangers in the Land*, 112.

22. *Eastern Argus*, January 22, 1900, 8.

23. Ibid. See also Babcock, "The Rise and Fall of Portland's Waterfront, 1850–1920," 77–78, and footnote 30. For a further reference to the SS *Sarah Sands* and its maritime connection to Portland, see Babcock, "The Rise and Fall," 63. Coleman, *Going to America*, portrays the social conditions, especially of the Irish sailing from Liverpool.

24. *Eastern Argus*, January 22, 1900, 8.

25. Ibid.

26. Babcock, "Rise and Fall," 80 and passim.

27. Ibid.

28. Clark, *Maine*, 104–5, and 134. See Jones, *Portland Ships Are Good Ships*. For Bath Iron Works, see Eskew, *Cradle of Ships*; and Sanders, *The Yard*. See also Paine, *Down East*, 149–51.

29. *Eastern Argus*, January 1, 1900, 2.

30. Cogill, *When God Was an Atheist Sailor*.

31. Portland Port Commission, *Report of the Portland Port Commission*, 1935.

32. Roland, Bolster, and Keyssar, *Way of the Ship*, 1.

33. Oral interviews with Lawrence Welch, January 6, 1982; and Thomas Mulkern, January 22, 1982.

34. *Fifteenth Annual Labor Report, 1900*, 6, as cited in Scontras, *Organized Labor in Maine* (1985), 11.

35. *Eastern Argus*, April 2, 1900, 2; and ibid., May 14, 1902, 5, as cited in Scontras, *Organized Labor in Maine* (1985), 13–14.

36. See material on Irish emigration to Canada in Miller, *Emigrants and Exiles*, 193–97 and passim. See also Adams, *Ireland and Irish Emigration*; Hanna, *The Scotch Irish*; and Schrier, *Ireland and the Irish Emigration*. For specific information on Irish immigration to Maine, see several essays in Connolly, *They Change Their Sky*.

37. Connolly, "Irish Longshoremen of Portland." See appendices C, D, and E for graphs of PLSBS membership 1880–1980.

38. Although there were 868 dues-paying members in 1900, only 253 could be found who listed their occupation in the 1900 census specifically as "longshoreman." For the sake of accuracy, only these were used in the computer analysis. For a more

detailed analysis of these longshoremen and their families, see ibid., especially chap. 3, "A Day in the Life of the Folan Family," 108–45.

39. Nilsen, "Thinking of Monday"; and Nilsen, "'The Language That the Strangers Do Not Know.'"

40. Kenny, *American Irish*, 99, 132.

41. Nilsen, "Thinking of Monday," 8.

42. Oral interview with Lawrence Welch, January 6, 1982.

43. Oral interviews with Philip O'Donnell, January 13, 1982; Thomas Mulkern, January 22, 1982; and Royal Caleb, February 5, 1982.

44. Oral interview with Stephen Concannon, February 3, 1983.

45. McCaffrey, *The Irish Diaspora in America*; Meagher, *From Paddy to Studs*; and Kenny, *American Irish*.

Chapter 4. Lost Strikes and Union Affiliation

1. A version of part of this chapter appeared in Connolly, "To 'Make This Port Union All Over': Longshore Militancy in Portland, 1911–1913," in *Maine History* 41, no. 1 (Spring 2002): 41–60. Used here with their kind permission.

2. Connolly, "Irish Longshoremen of Portland," appendices C and M.

3. Armstrong, "The Role of Short-Sea, Coastal, and Riverine Traffic," 126.

4. Montgomery, *Fall of the House of Labor*, 102–3.

5. Connolly, "Black Fades to Green," 357–73.

6. The records of the PLSBS (ILA local 861) together with some volumes of the predominantly Italian Freight Handlers' Union (ILA local 912) total more than ninety volumes and are housed at the Maine Historical Society in Portland, Maine, in Manuscript Collections 359 (MS 85–15) and 360.

7. For a discussion of a port-wide strike in Boston from January 5 to February 14, 1912, see McLaughlin, "Industrial Relations in the Boston Longshore Industry," 43–55.

8. Fowler, *Boston Looks Seaward*, 187–88, and 217–18. For a state of Maine perspective on labor activities in this period, see several books by Charles A. Scontras, all published by the Bureau of Labor Education at the University of Maine (Orono) including: *Organized Labor in Maine*; *Socialist Alternative*; and *Collective Efforts among Maine Workers*, among many others.

9. Winslow, "'Men of the Lumber Camps,'" 64.

10. Pilcher, *Portland Longshoremen*, 123.

11. Winslow, "'Men of the Lumber Camps,'" 70.

12. Ibid., 74. Coal played a major role in waterfront labor in other settings. See Armstrong, "Role of Short-Sea," 115–29; and Hudelson and Ross, *By the Ore Docks*.

13. PLSBS *Records and Minutes*, Records, vol. 5, January 31, 1911, 352.

14. Ibid., February 7, 1911, 353.

15. Ibid., February 14, 1911, 354.

16. Larrowe, *Shape-Up and Hiring Hall*, 27.

17. PLSBS *Records and Minutes*, Records, vol. 5, February 21, 1911, 355.

18. Quoted in Grace, "Irish in Mid-Nineteenth-Century Canada," 536–38. I am indebted to Fidelma McCarron of Portland, Maine, for this reference.

19. *Weekly Eastern Argus*, December 1, 1887, 4. Thanks for this reference to William David Barry of the Maine Historical Society.

20. PLSBS *Records and Minutes*, Records, vol. 5, September 12, 1911, 386. This wage schedule was published in the *Portland Evening Express*, November 1, 1911, 1. See PLSBS *Records and Minutes*, Records, vol. 4, July 29, 1902, 165; McLaughlin, "Replacement of the Knights of Labor."

21. McLaughlin, "Industrial Relations in the Boston Longshore Industry," 43–45.

22. PLSBS *Records and Minutes*, Records, vol. 5, October 24, 1911, 393.

23. *Portland Board of Trade Journal* 10 (December 1897): 230 as cited in Babcock, "Rise and Fall of Portland's Waterfront," 77.

24. *Portland Evening Express*, November 1, 1911, 1.

25. See Rosenberg, *New Orleans Dockworkers*, 51–57.

26. *Portland Evening Express*, November 2, 1911, 2.

27. PLSBS *Records and Minutes*, Records, vol. 5, October 31, 1911, 394.

28. *Portland Evening Express*, November 1, 1911, 1.

29. McLaughlin, "The Replacement of the Knights of Labor."

30. *Eastern Argus*, November 7, 1911, 16.

31. McLaughlin, "Industrial Relations," 47 and passim.

32. *Portland Evening Express*, November 1, 1911, 1.

33. *Eastern Argus*, November 8, 1911, 16.

34. Montgomery, *Fall of the House of Labor*, 103.

35. Winslow, "'Men of the Lumber Camps Come to Town,'" 86. The other great Irish labor leader besides James Connolly, James Larkin, is mentioned in connection with a longshore strike in Philadelphia in 1915 in Cole, *Wobblies on the Waterfront*, 64.

36. McLaughlin, "Replacement of the Knights of Labor."

37. Winslow, "'Men of the Lumber Camps Come to Town,'" 85.

38. For a discussion of the use of strikebreakers (scabs) in the port of New Orleans, see Rosenberg, *New Orleans Dockworkers*, 78–81, 89–90, 124–27, 130–33, and 170–74.

39. See Jacobson, *Whiteness of a Different Color*, 56–62. An additional and thorough discussion of the status of Italian and other "new immigrants" may be found in Barrett and Roediger, "Inbetween Peoples."

40. "The Annual Report of the Commissioner of Industrial and Labor Statistics,"

1887, 106. I am indebted to Charles A. Scontras of the Bureau of Labor Education at the University of Maine (Orono) for this reference.

41. Brody, *Workers in Industrial America*, 15.

42. Kenny, *American Irish*, 186. Kenny cites historians Kerby Miller and P. J. Drudy, and this thesis has long been maintained by the Chicago-based historian Lawrence McCaffrey.

43. Larrowe, *Shape-up and Hiring Hall*, 71, reports that several waterfront scholars had cited these "ethnic barriers" as "an important obstacle to the establishment of a centralized hiring system." See Montgomery, *Fall of the House of Labor*, 103.

44. Oral interview with Philip O'Donnell, January 13, 1982.

45. Cole, *Wobblies on the Waterfront*, 29; Bruce Nelson cited in ibid., 53.

46. Winslow, "'Men of the Lumber Camps,'" 74.

47. Cited in Gutman, *Work, Culture and Society in Industrializing America*, 152–53. Other very useful works on the subject of race and ethnicity and labor include Montgomery, *Fall of the House of Labor*, 96–109; Arnesen, *Waterfront Workers of New Orleans*; Rosenberg, *New Orleans Dockworkers*; Pilcher, *Portland Longshoremen*, 67–76; and Nelson, *Divided We Stand*, especially part 1, with chapters 1–3 devoted to the longshore industry. Race and labor relations between black and Irish waterfront workers in Philadelphia play a central part in Cole, *Wobblies on the Waterfront*, as well as several of Arnesen's essays regarding maritime labor in New Orleans. An excellent focused study, edited by Winslow, is *Waterfront Workers*. An essay that focuses on the role of Italian and other "new" immigrants is Barrett and Roediger, "Inbetween Peoples." Regarding the issue of race along Portland's nineteenth century docks, see Connolly, "Black Fades to Green."

48. Oral interviews with Stephen Concannon, February 3, 1983; and Royal Caleb, February 5, 1982.

49. PLSBS *Records and Minutes*, Records, vol. 6, September 13, 1914, 223; and ibid., September 15, 1914, 218.

50. Ibid., ms. coll. 360, four volumes, housed at the Maine Historical Society, Portland.

51. Cole, *Wobblies on the Waterfront*, 34.

52. Winslow, *Waterfront Workers*, 44, 62, and 69.

53. McLaughlin, "Replacement of the Knights of Labor."

54. PLSBS *Records and Minutes*, Records, vol. 6, November 14, 1911, 4.

55. McLaughlin, "Replacement of the Knights of Labor."

56. PLSBS *Records and Minutes*, Records, vol. 6, September 16, 1913, 130.

57. *Eastern Argus*, October 29, 1913, 3, carried this "P.L.S.B.S. Schedule of Wages," signed by the society president, Michael Keaney.

58. PLSBS *Records and Minutes*, Records, vol. 6, October 28, 1913, 138.

59. *Eastern Argus*, November 10, 1913, 12.

60. PLSBS *Records and Minutes*, Records, vol. 6, November 11, 1913, 142.

61. *Eastern Argus*, November 12, 1913, 12.

62. Ibid., November 13, 1913, 1.

63. PLSBS *Records and Minutes*, Records, vol. 6, November 13, 1913, 143. The PLSBS quickly dispatched their financial secretary to check on the wage scale currently in effect in Boston.

64. *Eastern Argus*, November 14, 1913, 1.

65. McLaughlin, "Industrial Relations in the Boston Longshore Industry," 43 and 53.

66. *Eastern Argus*, November 15, 1913, 12.

67. Ibid., November 17, 1913, 1.

68. Ibid., November 20, 1913, 1 and 5.

69. Ibid., 16.

70. Ibid., November 21, 1913, 1.

71. Ibid., 16.

72. *Portland Evening Express*, November 21, 1913, 1.

73. PLSBS *Records and Minutes*, Records, vol. 6, November 21, 1913, 146.

74. *Eastern Argus*, November 21, 1913, 1.

75. *Portland Evening Express*, November 21, 1913, 1.

76. *Eastern Argus*, November 21, 1913, 1.

77. PLSBS *Records and Minutes*, Records, vol. 6, November 21, 1913, 146.

78. *Eastern Argus*, November 22, 1913, 1.

79. PLSBS *Records and Minutes*, Records, vol. 6, November 25, 1913, 149.

80. *Eastern Argus*, November 25, 1913, 1.

81. PLSBS *Records and Minutes*, Records, vol. 6, November 25, 1913, 148; and ibid., December 2, 1913, 150.

82. Ibid., December 30, 1913, 156.

83. McLaughlin, "Industrial Relations in the Boston Longshore Industry," 54.

84. Larrowe, *Shape-Up and Hiring Hall*, 7. See also Winslow, *Waterfront Workers*.

85. McLaughlin, "Industrial Relations in the Boston Longshore Industry," 40.

86. McLaughlin, "Replacement of the Knights of Labor."

87. Ibid.

88. PLSBS *Records and Minutes*, Records, vol. 6, December 16, 1913, 153.

89. For more information on O'Connor and the role of the ILA in these years of controversy and growth, see Winslow, *Waterfront Workers*; Arnesen, "Biracial Waterfront Unionism"; Kimeldorf, "Radical Possibilities?"; and Cole, *Wobblies on the Waterfront*.

90. PLSBS *Records and Minutes*, Records, vol. 6, January 6, 1914, 159.

91. Ibid., February 10, 1914, 166.

92. Montgomery, *Fall of the House of Labor*, 104.

93. *Eastern Argus*, February 11, 1914, 12.

94. PLSBS *Records and Minutes*, Records, vol. 6, April 14, 1914, 180.
95. Montgomery, *Fall of the House of Labor*, 104.
96. PLSBS Records and Minutes, Records, vol. 6, May 19, 1914; and July 7, 1914.
97. Larrowe, *Shape-Up and Hiring Hall*, 7–9.
98. McGirr, "Black and White Longshoremen in the IWW," 379–81. The most comprehensive and current work on Philadelphia's longshoremen is Cole, *Wobblies on the Waterfront*.
99. Rubin, *The Negro in the Longshore Industry*, 48–75.
100. McGirr, "Black and White Longshoremen in the IWW," 377–78.
101. Larrowe, *Shape-Up and Hiring Hall*, 7–9, 225–26.
102. For a discussion of the contemporary conditions along the waterfront, see "The Wharves of Portland, Maine," 181–82.
103. Larrowe, *Shape-Up and Hiring Hall*, 3.
104. PLSBS *Records and Minutes*, Records, vol. 6, October 6, 1914, 229.
105. Oral interview with Lawrence Welch, January 6, 1982.
106. Montgomery, *Fall of the House of Labor*, 99.
107. *Eastern Argus*, April 3, 1917, 12, and April 6, 1917, 1.
108. Oral interviews with Thomas Mulkern, January 22, 1982; and Philip O'Donnell, January 13, 1982.
109. Connolly, *Irish Longshoremen of Portland, Maine 1880–1923*, appendices C and E. Also see Babcock, "Rise and Fall of Portland's Waterfront," 91–92.

Chapter 5. Apex of the Union and Catholic Hierarchical Influence

1. Connolly, "The Next Parish West of Galway," 6–9. See also Grimes and Connolly, "Migration Link between Cois Fharraige and Portland," 22–30.
2. Montgomery, *Fall of the House of Labor*, 309. See also the entire section titled "Party and Church," 302–10.
3. Thibodeau, "The French Catholics in Maine," 200–210. Also see Guignard, "Maine's Corporation Sole Controversy," 113–30.
4. Foley, *Bishop Healy, Beloved Outcaste*, 169.
5. O'Toole, *Passing for White*, chaps. 8 and 10. A new book deals with Healy's brother Michael. See Noble and Strobridge, *Captain "Hell Roaring" Mike Healy*.
6. Scontras, *Collective Efforts among Maine Workers*, 184; O'Toole, *Passing for White*, 144.
7. Browne, *Catholic Church and the Knights of Labor*, 128. Regarding Bishop Healy's difficult and costly conflict with the French-born priest of Biddeford, Maine, Father Jean Francois Ponsardin, see Foley, *Bishop Healy*, 128–40; and regarding the KOL, see ibid., 166–69. See also Kelly, *Dark Shepherd*, 125–28; Lucey, *Catholic Church in Maine*, 209–41; and Connolly, *Irish Longshoremen of Portland*, 89–94. An excellent account of the Healy versus Powderly conflict from the Maine labor

perspective may be found in Scontras, *Two Decades of Organized Labor and Labor Politics in Maine*, chap. 3, and 33–53. The best recent research on this topic may be found in O'Toole, *Passing for White*, 143–46, and for background all of chap. 7.

8. Powderly, *The Path I Trod*, 346.

9. Montgomery, *Fall of the House of Labor*, 303. See also Fremantle, *Papal Encyclicals in Their Historical Context*, 135–52.

10. Browne, *Catholic Church and the Knights of Labor*, 129.

11. Powderly, *The Path I Trod*, 371–72.

12. Browne, *Catholic Church and the Knights of Labor*, 128.

13. O'Toole, *Passing for White*, 147.

14. Foley, *Bishop Healy*, 151.

15. O'Toole, *Passing for White*, 146–47.

16. Foley, *Bishop Healy*, 169.

17. Lucey, *Catholic Church in Maine*, 235.

18. Montgomery, *Fall of the House of Labor*, 306.

19. *Daily Eastern Argus*, September 27, 1897, 5. Thanks to William David Barry of Maine Historical Society for this reference.

20. O'Toole, *Passing for White*, 147–51.

21. Connolly, *Irish Longshoremen of Portland*, 90. See also ibid., 87–94, for a wider analysis of the PLSBS in this period in relationship to the KOL and other local and national labor organizations.

22. O'Toole, *Militant and Triumphant*. I am indebted to William B. Jordan Jr. for this reference and for the use of this source. See also Lucey, *Catholic Church in Maine*, 272–82. Regarding the swing toward conservatism in 1899, see O'Toole, *Passing for White*, 147.

23. O'Toole, *Militant and Triumphant*, 38.

24. Ibid., 46.

25. Ibid., 40.

26. Connolly, *Irish Longshoremen of Portland*, 155. Mayor Baxter's journals are housed at the Baxter Memorial Library, Gorham, Maine.

27. O'Toole, *Militant and Triumphant*, 41.

28. Lucey, *Catholic Church in Maine*, 276.

29. O'Toole, *Militant and Triumphant*, 160–61.

30. Ibid., 162. For a discussion of IWW activities in Maine, especially in the lumber industry, see Scontras, *Organized Labor in Maine* (2002), 161–86.

31. Lucey, *Catholic Church in Maine*, 280.

32. See "Portland Site Number 31" at the Maine Irish Heritage Trail Web site, http://www.maineirishheritagetrail.org/workingmens-club_031.shtml. This is one entry in Matthew Jude Barker's Web site describing places of interest to Irish heritage in Portland. For additional information regarding moral reform movements in early-twentieth-century Portland, see Solomon, "Combating the 'Social Evil.'"

33. O'Toole, *Militant and Triumphant*, especially chap. 8, "Scandal and Survival."

34. Montgomery, *Fall of the House of Labor*, 306.

35. Ibid.

36. *The Connolly-Walker Controversy: On Socialist Unity in Ireland*, pamphlet reprinted by the Cork Workers' Club (Historical Reprint No. 9), November 1974 (in the author's possession).

37. *The Issue*, April 1913, 2, cited in Scontras, *The Socialist Alternative*, 159; and Scontras, *Organized Labor in Maine* (2002), especially chap. 2 on the role of the clergy in social reform in Maine.

38. Scontras, *The Socialist Alternative*, 159–60. These were reported in *The Issue*, June 1913, 4, and July 1913, 2. Volume 1, no. 1 (January 1911) is available in the Portland Room of the Portland Public Library (Cupboard #10, Drawer 1, No. 15). Thanks to William David Barry and Jamie Kingman Rice of the Maine Historical Society, and to Abraham Schecter of the Portland Public Library, for assistance in locating this source.

39. Ibid., 160n123. These were reported in the *Daily Eastern Argus*, March 2, 1915, 1.

40. Lucey, *Catholic Church in Maine*, 306.

41. Ibid., 295.

42. Brody, *Workers in Industrial America*, 44. See also Kirkpatrick, "Influenza 1918," 162–77.

43. Montgomery, *Workers' Control in America*, 96.

44. Bernstein, *The Lean Years*, 84. See also Allen, *Only Yesterday*.

45. Scontras, *Organized Labor in Maine* (2002), 31. See especially chap. 2, "Bolshevism and the 'Red Scare.'"

46. Montgomery, *Fall of the House of Labor*, 403.

47. *ILA Newsletter*, vol. 12, no. 1 (July/August 1992): 1. Kindly supplied by Jack Humeniuk, business agent of ILA Local 861.

48. Ryan was first mentioned in the PLSBS *Records and Minutes*, Records, vol. 7, April 19, 1921, 350.

49. PLSBS *Records and Minutes*, Records, vol. 7, March 3, 1921, 339.

50. *Portland Press Herald*, December 3, 1921, 1.

51. PLSBS *Records and Minutes*, Records, vol. 7, December 1, 1921, 392.

52. *Portland Press Herald*, December 3, 1921, 1 and 11.

53. PLSBS *Records and Minutes*, Records, vol. 7, December 2, 1921, 393.

54. Wright, "'Methods of Friendly Approach'"; Babcock, "Economic Development in Portland"; and Babcock, "The Rise and Fall of Portland's Waterfront."

55. *Portland Press Herald*, December 3, 1921, 11.

56. Montgomery, *Fall of the House of Labor*, 106.

57. PLSBS *Records and Minutes*, Records, vol. 7, December 3, 1921, 393.

58. *Portland Press Herald*, December 22, 1921, 1 and 4.
59. *Portland Press Herald*, December 23, 1921, 1.
60. PLSBS *Records and Minutes*, Records, vol. 7, December 23, 1921, 401.
61. *Portland Press Herald*, December 24, 1921, 1 and 2.
62. Ibid.
63. Connolly, *Irish Longshoremen of Portland*. See "Total Tonnage Handled in Portland (1890–1935)" in appendix M.
64. *Portland Press Herald*, December 24, 1921, 2.
65. Ibid.
66. PLSBS *Records and Minutes*, Records, vol. 7, December 26, 1921, 402.
67. See *Portland Press Herald*, December 27, 1921, 1.
68. For an analysis of the continued links between the PLSBS and Irish nationalism into the twentieth century, see Connolly, "Nationalism among Early Twentieth Century Irish Longshoremen in Portland, Maine," 277–96.
69. Bishop Louis S. Walsh, "Diaries," December 21, 1921. My thanks go to Sister Melissa Petrie, formerly of Saint Joseph's College, Standish, Maine, for reference to this material in the Walsh diaries.
70. Ibid., December 23, 1921.
71. Ibid., December 26, 1921.
72. *Portland Press Herald*, December 26, 1921, 1; and ibid., December 27, 1921, 1.
73. Ibid., December 28, 1921, 1. Concerning the extensive role of the U.S. Shipping Board in this year of strikes, see Montgomery, *Fall of the House of Labor*, 403.
74. Walsh, "Diaries," December 27, 1921.
75. Ibid., December 28, 1921.
76. PLSBS *Records and Minutes*, Records, vol. 7, December 28, 1921, 405.
77. Walsh, "Diaries," December 28, 1921.
78. *Portland Press Herald*, December 29, 1921, 2.
79. Oral interviews with Philip O'Donnell, January 13, 1982; and Lawrence Welch, January 6, 1982.
80. Walsh, "Diaries," December 29, 1921.
81. *Portland Press Herald*, December 29, 1921, 2.
82. Ibid.
83. PLSBS *Records and Minutes*, Records, vol. 7, October 27, 1922, 474.
84. Brody, *Workers in Industrial America*, 27 and 41. See also Reed, "Lumberjacks and Longshoremen," 41–59; Renshaw, *The Wobblies*; Kornbluh, *Rebel Voices*; Chaplin, *Wobbly*; Foner, "Industrial Workers of the World;" and Cole, *Wobblies on the Waterfront*.
85. Oral interview with Lawrence Welch, February 3, 1983.
86. Montgomery, *Fall of the House of Labor*; and Bernstein, *Lean Years*.
87. Portland Port Commission, *Report*, Plate III.
88. Babcock, "Economic Development"; and Babcock, "Rise and Fall of Portland's Waterfront."

89. Oral interview with Royal Caleb, February 5, 1982.
90. Oral interview with Lawrence Welch, January 6, 1982.
91. Eastman, "From Declining Seaport to Liberty City," 275–76.
92. Montgomery, *Fall of the House of Labor*, 461.
93. Ibid., 460–63. See also Syrett, "Principle and Expediency," 214–39; and Breton, "Red Scare."
94. Lee, "'What They Lack in Numbers,'" 236–37.
95. Ibid., 234–35.
96. Oral interview with Lawrence Welch, January 6, 1982.
97. Price and Talbot, *Maine's Visible Black History*, 148–52. See also Lee, "'What They Lack in Numbers,'" 218–46.
98. Lee, "What They Lack in Numbers,'" 232.
99. Lucey, *Catholic Church in Maine*, 304.
100. Oral interviews with Royal Caleb, February 5, 1982; and Thomas Mulkern, January 22, 1982.
101. Conforti, *Creating Portland*, xxv–xxvi.
102. Lucey, *Catholic Church in Maine*, 325.
103. O'Toole, *Militant and Triumphant*, 159.

Chapter 6. Longshore Culture and the Decline of the Port of Portland in the Mid- to Late Twentieth Century

1. *Portland Press Herald*, December 7, 1921, 1.
2. Oral interview with Philip O'Donnell, January 13, 1982.
3. Oral interview with Thomas Mulkern, January 22, 1982.
4. Oral interviews with Stephen Concannon, February 3, 1983; and Thomas Mulkern, January 22, 1982.
5. Oral interviews with Royal Caleb, February 5, 1982; and Thomas Mulkern, January 22, 1982.
6. Oral interview with Lawrence Welch, January 6, 1982.
7. Oral interviews with Thomas Mulkern, January 22, 1982; and Philip O'Donnell, January 13, 1982.
8. Oral interviews with Lawrence Welch, January 6, 1982; Thomas Mulkern, January 22, 1982; and Philip O'Donnell, January 13, 1982.
9. Saunders, *Economic History of the Maritime Provinces*; E. R. Hayes, "Development of Courtney Bay"; Réal Bibeault, "Le Syndicat des Debardeurs de Montréal"; Rice, "History of Organized Labor in Saint John"; and Swankey, *Man along the Shore*.
10. Angus, "Politics of the 'Short Line'"; Bush, "Canadian 'Fast Line'"; Wright, "'Methods of Friendly Approach'"; Babcock, "Economic Development in Portland," and "Rise and Fall."
11. *Portland Press Herald*, January 3, 1923, 1 and 18.

12. Wright, "'The Methods of Friendly Approach,'" 135.
13. Ibid., 138.
14. Ibid., 139–40.
15. *Portland Press Herald*, January 2, 1923, 11.
16. Bernstein, *The Lean Years*, 50. See also Divine, *American Immigration Policy*; Higham, *Strangers in the Land*; and Barbara Solomon, *Ancestors and Immigrants*.
17. Connolly, "Irish Longshoremen of Portland," computer analysis for chap. 3, 107. See also Asher, "Union Nativism"; and Breton, "Red Scare."
18. *Portland Press Herald*, November 1, 1923, 1.
19. *Portland Press Herald*, November 3, 1923, 1.
20. See Connolly, "Nationalism among Early Twentieth Century Irish Longshoremen."
21. Bernstein, *Lean Years*, 50.
22. Ibid., 66.
23. Velie, "Big Boss of the Big Port"; and Vorse, "Pirate's Nest of New York."
24. PLSBS *Records and Minutes*, Records, vol. 8, May 28, 1928, 400.
25. PLSBS *Records and Minutes*, Records, vol. 9, for the meetings of June 10, 1930; March 11, 1932; and October 14, 1932.
26. Oral interview with Lawrence Welch, January 6, 1982.
27. McLaughlin, "Boston Longshoremen's Strike of 1931," 6.
28. Ibid.
29. O'Leary, "History of Organized Labor in Maine."
30. PLSBS *Records and Minutes*, Records, vol. 9, November 20, 1934, 442.
31. The best comprehensive source on maritime labor in the 1930s is Bruce Nelson, *Workers on the Waterfront*. Two sympathetic sources on this episode in American labor history are Quin, *The Big Strike*; and Larrowe, *Harry Bridges*. See also Kerr, *Collective Bargaining on the Pacific Coast*; Larrowe, "The Great Maritime Strike of '34," and "The Great Maritime Strike of '34, Part II;" Malm, "Wage Differentials"; Mezy, "West Coast Waterfront Showdown;" and Roland, Bolster, and Keyssar, *Way of the Ship*, especially chap. 34, "A Tale of Two Harrys." Of related interest is a book dealing with longshore activities on the Gulf Coast and elsewhere from a radical and personal perspective by Mers, *Working the Waterfront*.
32. For additional literature on Bridges and the Pacific Coast longshoremen, see O'Connor, *Revolution in Seattle*; Radin, "Case of Harry Bridges," and "Harry Bridges Case Again," 541, and "Unfinished Case of Harry Bridges," 485; Sarbaugh, "Father Yorke and the San Francisco Waterfront"; Schneiderman, *Pacific Coast Maritime Strike*; Schwartz, *The March Inland*; Seidman, London, and Karsh, "Leadership in a Local Union;" Swados, "West-coast Waterfront"; Taylor and Gold, "San Francisco and the General Strike"; Theriault, *Longshoring on the San Francisco Waterfront*; Travers, *A Funeral for Sabella*; Vorse, *Labor's New Millions*, 210–20, and chapter 21; and Ward, *Harry Bridges on Trial*.
33. *Portland Press Herald*, July 6, 1934, 1. See also Roland, Bolster, and Keyssar,

Way of the Ship, chap. 34, "A Tale of Two Harrys: Radicalization of West Coast Labor," esp. 284 and 289.

34. Roland, Bolster, and Keyssar, *Way of the Ship*, 289.

35. PLSBS *Records and Minutes*, Records, vol. 10, January 8, 1935, 2.

36. Perhaps the best source for contrasting the two types of labor organizations represented by these leaders is a seminal work by Larrowe, *Shape-Up and Hiring Hall*. In this book the author compares the ILA's shape-up in New York City with the ILWU's hiring hall in Seattle, Washington.

37. Roland, Bolster, and Keyssar, *Way of the Ship*, 288 and 291. Scontras deals with the rise of the CIO in Maine in *Organized Labor in Maine* (2002), 223–50.

38. PLSBS *Records and Minutes*, Records, vol. 10, December 29, 1936, 132.

39. Hudelson and Ross, *By the Ore Docks*, 236–38.

40. Brian J. Cudahy, *Box Boats*, 247.

41. Rosenbaum, "Expulsion of the I.L.A. from the A.F. of L."

42. Oral interview with Lawrence Welch, January 6, 1982.

43. Bell, "The Racket-ridden Longshoremen;" Carter, "Behind the Waterfront Rackets;" Joyce Clements, "San Francisco Maritime and General Strikes"; Eliel, "Labor Peace in Pacific Coast Ports," and *Waterfront and General Strikes*; Hagel and Goldblatt, *Men and Machines*; and Harris, "The Trouble with Harry Bridges."

44. Theses and dissertations include the following: Buchanan, "History of the 1934 Waterfront Strike"; Francis, "History of Labor"; Hardt, "Port Changes in Pacific Coast Ports"; Liebes, "Longshore Labor Relations"; Palmer, "Pacific Coast Maritime Labor"; and Robinson, "Maritime Labor in San Francisco."

45. Oral interviews with Steven Concannon, February 3, 1983; Philip O'Donnell, January 13, 1982; Royal Caleb, February 5, 1982; and Thomas Mulkern, January 22, 1982.

46. Oral interview with Lawrence Welch, January 6, 1982. Welch's wife, Ethel, reportedly shuttled Harry Bridges around Boston on occasion without ever being discovered or suspected.

47. Cudahy, *Box Boats*, 247.

48. Roland, Bolster, and Keyssar, *Way of the Ship*, 291, 364.

49. Eastman, "From Declining Seaport to Liberty City," 279.

50. Ibid., 278–79.

51. Scontras, *Labor in Maine* (1985), 141. See chap. 5, "Maine's 'Rosie the Riveter.'"

52. Paine, *Down East*, 149–51.

53. Portland Port Commission, *Report*, Plate III.

54. Paine, *Down East*, 155.

55. Roland, Bolster, and Keyssar, *Way of the Ship*, 407.

56. PLSBS *Records and Minutes*, Records, vol. 11, October 19, 1945, 137. See also National Maritime Union, "N.M.U.—40 Years on a True Course"; and Lampman, "Collective Bargaining of West Coast Sailors."

57. Oral interview with Lawrence Welch, January 6, 1982.
58. Ibid.
59. PLSBS *Records and Minutes*, Records, vol. 11, June 18, 1948, 261.
60. Roland, Bolster, and Keyssar, *Way of the Ship*, 364.
61. Ibid.
62. *Portland Press Herald*, September 13, 1948, 2.
63. PLSBS *Records and Minutes*, Records, vol. 11, April 7, 1948, 249.
64. *Portland Press Herald*, September 13, 1948, 2.
65. Ibid., September 14, 1948, 1.
66. See Scontras, *Labor in Maine* (2002), especially "Reaction Reaches Maine," in chap. 10, 279–89, and chap. 11 "Organized Labor's Struggle for Survival." On page 302 there is a labor political advertisement asking supporters to vote "Against Both Measures."
67. Crosby, *God, Church, and Flag*; Holmes, *Specter of Communism in Hawaii, 1947–1953*; and Rovere, *Senator Joe McCarthy*. For a recent study of McCarthyism in New England, see Connolly, "Showing More Profile Than Courage."
68. PLSBS *Records and Minutes*, Records, vol. 11, June 15, 1949, 322.
69. PLSBS *Records and Minutes*, Records, February 13, 1957.
70. PLSBS *Records and Minutes*, Records, vol. 12, November 14, 1959, 83 (this volume is still in possession of the PLSBS Local 861).
71. Albion, "Port of Portland, Maine"; Albion, Baker, and Labaree, *New England and the Sea*; Peck, *Seaports in Maine*; "Union Labor: Less Militant, More Affluent"; and Pilcher, *Portland Longshoremen*.
72. Jensen, *Strife on the Waterfront*; Josephson, "Red Skies over the Waterfront"; Kerr and Fisher, "Conflict on the Waterfront;" and Lamson, "1951 New York Wildcat Dock Strike," 28.
73. Ball, *Government-Subsidized Union Monopoly*; Coffey, "Rise and Decline of the Port of Newburyport"; Evans, *Technical and Social Changes in the World's Ports*; Fairley, *Facing Mechanization*; Fairley, "Longshore Contract," 186; Finlay, "One Occupation, Two Labor Markets;" Goldberg, "Longshoremen and the Mechanization"; Gubin, "Technical Changes and Trade Union Policy"; Hayut, "Containerization and the Load Center Concept"; and Thoman, "Portland, Maine."
74. Finamore, *Maritime History as World History*. See essay by Armstrong, "The Role of Short-Sea, Coastal, and Riverine Traffic in Economic Development since 1750," 115–29.
75. Roland, Bolster, and Keyssar, *Way of the Ship*, 362. See especially chaps. 40 and 42 on Malcolm McLean and the container revolution in shipping and its effect on longshoremen. Other very useful and more comprehensive recent studies on this subject include Cudahy, *Box Boats*; Donovan and Bonney, *The Box That Changed the World*; and Levinson, *The Box*.
76. Rinaldi, *Containerization*, 55.
77. Roland, Bolster, and Keyssar, *Way of the Ship*, appx. C, 438.

78. Ibid., 343–46, 493.
79. Ibid., 38; and Finamore, ed., *Maritime History as World History*, 103.
80. Roland, Bolster, and Keyssar, *Way of the Ship*, 346–50.
81. DiFazio, *Longshoremen*; Hill, *The Dockers*; Lovell, *Stevedores and Dockers*; Lowndes, *Technical Innovation, Capital and Labour*; McKelvey, *Dock Labor Disputes in Great Britain*; Mellish, *Docks after Devlin*; Oram and Baker, *Efficient Port*; Swanstrom, *Waterfront Labor Problem*; and Taplin, *Dockers' Union*.
82. Dawson, "Stabilization of Dockworkers' Earnings"; Jensen, *Decasualization and Modernization;* Jensen, *Hiring of Dock Workers*; Lascelles and Bullock, "Dock Labour and Decasualization;" O'Brien, "Longshoremen Stabilize Their Jobs;" and Whyte, *Decasualization of Dock Labor*.
83. Roland, Bolster, and Keyssar, *Way of the Ship*, 366.
84. Ibid., 351, 365–67.
85. *Portland Press Herald*, May 3, 1983, 12.
86. Oral interview with Jack Humeniuk, May 19, 2008. Humeniuk joined the PLSBS in 1975, became the business agent for Local 861 in 1981, and has been an international ILA representative for this port since 1983.
87. Oral interviews with Philip O'Donnell, January 13, 1982; and Thomas Mulkern, January 22, 1982.
88. Jordan, "Jordan's Meats," 17. This source was made available by William David Barry of the Maine Historical Society.
89. *Portland Evening Express*, January 9, 1988, 1 and 12.
90. Oral interview with Lawrence Welch, January 6, 1982.

Conclusion: The Port of Portland in the Twenty-First Century and Its Maritime Future

1. Janzen, "A World-Embracing Sea," 104.
2. Rowe, *Maritime History of Maine*, 295. The story is found in Colcord, *Sea Language Comes Ashore*, and originally in Chase, *Sea Terms Come Ashore*.
3. Mooney, *Nine Years in America*, 126–27.
4. Babcock, "Economic Development in Portland," 29–30.
5. Duncan, *Coastal Maine*, 536–37. See also chap. 33, "History Hot Off the Stove," for a discussion of marine-related issues and developments up to 1992.
6. Roland, Bolster, and Keyssar, *Way of the Ship*, 414.
7. Maine DOT, "Port of Portland Cargo and Passenger Study," 11–17.
8. *Portland Press Herald*, August 7, 2007, C4.
9. Roland, Bolster, and Keyssar, *Way of the Ship*, 438.
10. *The Cat* arrived at Ocean Gateway for the first time on May 28, 2008, and made its first voyage to Yarmouth, Nova Scotia, from the new facility on May 30, 2008. *Portland Press Herald*, May 29, 2008, B1.
11. *Portland Press Herald*, October 9, 2008, B1,10; and October 10, 2008, A12.

12. Oral interview with Jack Humeniuk, May 19, 2008. Supported by Bouchard, "City to State."

13. Bell, "The Port Shapes Up."

14. Oral interview with Jack Humeniuk, May 19, 2008.

15. Woodard, "Chump Change," 14–18.

16. Ibid., in two addenda to the featured article, "Know your boats," 20; and "Well contained," 21.

17. Outwin, "Thriving and Elegant Town," 38.

18. Oral interview with Jack Humeniuk, May 19, 2008.

19. Conforti, *Creating Portland*, xvii.

Bibliography

Primary Sources

"The Annual Report of the Commissioner of Industrial and Labor Statistics, 1887." Augusta, Maine: Kennebec Journal Printing Company, 1887.

Baxter, James Phinney. *James Phinney Baxter Journals (1859–1920)*. Gorham, Maine: Baxter Memorial Library, Archives Collection.

Bureau of the Statistics of Labor. "Annual Reports of the Bureau of Industrial and Labor Statistics for the State of Maine." 1887–1907.

"Constitution and By-Laws of the Irish-American Relief Association of Portland Organized May 4, 1863." Portland, Maine: David Tucker, Printer, 1867.

"Constitution and By-Laws of the Portland Catholic Union Organized January, 1874." Portland, Maine: Stephen Berry Printer, 1874.

"Constitution and By-Laws of the St. Patrick's Benevolent Society, Portland, Maine." Portland, Maine: Stephen Berry, Printer, 1871.

Directors of the Port of Portland. "'America's Sunrise Gateway': Port of Portland, State of Maine and Its Hinterland." 1923.

Maine Alliance. "Charting Maine's Economic Future." Maine Chamber of Commerce and Industry, January 1994.

———. "Charting Maine's Economic Future." Maine Chamber of Commerce and Industry, Marine Science and Technology Foundation, October 1994.

———. "The Course for 1995 & Beyond: An Implementation Strategy for Charting Maine's Economic Future." Maine Chamber of Commerce and Industry, April 1995.

Maine Department of Transportation (DOT). "Feasibility Study of the Development of Cargo Handling Facilities at Maine Ports." Boston: Faye, Spofford & Thorndyke, January 1978.

———. "Feasibility Study of General Cargo Port Facilities in Maine." Bethesda, Md.: Booz, Allen & Hamilton, March 1980.

———. "Maine Department of Transportation Cargo Port Alternatives" (and Supplement of Report). Boston: Faye, Spofford & Thorndyke, September 1978.

———. "Maine Port Development Studies: Executive Summary." 1978.

———. "Maine Ports: Better Service via the Shortest U.S. Routes to Europe." Augusta, Maine: 1983.

———. "Port of Portland Cargo and Passenger Study: A Plan for Three Facilities." TAMS Consultants, May 1998. Maine State Library, Augusta, Maine.

Maine State Harbor Commission. "Report of the State Harbor Commission upon the Advisability of Building a Public Pier at Portland, Maine." December 31, 1918.

Muskie, Edmund S. Institute of Public Affairs. "The Port of Portland: Its Value to the Region." Portland, Maine: Portland Regional Chambers of Commerce, October 1993.

Office of Naval Intelligence. "Investigation of the Marine Transport Workers and the Alleged Threatened Combination Between Them and the Bolsheviki and Sinn Feiners," December 23, 1918, 31, file series 10110–567. R.G. 165, U.S. Military Intelligence Reports. Surveillance of Radicals in the United States, 1917–1941 (microfilm, University Publications of America, 1984).

Portland, Maine (City of). "Annual Reports of the City of Portland." 1847–1938.

———. Portland Planning Office. *City Edges.* 1975.

———. *"Report on Port Development Activities, Cities of Portland and South Portland for the Year 1938,"* ed. Charles H. Priest, 1938.

———. "Strategies for the Development and Revitalization of the Portland Waterfront." Progress Report, January 1985.

Portland City Directories. "City Directory of Portland, Maine." 1823–present. Portland: B. Thurston and Company.

"Portland Custom House and its Collectors." *Portland Board of Trade Journal* 12 (1899): 38.

Portland Harbor Commission. "Reports of the Commissioners of Portland Harbor." 1855.

Portland Longshoremen's Benevolent Society (PLSBS). *Records and Minutes.* Maine Historical Society Manuscript Collections 359 (MS 85–15, Local 861 ILA) and 360 (Italian Freight Handlers Union, Local 912 ILA).

"Portland in a Nutshell." *Portland Board of Trade Journal* V, no.1 (May 1892).

Portland Port Commission. "Report of the Portland Port Commission Appointed by Governor Louis S. Brann to Study Conditions Affecting the Port of Portland, Maine, 1935." Portland Room, Portland Public Library.

Roman Catholic Diocese of Portland (Maine). "Diaries of Bishop James A. Healy (1875–1900)"; and "Diaries of Bishop Louis S. Walsh (1909–1924)." Portland, Maine: Chancery Archives.

U.S. Census Office (Bureau of the Census). Fifth (1830); Sixth (1840); Seventh (1850); Eighth (1860); Ninth (1870); Tenth (1880); Eleventh (1890); Twelfth (1900); Thirteenth (1910); Fourteenth (1920) Census.

U.S. Department of Labor, Bureau of Labor Statistics. "Wage Chronology: North Atlantic Shipping Associations and the International Longshoremen's Association, 1934–1980" (Doc. # L2.3:2063).

Walsh, Louis S. "Diaries." Chancery Office of the Roman Catholic Diocese of Portland, Maine.

Waterfront Alliance. "Portland Harbor: A Vision." April 1996.

Waterfront Task Force. "Port of Portland: Imagine a Great Seaport." Portland, Maine: Chamber of Commerce of the Greater Portland Region, 1997.

Oral Histories (By the author and in his possession)

Royal Caleb (2/5/82); Stephen Concannon (2/3/83 and 12/15/85); Séamus Costello (12/15/85); Jack Humeniuk (1/31/83, 2/1/83, and 5/19/08); Patrick Malone (2/20/84); Thomas C. Mulkern (1/22/82); Philip O'Donnell (1/13/82); Patrick O'Malley (2/20/84); Patrick O'Toole (12/14/86); Lawrence F. Welch (1/6/82, 1/31/83, and 2/3/83).

Secondary Sources

Adams, William Forbes. *Ireland and Irish Emigration to the New World from 1815 to the Famine.* New York: Russell and Russell, 1932.

Albee, Parker B., Jr. *Letters from Sea, 1882–1901: Joanna and Lincoln Colcord's Seafaring Childhood.* Gardiner, Maine: Tilbury House Publishers, 1999.

Albion, Robert G. *Forests and Sea Power: The Timber Problem of the Royal Navy, 1652–1862.* Cambridge, Mass.: Harvard University Press, 1926.

———. "Introduction," in *The Revolutionary McLellans: A Bicentennial Project of the Portland Museum of Art*, edited by William David Barry and John Holverson. Portland, Maine: Portland Museum of Art, 1977.

———. "The Port of Portland, Maine." *Ships and the Sea* 4, no. 22 (August 1954): 44–50.

Albion, Robert G., William A. Baker, and Benjamin W. Labaree. *New England and the Sea.* Middletown, Conn.: Wesleyan University Press, 1972.

Allen, Fredrick L. *Only Yesterday: An Informal History of the Nineteen-Twenties.* New York: Harper and Row, 1964.

Anbinder, Tyler. *Five Points: The 19th-Century New York City Neighborhood That Invented Tap Dance, Stole Elections, and Became the World's Most Notorious Slum.* New York: The Free Press, 2001.

———. *Nativism and Slavery: The Northern Know Nothings and the Politics of the 1850s.* New York: Oxford University Press, 1992.

Anderson, Hayden L. V. *Canals and Waterways of Maine.* Portland: Maine Historical Society, 1982.

Andrews, Kenneth R., Nicholas P. Canny, and Paul E. H. Hair. *The Westward Enterprise: English Activities in Ireland, the Atlantic and America, 1480–1650.* Detroit: Wayne State University Press, 1979.

Angus, Murray E. "The Politics of the 'Short Line.'" Master's thesis, University of New Brunswick, 1958.

Anti-Negro Riots in the North, 1863. Salem, N.H.: Ayer Company Publishers, 1969. (Reprint of 1863 original)

Armstrong, John. "The Role of Short-Sea, Coastal, and Riverine Traffic in Economic Development since 1750." In *Maritime History as World History*, edited by Daniel Finamore, 115–29. Gainesville: University Press of Florida, 2004.

Arnesen, Eric. "Biracial Waterfront Unionism in the Age of Segregation." In *Waterfront Workers: New Perspectives on Race and Class*, edited by Calvin Winslow, 19–61. Urbana: University of Illinois Press, 1998.

———. "Following the Color Line of Labor: Black Workers and the Labor Movement before 1930." *Radical History Review* 55 (Winter 1993).

———. "'It Ain't Like They Do in New Orleans': Race Relations, Labor Markets, and Waterfront Labor Movements in the American South, 1880–1923." In *Racism and the Labor Market: Historical Studies*, edited by Calvin Winslow, 57–100. Bern, Switzerland: Peter Lang AG, 1995.

———. *Waterfront Workers of New Orleans: Race, Class and Politics, 1863–1923*. Urbana: University of Illinois Press, 1994.

Asher, Robert. "Union Nativism and the Immigrant Response." *Labor History* 23, no. 3 (1982): 325–48.

Babcock, Robert H. "Economic Development in Portland (ME) and Saint John (NB) during the Age of Iron and Steam, 1850–1914." *American Review of Canadian Studies* 9 (Spring 1979): 3–37.

———. "The Rise and Fall of Portland's Waterfront 1850–1920." *Maine Historical Society Quarterly* 22, no. 2 (Fall 1982): 63–98.

Baker, Emerson W. "Formerly Machegonne, Dartmouth, York, Stogummor, Casco, and Falmouth: Portland as a Contested Frontier in the Seventeenth Century." In *Creating Portland: History and Place in Northern New England*, edited by Joseph A. Conforti, 1–19. Durham: University of New Hampshire Press, 2005.

Baker, William A. *A Maritime History of Bath, Maine and the Kennebec River Region*. Bath, Maine: Marine Research Society of Bath, 1973.

Ball, Joseph H. *Government-Subsidized Union Monopoly: A Study of Labor Practices in the Shipping Industry*. Washington, D.C.: Labor Policy Association, 1966.

Banks, Ronald F., ed. *A History of Maine: A Collection of Readings on the History of Maine, 1600–1970*. Dubuque, Iowa: Kendall/Hunt Publishing, 1973.

———. *Maine Becomes a State: The Movement to Separate Maine from Massachusetts, 1785–1820*. Somersworth: New Hampshire Publishing, 1973.

———. *Maine during the Federal and Jeffersonian Period: A Bibliographical Guide Portland*. Portland: Maine Historical Society, 1974.

Barker, Matthew J. (Paul O'Neil, compiler). "A Collection of Brief Biographies of Early Portland Irish." *The Western Cemetery Project, 1997–2001, Irish-American History*. Portland, Maine: Ancient Order of Hibernians (Division 1), 2001.

———. *The Descendants of Patrick Graney of Cummer Parish: Galway, Ireland, 1800–1989*. South Portland, Maine: Matthew J. Barker, 1989.

———. "From Galway to Maine: The Story of an Immigrant Family." *Galway Roots/Clanna na Gaillimhe, Journal of the Galway Family History Society* 4 (1996): 21–22.

———, ed. "History of St. Dominic's Parish." *Saint Dominic's: 175 Years of Memories, 1822–1997*. Portland: Smart Marketing, Inc., 1997.

———. "The Irish Community and Irish Organizations of Nineteenth-Century Portland, Maine." In *They Change Their Sky: The Irish in Maine*, edited by Michael C. Connolly, 139–86. Orono: University of Maine Press, 2004.

———. "John Ford and the Feeney Family of Galway and Portland, Maine." *Galway Roots/Clanna na Gaillimhe* 5 (1998): 148–52.

———. "The Last Time We Shared Stone Soup." *Portland Monthly Magazine* (October 2000): 51–55.
———. "Munjoy Hill's Unsinkable Kitty Kentuck." *Portland Monthly Magazine* (December 1996): 24–29.
———. "The Shamrock Connection." Newsletter/Magazine (1995–98).
Barnes, Albert S., ed. *Greater Portland Celebration 350*. Portland, Maine: Gannett Books, 1984.
Barnes, Charles B. *The Longshoremen*. New York: Arno Press, 1977. (First published in 1915)
Barrett, James R., and David Roediger. "Inbetween Peoples: Race, Nationality and the 'New Immigrant' Working Class." *Journal of American Ethnic History* 16, no. 3 (Spring 1997): 3–44.
Barry, William D. *Bryce McLellan and His Children, 1720–1776*. Orono: University of Maine Press, 1973.
———. "A Concise History of the Portland Waterfront." *Portland Monthly Magazine* 13, no. 5 (July/August 1998): 24–41.
———. "Fires of Bigotry." *Down East* (October 1989): 44–47, 77–78.
———. "James Healy, We Hardly Knew You." *Portland Monthly Magazine* 9, no. 3 (May 1994): 9–17.
———. "Portland's Wackiest Fourth." *Down East* (July 1994): 47, 72–77.
———. *Rum, Riot and Reform: Maine and the History of American Drinking*. Portland: Maine Historical Society, 1998.
———. "A Vignetted History of Portland Business, 1632–1982." *Portland: The Newcomen Society in North America*, no. 1176, 1982.
Barry, William D., and Arthur J. Gerrier. *Munjoy Hill Historic Guide*. Portland, Maine: Greater Portland Landmarks, 1992.
Barry, William D., and John Holverson. *The Revolutionary McLellans: A Bicentennial Project of the Portland Museum of Art*. Portland, Maine: Portland Museum of Art, 1977.
Beck, John. "The Irish Roots of Great Lakes Waterfront Violence." Unpublished manuscript, East Lansing, Michigan, Michigan State University, 1994.
Bell, Daniel. "The Racket-ridden Longshoremen." *Dissent* 6 (Autumn 1959): 417–29.
Bell, Tom. "The Port Shapes Up as Cargo Ships Out." *Portland Press Herald*, October 5, 2007, A1, 12.
Belohlavek, John M. *Broken Glass: Caleb Cushing and the Shattering of the Union*. Kent, Ohio: Kent State University Press, 2005.
Berlin, Ira. *Slaves without Masters: The Free Negro in the Antebellum South*. New York: Pantheon Books, 1974.
Berlin, Ira, and Ronald Hoffman, eds. *Slavery and Freedom in the Age of the American Revolution*. Charlottesville: University of Virginia Press, 1983.
Bernstein, Irving. *The Lean Years: A History of the American Worker, 1920–1933*. Baltimore: Penguin Books, 1966.
Betts, John R. "The Negro and the New England Conscience in the Days of John Boyle O'Reilly." *Journal of Negro History* 51 (October 1966): 246–61.

Bibber, Joyce, and Earle G. Shettleworth Jr. *Portland* (Postcard History Series). Charleston, S.C.: Arcadia Publishing, 2007.

Bibeault, Réal. "Le Syndicat des Débardeurs de Montréal." Master's thesis, University of Montreal, 1954.

Billington, Ray Allen. *The Origins of Nativism in the United States, 1800–1844*. New York: Arno, 1974. (Reprint of 1933 thesis)

———. *The Protestant Crusade, 1800–1860: A Study of the Origins of American Nativism*. New York: Macmillan, 1938.

Blanshard, Paul. *The Irish and Catholic Power: An American Interpretation*. Boston: Beacon Press, 1953.

Boeze, Frank, ed. *Maritime History at the Crossroads: A Critical Review of Recent Historiography*. St. John's, Newfoundland: International Maritime Economic History Association, 1995.

Bolster, W. Jeffrey. *Black Jacks: African American Seamen in the Age of Sail*. Cambridge, Mass.: Harvard University Press, 1997.

———. *Cross-Grained and Wily Waters: A Guide to the Piscataqua Maritime Region*. Portsmouth, N.H.: Peter E. Randall, 2002.

———. "An Inner Diaspora: Black Sailors Making Selves." In *Through a Glass Darkly: Reflections on Personal Identity in Early America*, edited by Ronald Hoffman, Mechal Sobel, and Fredrika J. Teute, 419–48. Chapel Hill: University of North Carolina Press, 1997.

———. "'To Feel like a Man': Black Seamen in the Northern States, 1800–1860." *Journal of American History* 76 (March 1990): 1173–99.

Bouchard, Kelley. "City to State: Run Terminal." *Portland Press Herald*, April 1, 2008, A1, 8.

Boyle, Harold. "When the Klan Campaigned in Maine." *Maine Sunday Telegram*. April 23, 1978.

———. *The Best of Boyle*. Portland, Maine: Guy Gannett Publishing, 1980.

Bradford, James C., ed. *Crucible of Empire: The Spanish-American War and Its Aftermath*. Annapolis, Md.: Naval Institute Press, 1993.

Breton, Rita Mae. "Red Scare: A Study of Maine Nativism, 1919–1925." Master's thesis, University of Maine (Orono), 1972.

Brindle, Steven. *Brunel: The Man Who Built the World*. London: Weidenfeld & Nicolson, 2005.

Brody, David. *Workers in Industrial America: Essays on the Twentieth Century Struggle*. New York: Oxford University Press, 1980.

Brown, Thomas N. *Irish American Nationalism, 1870–1890*. Philadelphia: J. B. Lippincott, 1966.

———. "The Origin and Character of Irish-American Nationalism." In *Irish Nationalism and the American Contribution*, edited by Lawrence McCaffrey. New York: Arno Press, 1976.

Browne, Henry J. *The Catholic Church and the Knights of Labor*. Washington, D.C.: Catholic University Press, 1949.

Brundage, David. "American Labour and the Irish Question, 1916–1923." *Saothar: Journal of the Irish Labour History Society* 24 (1999).

———. "The 1920 New York Dockers' Boycott: Class, Gender, Race and Irish-American Nationalism." Unpublished manuscript (University of California, Santa Cruz, 1992).

Buchanan, Roger B. "History of the 1934 Waterfront Strike in Portland, Oregon." Master's thesis, University of Oregon (Eugene), 1964.

Buker, Margaret J. "The Irish in Lewiston, Maine: A Search for Security on the Urban Frontier, 1850–1880." *Maine Historical Society Quarterly* 13, no. 1 (special edition, 1973): 3–25.

Bunting, William H. *The Camera's Coast: Historical Images of Ship and Shore in New England*. Boston: Historical New England, 2006.

———. *A Day's Work: A Sampler of Historic Maine Photographs, 1860–1920*. Gardiner, Maine: Tilbury House Publishers, 1997.

———. *Live Yankees: The Sewalls and Their Ships*. Gardiner, Maine: Tilbury House Publishers, 2009.

———. *Portrait of a Port: Boston, 1852–1914*. Cambridge, Mass.: The Belknap Press of Harvard University Press, 1971.

———. *Sea Struck*. Gardiner, Maine: Tilbury House, 2004.

———. *Steamers, Schooners, Cutters, and Sloops: The Marine Photographs of N. L. Stebbins Taken from 1884–1907*. Boston: Houghton Mifflin, 1974.

Burlin, Paul T. *Imperial Maine and Hawai'i: Interpretive Essays in the History of Nineteenth Century American Expansion*. Lanham, Md.: Lexington Books, 2006.

Bush, Edward F. "The Canadian 'Fast Lane' on the North Atlantic, 1886–1915." Master's thesis, Carleton University, 1969.

Butler, Richard J. *Dock Walloper*. New York: G. P. Putnam's Sons, 1933.

Byrne, Frank L. *Prophet of Prohibition: Neal Dow and His Crusade*. Madison: University of Wisconsin, 1961.

Cahill, Thomas P. *A Short Sketch of the Life and Achievements of Captain Jeremiah O'Brien of Machias, Maine*. Worcester, Mass.: Harrigan Press, 1936.

Canny, Nicholas P. "The Ideology of English Colonization: From Ireland to America." *The William and Mary Quarterly* 30, no. 4 (October 1973): 575–98.

———. *Kingdom and Colony: Ireland in the Atlantic World, 1560–1800*. Baltimore, Md.: Johns Hopkins University Press, 1988.

Carter, Richard. "Behind the Waterfront Rackets." *Compass* (December 1951).

Catholic Diocese of Portland. "Memorable Events of the Catholic Church in Portland." *Maine Catholic Historical Magazine* 8 (1919–1928).

Chaplin, Ralph. *Wobbly*. Chicago: University of Chicago Press, 1948.

Chase, George Davis. *Sea Terms Come Ashore*. Orono: University of Maine Press, 1942.

Churchill, Edwin A. "The Historiography of the *Margaretta* Affair, Or, How Not to Let the Facts Interfere with a Good Story." *Maine Historical Society Quarterly* (Fall 1975): 60–74.

———. "Too Great the Challenge: The Birth and Death of Falmouth, Maine, 1624–1676." Ph.D. diss., University of Maine (Orono), 1979.

Clancy, Mary, John Cunningham, and Alf MacLochlain, eds. *The Emigrant Experience*. Galway, Ireland: Galway Labour History.

Clark, Charles E. *The Eastern Frontier: The Settlement of Northern New England, 1610–1763*. New York: Alfred A. Knopf, 1970.

———. *Maine: A Bicentennial History*. New York: Norton, 1977. (The States and the Nation Series)

———. *Maine during the Colonial Period: A Bibliographical Guide*. Portland: Maine Historical Society, 1974.

Clark, Charles E., James S. Leamon, and Karen Bowden, eds. *Maine in the Early Republic: From Revolution to Statehood*. Hanover, N.H.: University Press of New England, 1988.

Clark, Roy. *Longshoremen*. North Pomfret, Vt.: David and Charles, 1974.

Clayton, W. W. *History of Cumberland County Maine*. Philadelphia: Everts and Peck, 1880.

———. *History of York County, Maine*. Philadelphia: Everts and Peck, 1880.

Clements, Joyce. "The San Francisco Maritime and General Strikes of 1934 and the Dynamics of Repression," Ph.D. diss., University of California, Berkeley, 1975.

Coffey, Lorraine. "The Rise and Decline of the Port of Newburyport." Ph.D. diss., Boston University, 1975.

Coffin, Robert P. Tristram. *Captain Abby and Captain John*. New York: Macmillan, 1939.

———. *Kennebec: Cradle of Americans*. New York: Ferrar & Rinehart, 1937.

Cogill, Burgess. *When God Was an Atheist Sailor: Memories of a Childhood at Sea 1902–1910*. New York: W. W. Norton, 1985.

Colcord, Joanna Carver. *Sea Language Comes Ashore*. New York: Cornell Maritime Press, 1945.

Cole, Peter. "Shaping Up and Shipping Out: The Philadelphia Waterfront during and after the IWW Years, 1913–1940." Ph.D. diss., Georgetown University, 1997.

———. *Wobblies on the Waterfront: Interracial Unionism in Progressive-Era Philadelphia*. Urbana: University of Illinois Press, 2007.

Coleman, Terry. *Going to America*. Garden City, N.Y.: Anchor Books, 1973.

Commons, John R. "Types of American Labor Unions: The Longshoremen of the Great Lakes." *The Quarterly Journal of Economics* 20, no. 1 (November 1905): 59–85.

Conforti, Joseph A., ed. *Creating Portland: History and Place in Northern New England*. Durham: University of New Hampshire Press, 2005.

Connolly, Michael C. "Black Fades to Green: Irish Labor Replaces African-American Labor along a Major New England Waterfront, Portland, Maine, in the Mid-Nineteenth Century." *Colby Quarterly* 37, no.4 (December 2001): 357–73.

———. "The First Hurrah: James Michael Curley versus the 'Goo-Goos' in the Boston Mayoralty Election of 1914." *Historical Journal of Massachusetts* 30, no. 1 (Winter 2002): 50–74.

———. "The Irish Longshoremen of Portland, Maine 1880–1923." Ph.D. diss., Boston College, 1988.

———. "Nationalism among Early Twentieth Century Irish Longshoremen in Portland,

Maine." In *They Change Their Sky: The Irish in Maine*, edited by Michael C. Connolly, 277–96. Orono: University of Maine Press, 2004.

———. "The Next Parish West of Galway: The Irish Diaspora of Portland, Maine." *House Island Project*. Portland, Maine: Portland Performing Arts, 1996.

———. "Showing More Profile Than Courage: McCarthyism in Massachusetts and Its Challenge to the Young John Fitzgerald Kennedy." *Historical Journal of Massachusetts* 36, no. 1 (Winter 2008): 29–56.

———, ed. *They Change Their Sky: The Irish in Maine*. Orono: University of Maine Press, 2004.

———. "To 'Make This Port Union All Over': Longshore Militancy in Portland, 1911–1913." *Maine History* 41, no. 1 (Spring 2002): 41–60.

Connolly, Michael C., and Séamus Grimes. "Emigration from Connemara to America." *Galway Roots, the Journal of the Galway Historical Society* 2 (1994): 40–43.

Connolly, Michael C., and Kevin L. Stoehr, eds. *John Ford in Focus: Essays on the Filmmaker's Life and Work*. Jefferson, N.C.: McFarland, 2008.

Cook, Adrian. *The Armies of the Streets: The New York City Draft Riots of 1863*. Lexington: University Press of Kentucky, 1974.

Cousens, S. H. "Demographic Change in Ireland, 1851–1861." *Economic History Review* 14 (Spring 1961): 275–88.

———. "The Regional Variations in Population Changes in Ireland, 1860–1881." *Economic History Review*, no. xvii (1964).

Crapol, Edward P. *James G. Blaine: Architect of Empire*. Wilmington, Del.: Scholarly Resources, 2000.

Crosby, Donald F. *God, Church, and Flag: Senator Joseph R. McCarthy and the Catholic Church, 1950–1957*. Chapel Hill: University of North Carolina Press, 1978.

Cudahy, Brian J. *Box Boats: How Container Ships Changed the World*. New York: Fordham University Press, 2006.

Currie, Archibald W. *The Grand Trunk Railway of Canada*. Toronto: University of Toronto Press, 1957.

Curtis, L. Perry, Jr. *Apes and Angels: The Irishman in Victorian Caricature*. Washington, D.C.: Smithsonian Institution Press, 1971.

Davis, Colin. "'All I Got's a Hook': New York Longshoremen and the 1948 Dock Strike." In *Waterfront Workers: New Perspectives on Race and Class*, edited by Calvin Winslow, 131–54. Urbana: University of Illinois Press, 1998.

Davis, Harold A. "The Fenian Raid on New Brunswick." *Canadian Historical Review* 36 (December 1955): 316–34.

Dawson, A. A. P. "The Stabilization of Dockworkers' Earnings." *International Labour Review* 43 (March–April 1951).

Dean, Nicholas. *Lubec*. Cambridge, Mass.: Identity Magazine, 1966.

———. *Snow Squall: The Last American Clipper Ship*. Gardiner, Maine: Tilbury House, 2001.

Dean, Nicholas, and John K. Moulton. *The Portland Marine Society, 1796–1996: A Bicentennial History*. Portland, Maine: Portland Marine Society, 1996.

de Freine, Seán. *The Great Silence*. Cork, Ireland: Mercier Press, 1978.

Desmond, Lawrence A., and Donna M. Norell. *The Case for Fr. Charles Dominic Ffrench (1775-1851)*. Yorkton, Saskatchewan: Laverdure & Associates, 2004.

Detmer, J. H., and P. N. Pancoast. *Portland*. Portland, Maine: Greater Portland Landmarks, 1972.

DiFazio, William. *Longshoremen: Community and Resistance on the Brooklyn Waterfront*. South Hadley, Mass.: Bergin and Garvey, 1985.

Divine, Robert A. *American Immigration Policy, 1924-1952*. New Haven, Conn.: Yale University Press, 1957.

Dominic, Randolph, and William D. Barry. *Pyrrhus Venture*. Boston: Little, Brown, 1983.

Donohoe, J. M. *The Irish Catholic Benevolent Union: 1869-1893*. Washington, D.C.: Catholic University Press, 1951.

Donovan, Arthur, and Joseph Bonney. *The Box That Changed theWorld: Fifty Years of Container Shipping—An Illustrated History*. East Windsor, N.J.: Commonwealth Business Media, 2006.

Dow, Neal. *The Reminiscences of Neal Dow*. Portland, Maine: Evening Express Publishing, 1898.

Doyle, David N. *Irish America: Native Rights and National Empires, 1890-1901*. New York: Arno Press, 1976.

Doyle, David N., and Owen Dudley Edwards, eds. *America and Ireland, 1776-1976: The American Identity and the Irish Connection*. Westport, Conn.: Greenwood Press, 1976.

Doyle, Joe. "Striking for Ireland on the New York Docks." In *The New York Irish*, edited by Ronald H. Bayor and Timothy J. Meagher, 357-73. Baltimore: Johns Hopkins University Press, 1996.

Drudy, P. J., ed. *The Irish in America: Immigration, Assimilation, and Impact*. New York: Cambridge University Press, 1985.

Dunbaugh, Edwin L. *The New England Steamship Company*. Gainesville: University Press of Florida, 2005.

———. *Nightboat to New England, 1815-1900*. New York: Greenwood Press, 1992.

Duncan, Roger F. *Coastal Maine: A Maritime History*. New York: W. W. Norton, 1992.

Eagan, Eileen. "Working Portland: Women, Class, and Ethnicity in the Nineteenth Century." In *Creating Portland: History and Place in Northern New England*, edited by Joseph A. Conforti, 193-217. Durham: University of New Hampshire Press, 2005.

Eagan, Eileen, and Patricia Finn. "From Galway to Gorham's Corner: Irish Women in Portland, Maine." In *Of Place and Gender: Women in Maine History*, edited by Marli F. Weiner, 235-63. Orono: University of Maine Press, 2005.

———. "Mutually Single: Irish Women in Portland, Maine, 1875-1945." In *They Change Their Sky: The Irish in Maine*, edited by Michael C. Connolly, 257-75. Orono: University of Maine Press, 2004.

Eastman, Joel. "From Declining Seaport to Liberty City: Portland During Depression and War." In *Creating Portland: History and Place in Northern New England*, edited by Joseph A. Conforti, 274-94. Durham: University of New Hampshire Press, 2005.

Eckstorm, Fannie H. *Indian Place Names of the Penobscot Valley and Maine Coast.* Orono: University of Maine Press, 1941.

Eliel, Paul. "Labor Peace in Pacific Coast Ports." *Harvard Business Review* XIX (Summer 1941): 429–37.

———. *The Waterfront and General Strikes, San Francisco, 1934.* San Francisco: Hooper Printing Company, 1934.

Elwell, Edward H. *The Boys of Thirty-Five: A Story of a Seaport Town.* Boston: Lee and Shepard, 1884.

———. *Portland and Vicinity.* Portland, Maine: Greater Portland Landmarks, 1975.

Eskew, Garnet L. *Cradle of Ships.* New York: Putnam, 1958.

Evans, A. A. *Technical and Social Changes in the World's Ports.* International Labour Office (Studies and Reports, New Series, no.74), 1971.

Evans, E. Estyn. *Ireland and the Atlantic Heritage.* Dublin: Lilliput Press, 1996.

———. "Old Ireland and New England," in *Ireland and the Atlantic Heritage,* by E. Estyn Evans. Dublin: Lilliput Press, 1996.

Fair, Marvin L. *Port Administration in the United States.* Cambridge, Md.: Cornell Maritime Press, 1954.

Fairley, Lincoln. *Facing Mechanization: The West Coast Longshore Plan.* Los Angeles: U.C.L.A. Industrial Relations (Monograph #23), 1971.

———. "Longshore Contract." *Dissent* 9 (1962): 186.

Fallows, Marjorie R. *Irish Americans: Identity and Assimilation.* Englewood Cliffs, N.J.: Prentice Hall, 1979.

Fenning, Fr. Hugh. "The Conversion of Charles Ffrench." *The Watchman* 28, no.53 (Summer 1961): 34–39.

Ferland, Durwood, Jr. *Fortitudo et Spes: The Courage and Hope to Move a College.* Greenville, Maine: Moosehead Communication, 1999.

Fernández-Armesto, Felipe. "Maritime History and World History." In *Maritime History as World History,* edited by Daniel Finamore, 7–34. Gainesville: University Press of Florida, 2004.

Finamore, Daniel, ed. *Maritime History as World History.* Gainesville: University Press of Florida, 2004.

Fink, Leon. *Workingmen's Democracy: The Knights of Labor and American Politics.* Urbana: University of Illinois Press, 1983.

Finlay, William. "One Occupation, Two Labor Markets: The Case of Longshore Crane Operators." *American Social Review* 48, no.3 (1963): 306–15.

Foley, Albert S. "Bishop Healy and the Colored Catholic Congress." *Interracial Review* 28 (May 1954): 79–80.

———. *Bishop Healy, Beloved Outcaste: The Story of a Great Priest Whose Life Has Become a Legend.* New York: Ferrar, Straus and Young, 1954.

———. *Dream of an Outcaste: Patrick F. Healy.* Tuscaloosa, Ala.: Portals Press, 1989.

———. *God's Men of Color: The Colored Catholic Priests of the United States, 1854–1954.* New York: Farrar, Straus, 1955.

Foner, Eric. "Class, Ethnicity, and Radicalism in the Gilded Age: The Land League and Irish America." *Marxist Perspectives* 1, no. 2 (Summer 1978): 6–55.

Foner, Philip. "The Industrial Workers of the World." In *History of the Labor Movement in the United States*, vol. 4. New York: International Publishers, 1965.

Ford, Norman D. *Freighter Days: How to Travel by Freighter*. Greenlawn, N.Y.: Harian Publications, 1969.

Foulke, Robert D. "Odysseus's Oar: Archetypes of Voyaging." In *Maritime History as World History*, edited by Daniel Finamore, 183–202. Gainesville: University Press of Florida, 2004.

Fowler, W. M., Jr., ed. *Boston Looks Seaward: The Story of the Port, 1630–1940*, Writers' Project of the WPA. Boston: Northeastern University Press, 1985. (First published in 1941)

Francis, Robert C. "A History of Labor on the San Francisco Waterfront." Ph.D. diss., University of California, 1934.

Frappier, William J. *Steamboat Yesterdays on Casco Bay: The Steamboat Era in Maine's Calendar Island Region*. Toronto: Stoddart Publishing, 1993.

Fremantle, Anne, ed. *The Papal Encyclicals in Their Historical Context*. New York: New American Library, 1956.

Gallagher, Thomas. *Paddy's Lament: Ireland 1846 to 1847; Prelude to Hatred*. San Diego: Harcourt, Brace, Jovanovich, 1982.

Garin, Kristoffer A. *Devils on the Deep Blue Sea: The Dreams, Schemes, and Showdowns that Built America's Cruise-ship Empires*. New York: Viking, 2005.

Gibbs, C. R. Vernon. *Passenger Liners of the Western Ocean*. London: Staples Press, 1957.

Gilje, Paul A. *Liberty on the Waterfront: American Maritime Culture in the Age of Revolution*. Philadelphia: University of Pennsylvania Press, 2004.

Goldberg, Joseph P. "Longshoremen and the Mechanization of Cargo Handling in the United States." *International Labor Review* 28, no. 3 (1973): 253–79.

Goold, William. *Portland in the Past with Historical Notes of Old Falmouth*. Portland: B. Thurston, 1886.

Grace, Robert John. "The Irish in Mid-Nineteenth-Century Canada and the Case of Quebec: Immigration and Settlement in a Catholic City." Ph.D. diss., Université Laval, Québec, 1999.

Greater Portland Landmarks, *Portland*. Portland, Maine: Greater Portland Landmarks, 1972.

Greene, Lorenzo J. *The Negro in Colonial New England*. New York: Atheneum Publishers, 1968.

Grimes, Séamus, and Michael C. Connolly. "Emigration from Connemara to America." *Galway Roots, the Journal of the Galway Historical Society* 2 (1994): 40–43.

———. "The Migration Link between Cois Fharraige and Portland, Maine, 1880s to 1920s." *Irish Geography* 22 (1989): 22–30.

Gubin, Sidney N. "Technical Changes and Trade Union Policy," Ph.D. diss., University of California, 1938.

Guignard, Michael J. "Maine's Corporation Sole Controversy." *Maine Historical Society Quarterly* 12, no. 3 (Winter 1973): 113–30.

Gutman, Herbert. *Work, Culture and Society in Industrializing America: Essays in American Working-Class and Social History*. New York: Alfred A. Knopf, 1976.
Hachey, Thomas, and Lawrence McCaffrey. *Perspectives on Irish Nationalism*. Lexington: University Press of Kentucky, 1989.
Hagel, Otto, and Louis Goldblatt. *Men and Machines*. San Francisco: International Longshoremen's and Warehousemen's Union and the Pacific Maritime Association, 1963.
Handlin, Oscar. *Boston's Immigrants: A Study in Acculturation*. New York: Atheneum, 1997.
———, ed. *The Children of the Uprooted*. New York: G. Braziler, 1966.
Hanna, Charles A. *The Scotch Irish*. New York: G. P. Putnam's Sons, 1902.
Hansen, Marcus L. *The Atlantic Migration, 1607–1860*. New York: Harper, 1961.
———. *The Immigrant in American History*. New York: Harper & Row, 1964.
Hardt, John P. "Port Changes in Pacific Coast Ports." Master's thesis, University of Washington, 1948.
Harris, Ed. "The Trouble with Harry Bridges." *International Socialist Review* 34 (September 1973): 6–11, 39.
Hatch, Louis C. *Maine: A History*. Somersworth: New Hampshire Publishing Company, 1974.
Hayes, Ernest R. "The Development of Courtney Bay, Saint John, New Brunswick, 1908–1918." Master's thesis, University of New Brunswick, 1969.
Hayut, Yehuda. "Containerization and the Load Center Concept." *Economic Geography* 57, no.2 (1981): 160–76.
Headley, Joel. *The Great Riots of New York: 1712–1873*. New York: Irvington Publishers, 1970.
Higham, John. "Another Look at Nativism." *Catholic Historical Review* 44, no. 2 (1958): 147–58.
———. *Strangers in the Land: Patterns of American Nativism, 1860–1925*. New Brunswick, N.J.: Rutgers University Press, 1955.
Hill, Stephen. *The Dockers: Class and Tradition in London*. London: Heinemann, 1976.
Hoffer, Eric. *Working and Thinking on the Waterfront*. New York: Harper & Row, 1969.
Hoffman, Miles E. *International Longshoremen's Association: A Contemporary Analysis of a Labor Union*. Philadelphia: Temple University Press (Labor Monograph #7), 1966.
Holmes, Thomas. "*The Specter of Communism in Hawaii, 1947–1953*." Dissertation Abstracts International, vol. 36, 1976.
Holt, Jeff. *The Grand Trunk in New England*. Toronto: Railfare Enterprises, 1986.
Horton, James O., and Lois E. Horton. *Black Bostonians: Family Life and Community Struggle in the Antebellum North*. New York: Holmes and Meier, 1979.
Hudelson, Richard, and Carl Ross. *By the Ore Docks: A Working People's History of Duluth*. Minneapolis: University of Minnesota Press, 2006.
Hull, John T., ed. *Centennial Celebration 1786–1886, Portland, Maine*. Portland: Owen, Strout and Company, 1886.
Ignatiev, Noel. *How the Irish became White*. New York: Routledge, 1995.
ILWU Local 500 Pensioners. *Man Along the Shore: The Story of the Vancouver Waterfront*

as Told by the Longshoremen Themselves 1860s–1975. Vancouver: ILWU Local 500, 1975.

Ireland, Tom. *The Great Lakes—St. Lawrence Deep Waterway to the Sea*. New York: G. P. Putnam's Sons, 1934.

Jacobs, Donald M. "A Study of the Boston Negro from Revolution to Civil War." Ph.D. diss., Boston University, 1968.

Jacobson, Matthew Frye. *Whiteness of a Different Color: European Immigrants and the Alchemy of Race*. Cambridge, Mass.: Harvard University Press, 1998.

Janzen, Olaf, ed. *Merchant Organization and Maritime Trade in the North Atlantic, 1660–1815*. St. John's, Newfoundland: International Maritime Economic History Association, 1998.

———. "A World-Embracing Sea: The Oceans as Highway, 1604–1815." In *Maritime History as World History*, edited by Daniel Finamore, 102–114. Gainesville: University Press of Florida, 2004.

Jay, Margaret Buker. "The Irish Experience in Lewiston, 1850–1880." In *They Change Their Sky: The Irish in Maine*, edited by Michael C. Connolly, 187–212. Orono: University of Maine Press, 2004.

Jennings, Francis. *The Invasion of America: Indians, Colonialism, and the Cant of Conquest*. Chapel Hill: University of North Carolina Press, 1975.

Jensen, Vernon H. *Decasualization and Modernization of Dock Work in London*. New York: New York School of Industrial Relations (I.L.R. Paperback Series: no.9), 1971.

———. *Hiring of Dock Workers and Employment Practices in the Ports of New York, Liverpool, London, Rotterdam and Marseilles*. Cambridge, Mass.: Harvard University Press, 1964.

———. *Strife on the Waterfront: The Port of New York Since 1945*. Ithaca, N.Y.: Cornell University Press, 1974.

Johnson, Arthur L. "Boston and the Maritimes: A Century of Steam Navigation." Ph.D. diss., University of Maine (Orono), 1971.

Jones, Herbert G. *Portland Ships Are Good Ships*. Portland, Maine: Machigonne Press, 1945.

Jordan, Bruce M. "A *Historical Synopsis of Economic Development in Portland, Maine, 1623–1923*." B.A. thesis, Portland University College of Business Administration, 1958.

Jordan, Joseph. "Jordan's Meats: A Thriving Business in Its Third Generation . . . Built Primarily on Hot Dogs." New York: The Newcomen Society of the United States, no. 1389 (January 1993): 5–24.

Jordan, William B., Jr. *Burial Records of Eastern Cemetery, 1717–1962 of the Eastern Cemetery, Portland, Maine*. Bowie, Md.: Heritage Books, 1987.

———. *Burial Records of Western Cemetery, 1811–1980 of the Western Cemetery, Portland, Maine*. Bowie, Md.: Heritage Books, 1987.

———. *Civil War Journals of John Mead Gould, 1861–1866*. Baltimore: Butternut and Blue, 1997.

———. *A History of Cape Elizabeth, Maine*. Bowie, Md.: Heritage Books, 1987. (Reprint of 1965 edition)

———. *Index to Portland Newspapers 1785–1835*. Bowie, Md.: Heritage Books, 1994.

———. *Red Diamond Regiment: The Seventeenth Maine Infantry, 1862–1865*. Shippensburg, Pa.: White Mane Publishers, 1996.

Jordan, Winthrop D. *White over Black: American Attitudes toward the Negro, 1550–1812*. Chapel Hill: University of North Carolina Press, 1968.

Josephson, Mathew. "Red Skies over the Waterfront." *Colliers* 118 (October 5, 1946): 17, 88–90.

Judd, Richard W., Edwin Churchill, and Joel Eastman, eds. *Maine: The Pine Tree State from Prehistory to the Present*. Orono: University of Maine Press, 1995.

Kelley, James. *Labor Problems of the Longshoremen in the United States*. Ph.D. diss., Boston University, 1941.

Kellogg, Elijah. *A Strong Arm and a Mother's Blessing*. Boston: Lothrop, Lee, and Shepherd Publishers, 1880.

Kelly, Andrew, and Melanie Kelly, eds. *Brunel, in Love with the Impossible*. Bristol, U.K.: Bristol Cultural Development Partnership, 2006.

Kelly, Josephine. *Dark Shepherd*. Paterson, N.J.: St. Anthony Guild Press, 1967.

Kenny, Kevin. *The American Irish: A History*. New York: Pearson Education Inc., 2000.

———. *Making Sense of the Molly Maguires*. New York: Oxford University Press, 1998.

Kerr, Clark. *Collective Bargaining on the Pacific Coast*. Berkeley: University of California Press, 1948.

Kerr, Clark, and Lloyd Fisher. "Conflict on the Waterfront." *Atlantic Monthly* 184 (September 1949): 17–23.

Kimeldorf, Howard. "Radical Possibilities? The Rise and Fall of Wobbly Unionism on the Philadelphia Docks." In *Waterfront Workers: New Perspectives on Race and Class*, edited by Calvin Winslow, 97–130. Urbana: University of Illinois Press, 1998.

———. *Reds or Rackets? The Making of Radical and Conservative Unions on the Waterfront*. Berkeley: University of California Press, 1988.

Kimeldorf, Howard, and Robert Penney. "Excluded by Choice: Dynamics of Interracial Unionism on the Philadelphia Waterfront 1910–1930." *International Labor and Working-Class History* 51 (Spring 1997): 50–71.

Kinealy, Christine. *The Great Famine: Impact, Ideology and Rebellion*. New York: Palgrave, 2002.

Kirkland, Edward Chase. *Men, Cities, and Transportation: A Study in New England History*. Cambridge, Mass.: Harvard University Press, 1948.

Kirkpatrick, Gabriel W. "Influenza 1918: A Maine Perspective." *Maine Historical Society Quarterly* 25, no.3 (Winter 1986): 162–77.

Knights, Peter R. *Plain People of Boston, 1830–1860*. New York: Oxford University Press, 1971.

Knobel, Dale T. *Paddy and the Republic*. Middletown, Conn.: Wesleyan University Press, 1986.

Kohl, Lawrence F., ed. *Irish Green and Union Blue: The Civil War Letters of Peter Welch*. Bronx, New York: Fordham University Press, 1986.

Kornbluh, Joyce L., ed. *Rebel Voices: An I.W.W. Anthology*. Ann Arbor: University of Michigan Press, 1964.

Lampman, Robert J. "Collective Bargaining of West Coast Sailors, 1885–1947: A Study in Unionism." Ph.D. diss., University of Wisconsin, 1950.

Lamson, R. "1951 New York Wildcat Dock Strike." *Social Science Quarterly* 34 (1954): 28.

Langlois, Edward (Jedediah Scott, pseudonym), ed. *Port of Portland, Maine*. Portland, Maine: Chamber of Commerce of the Greater Portland Region, 1980.

Larrowe, Charles P. "The Great Maritime Strike of '34." *Labor History* 11, no.4 (Fall 1970): 403–51.

———. "The Great Maritime Strike of '34, Part II." *Labor History* 12, no.1 (Winter 1971): 3–37.

———. *Harry Bridges: The Rise and Fall of Radical Labor in the United States*. New York: Lawrence Hill Publishers, 1972.

———. "Maritime Labor Relations on the Great Lakes." Michigan State University Labor and Industrial Relations Center, 1955.

———. *Shape-up and Hiring Hall: A Comparison of Hiring Methods and Labor Relations on the New York and Seattle Waterfronts*. Westport, Conn.: Greenwood Press, 1976. (Reprint of 1955 Berkeley edition)

Lascelles, E. C., and S. S. Bullock. "Dock Labour and Decasualization." *Studies in Economics and Political Sciences*, no.75, London School of Economics and Political Science, 1924.

Leamon, James S. "Falmouth, the American Revolution, and the Price of Moderation." In *Creating Portland: History and Place in Northern New England*, edited by Joseph A. Conforti, 44–71. Durham: University of New Hampshire Press, 2005.

———. *Revolution Downeast: The War for American Independence in Maine*. Amherst: University of Massachusetts Press, 1993.

Leamon, James S., and Karen Bowden, eds. *Maine in the Early Republic: From Revolution to Statehood*. Hanover, N.H.: University Press of New England, 1988.

Leamon, James S., Richard R. Wescott, and Edward O. Schriver. "Separation and Statehood, 1783–1820." In *Maine: The Pine Tree State from Prehistory to the Present*, edited by Richard W. Judd, Edwin Churchill, and Joel Eastman. Orono: University of Maine Press, 1995.

Lee, Joseph. *Ireland, 1945–1970*. Dublin: Gill and Macmillan, 1979.

Lee, Maureen Elgersman. *Black Bangor: African Americans in a Maine Community, 1880–1950*. Durham: University of New Hampshire Press, 2005.

———. "'What They Lack in Numbers': Locating Black Portland, 1870–1930." In *Creating Portland: History and Place in Northern New England*, edited by Joseph A. Conforti, 218–46. Durham: University of New Hampshire Press, 2005.

Lemke, William. *Wild, Wild East: Unusual Tales of Maine History*. Camden, Maine: Yankee Books, 1990.

Levinsky, Allan. *A Short History of Portland*. Beverly, Mass.: Commonwealth Editions, 2007.

Levinson, Marc. *The Box: How the Shipping Container Made the World Smaller and the World Economy Bigger*. Princeton, N.J.: Princeton University Press, 2006.

Liebes, Richard A. "Longshore Labor Relations on the Pacific Coast, 1934–1942." Ph.D. diss., University of California, 1942.

Litwack, Leon F. *North of Slavery: The Negro in the Free States, 1790–1860*. Chicago: University of Chicago Press, 1965.

Long, David F. "'Martial Thunder': The First Official American Armed Intervention in Asia." *The Pacific Historical Review* 42, no. 2 (May 1973): 143–62.

Longfellow, Henry Wadsworth. *Henry Wadsworth Longfellow Poems*. Secaucus, N.J.: Longriver Press, 1976.

Loveitt, Lillian F. "The Social History of Portland, Maine from 1820–1840." The Special Collection, Fogler Library, University of Maine (Orono).

Loveitt, Rosella A. "The Social History of Portland, Maine from 1840–1860." The Special Collection, Fogler Library, University of Maine (Orono).

Lovell, John C. *Stevedores and Dockers: A Study of Trade Unionism in the Port of London, 1870–1914*. New York: A. M. Kelley, 1969.

Lowndes, Richard. *Technical Innovation, Capital and Labour: Two Case Histories of the Port Industry of California*. Romford, England: Anglican Regional Management Centre, 1976.

Lucey, William Leo. *The Catholic Church in Maine*. Francestown, N.H.: Marshall Jones, 1957.

———. "Two Irish Merchants of New England." *The New England Quarterly* XIV, no. 4 (December 1941): 633–45.

MacWilliams, J. Donald. *A Time of Men*. Lewiston, Maine: Twin City Printery, 1967.

Madore, Nelson, and Barry Rodrigue, eds. *Voyages: A Maine Franco-American Reader*. Gardiner, Maine: Tilbury House, 2007.

Magden, Ronald, and A. D. Martinson. *The Working Waterfront: The Story of Tacoma's Ships and Men*. Tacoma, Wash.: ILWU Local 23, 1982.

Maine Historical Society. *Sacred Heart Parish: Seventy-Fifth Anniversary*. Portland: Maine Historical Society, 1972.

Malm, F. T. "Wage Differentials in Pacific Coast Longshoring." *Industrial and Labor Relations Review* 5 (October 1951): 33–49.

Mannion, John, and Fidelma Maddock. "Old World Antecedents, New World Adaptations: Inistioge Immigrants in Newfoundland." In *Kilkenny History and Society: Interdisciplinary Essays on the History of an Irish County*, edited by William Nolan and Kevin Whelan, 345–404. Dublin: Geography Publications, 1990.

McCaffrey, Lawrence J. *The Irish Diaspora in America*. Bloomington: Indiana University Press, 1976.

———, ed. *The Irish in Chicago*. Urbana: University of Illinois Press, 1987.

———, ed. *Irish Nationalism and the American Contribution*. New York: Arno Press, 1976.

———. *Textures of Irish America*. Syracuse, N.Y.: Syracuse University Press, 1992.

McCarron, Edward T. "A Brave New World: The Irish Agrarian Colony of Benedicta, Maine in the 1830s and 1840s." *Records of the American Catholic Historical Society of Philadelphia* 105 (Spring–Summer 1994): 1–15.

———. "A Brave New World: The Irish Agrarian Colony of Benedicta, Maine." In *They Change Their Sky: The Irish in Maine*, edited by Michael C. Connolly, 121–37. Orono: University of Maine Press, 2004.

———. "Facing the Atlantic: The Irish Merchant Community of Lincoln County, 1780–1820." In *They Change Their Sky: The Irish in Maine*, edited by Michael C. Connolly, 61–95. Orono: University of Maine Press, 2004.

———. "Irish Migration and Settlement on the Eastern Frontier: The Case of Lincoln County, Maine, 1760–1820." *Retrospection: The New England Graduate Review in American History II* (1989): 21–31.

———. "In Pursuit of the 'Maine' Chance: The North Family of Offaly and New England, 1700–1776." In *Offaly History and Society: Interdisciplinary Essays on the History of an Irish County*, edited by William Nolan and Timothy P. O'Neill, 339–70. Dublin: Geography Publications, 1998.

———. *The World of Kavanagh and Cottrill: A Portrait of Irish Emigration, Entrepreneurship, and Ethnic Diversity in Mid-Maine, 1760–1820*. Ph.D. diss., University of New Hampshire, 1992.

McCarron, Fidelma. "Ireland along the Passamaquoddy: Rathlin Islanders in Washington County, Maine." In *They Change Their Sky: The Irish in Maine*, edited by Michael C. Connolly, 97–119. Orono: University of Maine Press, 2004.

McGirr, Lisa. "Black and White Longshoremen in the IWW: A History of the Philadelphia Marine Transport Workers Industrial Union Local 8." *Labor History* 36, no. 3 (June 1995): 377–402.

McKelvey, Jean T. *Dock Labor Disputes in Great Britain: A Study in the Persistence of Industrial Unrest*. Ithaca, N.Y.: Cornell University (State School of Industrial and Labor Relations), 1953.

McKeon, Edward G. *In the Streets Half Heard: A Biographical Novel*. Bangor, Maine: Penobscot Press, 2004.

McLaughlin, Francis M. "The Boston Longshoremen's Strike of 1931." *Historical Journal of Massachusetts* (Summer, July 1998): 158–71.

———. "The Development of Labor Peace in the Port of Boston." *Industrial and Labor Relations Review* 20 (1967): 221–33.

———. "Industrial Relations in the Boston Longshore Industry." Ph.D. diss., Massachusetts Institute of Technology, 1964.

———. "The Replacement of the Knights of Labor by the International Longshoremen's Association in the Port of Boston." *Historical Journal of Massachusetts* (Winter, January 1998): 27–45.

Meagher, Timothy J., ed. *From Paddy to Studs: Irish American Communities at the Turn of the Century, 1880 to 1920*. Westport, Conn.: Greenwood Press, 1986.

———. *Inventing Irish America: Generation, Class, and Ethnic Identity in a New England City, 1880–1928*. Notre Dame, Ind.: University of Notre Dame Press, 2001.

Mellish, Michael. *The Docks after Devlin: A Study of the Effects of the Recommendations of the Devlin Committee on Industrial Relations in the London Docks*. London: Heinemann Educational Press, 1972.

Mers, Gilbert. *Working the Waterfront: The Ups and Downs of a Rebel Longshoreman.* Austin: University of Texas Press, 1988.

Mezy, Phiz. "West Coast Waterfront Showdown." *Nation* 16 (November 1948).

Miller, Kerby A. *Emigrants and Exiles: Ireland and the Irish Exodus to North America.* New York: Oxford University Press, 1985.

Miller, Kerby A., Arnold Schrier, Bruce D. Boling, and David N. Doyle. *Irish Immigrants in the Land of Canaan: Letters and Memoirs from Colonial and Revolutionary America, 1675–1815.* Oxford: Oxford University Press, 2003.

Miner, A. A. "Neal Dow and His Life Work." *The New England Magazine* 16, no. 4 (June 1894): 397–412.

Mitchell, Arthur. *Labour in Irish Politics 1890–1930.* Dublin: Irish University Press, 1974.

Mitchell, George J. *Making Peace.* Berkeley: University of California Press, 1999.

Mokyr, Joel. *Why Ireland Starved: A Quantitative and Analytical History of the Irish Economy, 1800–1850.* Winchester, Mass.: Allen and Unwin, 1983.

Montgomery, David. *Beyond Equality: Labor and the Radical Republicans, 1862–1872.* New York: Alfred A. Knopf, 1967.

———. *The Fall of the House of Labor.* New York: Cambridge University Press, 1987.

———. "The Irish and the American Labor Movement." In *America and Ireland, 1776–1976: The American Identity and the Irish Connection,* edited by David Doyle and Owen Dudley Edwards. Westport, Conn.: Greenwood Press, 1979.

———. *Workers' Control in America: Studies in the History of Work, Technology, and Labor Struggles.* Cambridge, Mass.: Cambridge University Press, 1979.

Mooney, Thomas. *Nine Years in America: A Series of Letters to His Cousin, Patrick Mooney, a Farmer in Ireland.* Dublin: James McGlashan Publishers, 1850.

Morison, Samuel Elliot. *The Maritime History of Massachusetts, 1783–1869.* Boston: Northeastern University Press, 1979.

Morris, James M. *Our Maritime Heritage: Maritime Developments and Their Impact on American Life.* Lanham, Md.: University Press of America, 1979.

Moulton, John K. *Captain Moody and His Observatory.* Portland, Maine: Mount Joy Publishing, 2000.

Mundy, James H. *Bygone Bangor.* Bangor, Maine: *Bangor Daily News,* 1976.

———. *Hard Times, Hard Men: Maine and the Irish 1830–1860.* Scarborough, Maine: Harp Publications, 1990.

Mundy, James H., and Earle G. Shettleworth Jr. *The Flight of the Grand Eagle.* Augusta, Maine: Maine Historic Preservation Commission, 1977.

Myers, John F. *Over to Bangor: The Emigration from the Maritimes to Eastern Maine, 1880–1910.* Orono: University of Maine.

Nash, Gary B. "Forging Freedom: The Emancipation Experience in the Northern Seaport Cities, 1775–1820." In *Slavery and Freedom in the Age of the American Revolution,* edited by Ira Berlin and Ronald Hoffman, 3–48. Charlottesville: University of Virginia Press, 1983.

———. *The Urban Crucible: Social Change, Political Consciousness and the Origins of the American Revolution.* Cambridge, Mass.: Harvard University Press, 1979.

National Maritime Union. "N.M.U.—40 Years on a True Course." *N.M.U. Pilot* 42 (May 1977): 12–13.

Neal, John. *Portland Illustrated*. Portland: W. S. Jones, 1874.

Nelson, Bruce. *Divided We Stand: American Workers and the Struggle for Black Equality*. Princeton, N.J.: Princeton University Press, 2001.

———. "The 'Lords of the Docks' Reconsidered: Race Relations among West Coast Longshoremen, 1933-61." In *Waterfront Workers: New Perspectives on Race and Class*, edited by Calvin Winslow, 155–92. Urbana: University of Illinois Press, 1998.

———. *Workers on the Waterfront: Seamen, Longshoremen, and Unionism in the 1930s*. Urbana: University of Illinois Press, 1988.

New York Committee of Merchants for the Relief of Colored People Suffering from the Late Riots, 1863 Report. Salem, N.H.: Ayer Company Publishers, 1969. (Reprint of the 1863 original)

Nilsen, Kenneth E. "Collecting Celtic Folklore in the United States." In *Proceedings of the First North American Congress of Celtic Studies, 1986*, edited by Gordon W. MacLennan, 55–74. Ottawa: University of Ottawa, 1988.

———. "Irish Gaelic Literature in the U.S. in the Nineteenth Century." In *American Babel: Literatures of the United States from Abnaki to Zuni*, edited by Marc Shell, 188–218. Cambridge, Mass.: Harvard University Press, 2002.

———. "The Irish Language in New York, 1850-1900." In *The New York Irish*, edited by Ronald H. Bayor and Timothy J. Meagher, 252–74. Baltimore: The Johns Hopkins University Press, 1996.

———. "The Irish Language in the U.S." *The Encyclopedia of the Irish in America*, edited by Michael Glazier, 470–74. Notre Dame, Ind.: Notre Dame Press, 1999.

———. "'The Language That the Strangers Do Not Know': The Galway Gaeltacht of Portland, Maine in the Twentieth Century." In *They Change Their Sky: The Irish in Maine*, edited by Michael C. Connolly, 297–339. Orono: University of Maine Press, 2004.

———. "Thinking of Monday: The Irish Speakers of Portland, Maine." *Eire/Ireland* 25, no. 1 (Spring 1990): 6–19.

Noble, Dennis L., and Truman R. Strobridge. *Captain "Hell Roaring" Mike Healy: From American Slave to Arctic Hero*. Gainesville: University Press of Florida, 2009.

Northrup, Herbert R. "New Orleans Longshoremen." *Political Science Quarterly* 57, no. 4 (December 1942): 526–44.

———. *Organized Labor and the Negro*. New York: Harper, 1944.

O'Brien, Francis M. *A Backward Look: 50 Years of Maine Books and Bookmen*. Portland, Maine: Anthoensen Press, 1986.

O'Brien, Michael J. "The Early Irish in Maine." *Journal of the American Irish Historical Society* 10 (1911): 162–70.

———. "The Lost Settlement of Cork, Maine." *Journal of the American Irish Historical Society VII* (1913): 175–84.

O'Brien, Simon P. "Longshoremen Stabilize Their Jobs." *American Federationist* 34 (May 1927).

O'Connor, Harvey. *Revolution in Seattle*. Seattle: Left Bank Books, 1981.

O'Connor, Thomas H. "The Irish in New England." *New England Historical and Genealogical Register* 139 (July 1985): 187–95.
O'Dwyer, George F. "Captain James Howard, Col. William Lithgow, Col. Arthur Noble, and Other Irish Pioneers in Maine." *Journal of the American Irish Historical Society* 19 (1920): 71–91.
O'Leary, Charles J. "A History of Organized Labor in Maine During the New Deal." The Special Collection, Fogler Library, University of Maine (Orono).
O'Leary, Wayne M. *The Maine Sea Fisheries, 1830–1890: The Rise and Fall of a Native Industry*. Boston: Northeastern University Press, 1996.
O'Neill, Kevin. *Family and Farm in Pre-Famine Ireland: The Parish of Killashandra*. Madison: University of Wisconsin Press, 1984.
Oram, R. B. *The Dockers Tragedy*. London: Hutchinson, 1970.
Oram, R. B., and C. C. Baker. *The Efficient Port*. Elmsford, N.Y.: Pergamon, 1971.
O'Toole, James M. *Militant and Triumphant: William Henry O'Connell and Catholicism in Boston, 1859–1944*. Notre Dame, Ind.: University of Notre Dame Press, 1992.
———. *Passing for White: Race, Religion, and the Healy Family 1820–1920*. Amherst: University of Massachusetts Press, 2002.
Ó Tuathaigh, Gearóid. *Ireland before the Famine, 1798–1848*. Dublin: Gill and Macmillan, 1972.
Outwin, Charles P. M. "Thriving and Elegant, Flourishing and Populous: A History of Falmouth in Casco Bay, 1760–1775." Ph.D. diss., University of Maine (Orono), 2008.
———. "Thriving and Elegant Town: Eighteenth-Century Portland as Commercial Center." In *Creating Portland: History and Place in Northern New England*, edited by Joseph A. Conforti, 20–43. Durham: University of New Hampshire Press, 2005.
Paine, Lincoln P. *Down East: A Maritime History of Maine*. Gardiner, Maine: Tilbury House, 2000.
———. *A Maritime History of the World*. New York: Alfred A. Knopf, forthcoming.
———. *Ships of the World: An Historical Encyclopedia*. Boston: Houghton Mifflin, 1997.
Palmer, Dwight L. "Pacific Coast Maritime Labor." Ph.D. diss., Stanford University, 1935.
Pancoast, John. "The Irish Are Coming." *Portland Landmarks Observer* (September–October 1979).
Peck, Henry A. *Seaports in Maine: An Economic Study*. Orono: University of Maine Studies (Second series, no. 2), 1955.
Peterson, Gardner, *Docker*. New York: Atheneum, 1980.
Pilcher, William W. *The Portland Longshoremen: A Dispersed Urban Community*. New York: Holt, Rinehart and Winston, 1972.
Pillsbury, David B. "The History of the Atlantic and St. Lawrence Railroad Company." The Special Collection, Fogler Library, University of Maine (Orono).
Poor, Laura E., ed. *The First International Railway and the Colonization of New England: Life and Writings of John Alfred Poor*. New York: G. P. Putnam's, 1892.
Potter, George. *To the Golden Door*. Westport, Conn: Greenwood Press, 1974.

Powderly, Terence V. *The Path I Trod.* Harry J. Carman, Henry David, and Paul N. Guthrie, editors. New York: Columbia University Press, 1940.

———. *Thirty Years of Labor 1859 to 1889.* Seaman, Ohio: Kelley Publications. (Reprint of 1890 original)

Price, Harriet H., and Gerald E. Talbot. *Maine's Visible Black History: The First Chronicle of its People.* Gardiner, Maine: Tilbury House, 2006.

Priest, Charles H. *Report on Port Development Activities, Cities of Portland and South Portland for the Year 1938.* Portland, Maine: Charles H. Priest, 1938.

Quin, Mike. *The Big Strike.* New York: International Publishers, 1979. Originally published by Olema Publishing Company, 1949.

Radin, M. "The Case of Harry Bridges: A Deportation Case." *Social Service Review* 14 (1940): 1.

———. "Harry Bridges Case Again." *Social Service Review* 16 (1942): 541.

———. "The Unfinished Case of Harry Bridges." *Social Service Review* 19 (1945): 485.

Reed, Merl E. "Lumberjacks and Longshoremen: The I.W.W. in Louisiana." *Labor History* 13, no.1 (Winter 1972): 41–59.

Reiche, Howard C., Jr. *Closeness: Memories of Mrs. Munjoy's Hill.* Falmouth, Maine: Long Point Press, 2002.

Renshaw, Patrick. *The Wobblies.* Garden City, N.J.: Doubleday, 1967.

Reynolds, Lloyd G. *Trade Union Publications: The Official Journals, Proceedings, and Constitutions of International Unions and Federations, 1850–1941.* Baltimore: Johns Hopkins University Press, 1944.

Rice, James R. "A History of Organized Labor in Saint John, New Brunswick, 1813–1890." Master's thesis, University of New Brunswick, 1968.

Rinaldi, Laurence J. *Containerization: The New Method of Intermodal Transport.* New York: Sterling Publishing, 1972.

Robinson, Robert M. "Maritime Labor in San Francisco, 1933–1937." Ph.D. diss., University of California, 1937.

Robinson, Tim. *Connemara.* Roundstone, Co. Galway, Ireland: Folding Landscapes, 1990.

———, ed. *Connemara after the Famine: Journal of a Survey of the Martin Estate.* Dublin: Lilliput Press, 1995. (Thomas Colville Scott original author)

———. *Mapping South Connemara.* Roundstone, Co. Galway, Ireland: Folding Landscapes, 1985.

———. *Stones of Aran: Pilgrimage.* New York: Penguin, 1990.

Roediger, David. *Towards the Abolition of Whiteness: Essays on Race, Politics, and Working-Class History.* London: Verso, 1994.

———. *The Wages of Whiteness: Race and the Making of the American Working Class.* New York: Routledge, 1991.

Roland, Alex W., W. Jeffrey Bolster, and Alexander Keyssar. *The Way of the Ship: America's Maritime History Reenvisioned, 1600–2000.* Hoboken, N.J.: John Wiley & Sons, 2008.

Rosenbaum, Edward. "The Expulsion of the I.L.A. from A.F. of L." Ph.D. diss., University of Wisconsin at Madison, 1955.

Rosenberg, Daniel. *New Orleans Dockworkers: Race, Labor, and Unionism, 1892–1920.* Albany, N.Y.: SUNY Press, 1988.

Ross, Steven J. *Workers on the Edge: Work, Leisure and Politics in Industrializing Cincinnati, 1788–1890.* New York: Columbia University Press, 1985.

Rovere, Richard H. *Senator Joe McCarthy.* New York: Harcourt, Brace, 1959.

Rowe, William Hutchinson. *The Maritime History of Maine: Three Centuries of Shipbuilding and Seafaring.* New York: W. W. Norton, 1948.

———. *Shipbuilding Days on Casco Bay, 1727–1890.* Yarmouth, Maine, 1929.

Royall, Anne. *The Black Book; or A Continuation of Travels in the United States 1826–1827.* Washington, D.C., 1828.

Rubin, Lester. *The Negro in the Longshore Industry.* Philadelphia: University of Pennsylvania Press, 1974; Kraus reprint.

Rubin, Lester, William S. Swift, and Herbert R. Northrup. *Negro Employment in the Maritime Industries: A Study of Racial Policies in the Shipbuilding, Longshore, and Offshore Maritime Industries.* Philadelphia: University of Pennsylvania, 1974.

Russell, Maud. *Men Along the Shore: The ILA and Its History.* New York: Brussel and Brussel, 1966.

Rutter, Owen. *The Pirate Wind: Tales of the Sea-Robbers of Malaya.* Singapore: Oxford University Press, 1986.

Saint Dominic's Parish. *Souvenir History of St. Dominic's Parish, 1822–1909.* Portland, Maine: Saint Dominic's Parish, 1909.

Sanders, Michael S. *The Yard: Building a Destroyer at Bath Iron Works.* New York: Harper Collins, 1999.

Sarbaugh, Timothy J. "Exiles of Confidence: The Irish-American Community of San Francisco, 1880 to 1920." In *From Paddy to Studs: Irish American Communities at the Turn of the Century, 1880 to 1920,* edited by Timothy J. Meagher, 161–79. Westport, Conn.: Greenwood Press, 1986.

———. "Father Yorke and the San Francisco Waterfront, 1901–1916." *Pacific History* 25, no.3 (1981): 28–35.

Saunders, S. A. *The Economic History of the Maritime Provinces.* Ottawa: Royal Commission on Dominion-Provincial Relations, 1939.

Schneiderman, William. *The Pacific Coast Maritime Strike.* San Francisco: Western Worker Publisher, 1937.

Schrier, Arnold. *Ireland and the Irish Emigration, 1815–1900.* Minneapolis: University of Minnesota Press, 1958.

Schwartz, Harvey. *The March Inland: Origins of the International Longshoremen's and Warehouse Division, 1934–1938.* Monograph Series #19. Los Angeles: UCLA Industrial Relations, 1978.

Scontras, Charles A. *Collective Efforts among Maine Workers: Beginnings and Foundations, 1820–1880.* Orono: Bureau of Labor Education, University of Maine, 1994.

———. *Labor in Maine: Building the Arsenal of Democracy and Resisting Reaction at Home, 1939–1952.* Orono: Bureau of Labor Education, University of Maine, 2006.

———. *Organized Labor and Labor Politics in Maine, 1880–1980.* University of Maine Studies, Series 2, no.83. Orono: University of Maine Press, 1966.

———. *Organized Labor in Maine: Twentieth Century Origins*. Orono: Bureau of Labor Education, University of Maine, 1985.

———. *Organized Labor in Maine: War, Reaction, Depression, and the Rise of the CIO 1914-1943*. Orono: Bureau of Labor Education, University of Maine, 2002.

———. *The Socialist Alternative: Utopian Experiments and the Socialist Party of Maine, 1895-1914*. Orono: Bureau of Labor Education, University of Maine, 1985.

———. *Time-Line of Selected Highlights of Maine Labor History: 1636-2003*. Orono: Bureau of Labor Education, University of Maine, 2003.

———. *Two Decades of Organized Labor and Labor Politics in Maine, 1880-1900*. Orono: Bureau of Labor Education, University of Maine, 1969.

Seidman, J., Jack London, and Bernard Karsh. "Leadership in a Local Union." *American Journal of Sociology* 56, no.3 (November 1950): 229-37.

Sheehy, Michael J. "John Alfred Poor and International Railroads: The Early Years to 1860." Master's thesis, University of Maine (Orono), 1974.

Sherman, Andrew M. *Life of Captain Jeremiah O'Brien, Machias, Maine*. Morristown, N.J.: The Jerseyman Office, 1902.

Sherman, Rexford B. "The Bangor and Aroostook Railroad and the Development of the Port of Searsport." The Special Collection, Fogler Library, University of Maine (Orono).

Shettleworth, Earl G., Jr., and William D. Barry. *Mr. Goodhue Remembers Portland: Scenes From the Mid-Nineteenth Century*. Augusta: Maine Historic Preservation Commission Publications, 1981.

Smith, David C. *A History of Lumbering in Maine, 1861-1960*. University of Maine Studies, no. 93. Orono: University of Maine Press, 1972.

Smith, Gene A. *For the Purposes of Defense: The Politics of the Jeffersonian Gunboat Program*. Newark: University of Delaware Press, 1995.

Smith, Joshua M. *Borderland Smuggling: Patriots, Loyalists, and Illicit Trade in the Northeast, 1783-1820*. Gainesville: University Press of Florida, 2006.

Smith, Mason Phillip. *Confederates Downeast*. Portland, Maine: Provincial Press, 1985.

Snow, Ralph Linwood, and Douglas K. Lee. *A Shipyard in Maine: Percy and Small and the Great Schooners*. Gardiner, Maine: Tilbury House, 1999.

Solomon, Barbara. *Ancestors and Immigrants: A Changing New England Tradition*. Cambridge, Mass.: Harvard University Press, 1956.

Solomon, Harold M. "Combating the 'Social Evil': Masculinity and Moral Reform in Portland, 1912-1914." *Maine History* 43 (January 2008): 139-65.

Stakeman, Randolph. "The Black Population of Maine 1764-1900." *New England Journal of Black Studies*, no. 8 (1989): 17-35.

———. "Slavery in Colonial Maine." *Maine Historical Society Quarterly* 27, no. 2 (Fall 1987): 58-81.

Stoehr, Kevin L., and Michael C. Connolly, eds. *John Ford in Focus: Essays on the Filmmaker's Life and Work*. Jefferson, N.C.: McFarland, 2008.

Sullivan, James. *History of the District of Maine*. Augusta: Maine State Museum, 1970. (Reprint of a 1795 edition)

Swados, Harvey. "West-coast Waterfront—The End of an Era." *Dissent* (Autumn 1961).

Swankey, Ben. *Man along the Shore: The Story of the Vancouver Waterfronts as Told by Longshoremen Themselves (1860–1975)*. Vancouver: International Longshoremen's and Warehousemen's Union, Local 500 Pensioners, 1975.

Swanstrom, Edward E. *The Waterfront Labor Problem*. New York: Fordham University Press, 1938.

Syrett, John. "Principle and Expediency: The Ku Klux Klan and Owen Brewster in 1924." *Maine History* 39, no. 4 (Winter 2000–2001): 214–39.

Taplin, Eric L. *The Dockers' Union: A Study of the National Union of Dockworkers, 1889–1922*. New York: St. Martin's Press, 1986.

Taylor, Alan. *Liberty Men and Great Proprietors: Revolutionary Settlement on the Maine Frontier, 1760–1820*. Chapel Hill: University of North Carolina Press, 1989.

Taylor, Paul S., and Normal Leon Gold. "San Francisco and the General Strike." *Survey Graphic* 23 (September 1934): 405–11.

Theriault, Reg. *Longshoring on the San Francisco Waterfront*. San Pedro, Calif.: Singlejack Books, 1978.

Thibodeau, Father Clement. "The French Catholics in Maine." In *Voyages: A Maine Franco-American Reader*, edited by Nelson Madore and Barry Rodrigue, 200–210. Gardiner, Maine: Tilbury House, 2007.

Thiesen, William H. *Industrializing American Shipbuilding: The Transformation of Ship Design and Construction, 1820–1920*. Gainesville: University Press of Florida, 2006.

Thoman, Richard. "Portland, Maine: An Economic-Urban Appraisal." *Economic Geography* 27 (1951): 349–67.

Tibbetts, Margaret Joy. "The Irish Neighborhood in Greenwood, Maine." *The Bethel Courier* (Journal of the Bethel Historical Society) 5, no. 1 (March 1981): 1–3.

Travers, Robert. *A Funeral for Sabella*. New York: Harcourt, Brace, 1952.

"Union Labor: Less Militant, More Affluent." *Time*, September 17, 1965, 42–43.

Velie, Lester. "Big Boss of the Big Port." *Colliers* 129 (9 February 1952).

Vorse, Mary Heaton. *Labor's New Millions*. New York: Arno Press, 1969.

———. "The Pirate's Nest of New York." *Harpers* 204 (April 1952).

Wallace, R. Stuart. "The Scotch-Irish of Provincial Maine: Purpooduck, Merrymeeting Bay, and Georgia." In *They Change Their Sky: The Irish in Maine*, edited by Michael C. Connolly, 41–59. Orono: University of Maine Press, 2004.

———. "The Scotch-Irish of Provincial New Hampshire." Ph.D. diss., University of New Hampshire, 1984.

Ward, Estolv E. *Harry Bridges on Trial*. New York: A.M.S. Press, 1976. (Reprint of 1940 edition)

Weiner, Marli F., ed. *Of Place and Gender: Women in Maine History*. Orono: University of Maine Press, 2005.

Wellman, David. *The Union Makes Us Strong: Radical Unionism on the San Francisco Waterfront*. New York: Cambridge University Press, 1995.

Wells, Dave, and Jim Stodder. "A Short History of New Orleans Dockworkers." *Radical America* 10 (January–February 1976).

"The Wharves of Portland, Maine." *Portland Board of Trade Journal* 179 (1912–13): 181–82.

Whitmore, Allan R. "'A Guard of Faithful Sentinels': The Know-Nothing Appeal in Maine, 1854–1855." *Maine Historical Society Quarterly* 20, no. 3 (Winter 1981): 151–97.

Whyte, W. Hamilton. *Decasualization of Dock Labor.* Bristol, England: Arrowsmith, 1934.

Williamson, William D. *The History of the State of Maine: From Its First Discovery,* A.D. *1602, to the Separation,* A.D. *1820, Inclusive.* Freeport, Maine: Cumberland Press, 1966. (Originally published in 1832)

Willis, William. *The History of Portland.* Portland: Maine Historical Society, 1972. (Reprint of the 1865 edition)

———. "Scotch Irish Immigration to Maine, and a Summary History of Presbyterianism." Collection of Maine Historical Society 6. Portland: Maine Historical Society, 1859: 1–37.

Wilson, Hazel. *Tall Ships.* Boston: Little, Brown, 1958.

Wilson, William Julius. *The Declining Significance of Race: Blacks and Changing American Institutions.* Chicago: University of Chicago Press, 1978.

Winks, Robin. "Raid at St. Albans." *Vermont Life* 15 (Spring 1961): 40–46.

Winslow, Calvin. "'Men of the Lumber Camps Come to Town': New York Longshoremen in the Strike of 1907." In *Waterfront Workers: New Perspectives on Race and Class,* edited by Calvin Winslow, 62–96. Urbana: University of Illinois Press, 1998.

———. "On the Waterfront: Black, Italian, and Irish Longshoremen in the New York Harbor Strike of 1919." In *Protest and Survival: Essays for E. P. Thompson,* edited by John Rule and Robert Malcolmson. New York: New Press, 1993.

———, ed. *Waterfront Workers: New Perspectives on Race and Class.* Urbana: University of Illinois Press, 1998.

Wood, Richard G. *A History of Lumbering in Maine, 1820–1861.* University of Maine Studies, no. 33. Orono: University of Maine Press, 1961.

Woodard, Colin. "Chump Change: Why Cruise Ships Are a Bad Deal for Portland." *The Bollard.* (June 2008): 14–18, 20–21.

Woodham-Smith, Cecil. *The Great Hunger; Ireland, 1845–1849.* New York: Harper and Row, 1962.

Wright, Allan J. "'The Methods of Friendly Approach': Portland, Maine as Canada's Winter Port." Master's thesis, University of New Brunswick, 1976.

Writer's Project of the WPA. *Maine: A Guide "Down East."* St. Clair Shores, Mich.: Scholarly Press, 1976.

———. *Portland City Guide.* Portland, Maine: Forest City Printing, 1940. (The American Guide Series)

Yerxa, Donald A. "The Burning of Falmouth, 1775: A Case Study in Imperial Pacification." *Maine Historical Society Quarterly* 13 (Winter 1975): 119–61.

Index

Page references in italics refers to illustrations.

Abyssinian Church/Meeting House, xix, 40, 44, 138, 223n9
Adams, John, 11
Adams, Silas B., 101, 102
African Americans: black community at base of Munjoy Hill ("Nigger Hill"), 19, 40–41, 44–45, 137–38; black longshoremen displaced by Irish in Portland, 55–57, 64, 86, 137; blacks as targets of Ku Klux Klan, 137; dockworkers in the 19th century, 40–53; ethnic tensions with Irish dockworkers, 36–64; first recorded strike in Maine (1866), 47; Healy as first African American Catholic bishop, xx, 114, 118; Philadelphia black longshoremen, 108–9; segregated education for colored children, 40; slavery abolished in Maine, 40; slavery issue, 40, 53; union membership exclusions, 47, 95, 96
Alabama claims, 67
Allan, Andrew A., 100
Allan, Hugh, 100
Allan Line, 32, 48, 59, 73, 100
Alongshoremen's United Benefit Society, 104
American Federation of Labor (AFL): and CIO split, 160, 162; emergence of, 115, 116; exclusion of blacks from, 95; expulsion of communist organizations, 134
"Americanization" policy, 113
Anchor-Donaldson Line, 133, 154
Anchor Line, 39
Ancient Order of Hibernians, 115
Annie C. Maguire (bark), wreck of, xx, 67
Antilabor legislation: Labor Disputes Act (1946), 167; Taft-Hartley Act (1947), xxii, 142, 167

Arrival of the SS Oregon, *Portland ME, January 21, 1884*, pencil sketch by Goth, 32, *33*
A.R. Wright Coal Company, 147, 169
Atlantic and St. Lawrence Railroad (A&StLRR), xx, 29, 31, 42, 45. *See also under its later name* Grand Trunk Railway (GTR)

Babcock, Robert H., 2, 74, 112, 183
Bagnall, Robert, 137, 138
Bailey, William, 99
Baltimore: Inner Harbor waterfront development, 177; shipping tonnage (1855), 16; strikes (1900), 96; strikes (1912), 96
Bangor (steamship), 26
Barrett, Patrick, 107
Barry, William David, 23, 223n12
Bassett, Jeremiah, 48
Bath Iron Works (BIW), 75, 163, 174–75, 177
Baxter, James Phinney (Portland mayor), 38, 55, 120
Bay Ferries Limited, 188
Benevolent societies, 104
Berlin and Milan decrees (1806), 16, 18
Bermuda Star Cruise Line, 177
Bernstein, Irving, 152, 154
Black Americans. *See* African Americans
Black churches, 40–41, 44
Black population: Boston (1840 to 1860), 44–45, 44 table; Massachusetts dock laborers (1910), 109; New Orleans (1900), 47; Philadelphia (1896), 108; Philadelphia (1910), 108; Portland, Maine, 223n12; Portland, Maine (1840 to 1860), 44–45, 44 table; Portland, Maine (1860 to 1900), 50; Portland, Oregon (1941), 50

Blaine, James G., 68
Blyth, Cdr. Samuel, 19
Board of Trade. *See* Portland Board of Trade
Bohemian (Royal Mail Steamer): sinking of, xv, 59, 67
Boothby, Frederick E. (Portland mayor), 72
Boston: black population (1840 to 1860), 44–45, 44 table; longshore strike (1931), 156–57; longshoremen affiliation with ILA, 104; maritime strike (1909), 86; maritime strike (1911), 90; maritime strike (1912), 90, 103; New Quincy Market and harbor development, 177; port development, 4; shipping from Falmouth, Maine, 9; shipping tonnage (1855), 16; shipping tonnage (1860), 25; wage scale, 99
Boston Dock Workers Federation, 157
Boston Port Act (1774), 11
Bowers, John: ILA presidency, xxii, 125
Boxer (HMS): defeated by *Enterprise* (USS), xix, 19–20
Bradley, William: ILA presidency, xxii, 125
Brann, Louis (Maine governor), 151
Brennan, Catherine (*nee* Mulkerrin), xiii
Brennan, John J., xiii
Brennan, Joseph (Maine governor): cargo facility bond referendum, 175–76; on Portland's legacy, xiii–xiv; profile of, 184
Brewster, Ralph Owen (Maine governor): KKK support for, 139
Bridges, Harry: and the West Coast labor militancy model, 158–62; ILWU leader, xxi, 1, 134, 141; McCarthyism and communist sympathies, 168–69; personality struggle with Ryan, 159–61; photo of, *159*; Welch's positive views on, 161–62
"Broaching" or "pilfering," 132–33
Brotherhood of Locomotive engineers, 115
Brown, James, 199
Brown, John, 102
Brown, John Bundy, xx, 28, 38, 42–43
Brunel, Isambard Kingdom, 29
Bryan, William Jennings, 69
Burnham, George, 27
Burnham and Morrill Company, 145–46
Burns, Roy C., 101–2
Burrows, Lt. William, 19
Butts, Samuel, 15

Caldwell, Bill, 174
Caleb, Royal "Roy": on Portland longshoremen, 81, 95, 136, 139, 145, 161; oral history of, 201; photo of, *143*; retirement from PLSBS, 199
Caleb Cushing (U.S. Revenue Cutter): seized by Confederate raiders, xx, 67
Canada. *See* Halifax, Nova Scotia; Saint John, New Brunswick
Canadian export policy, 183
Canadian grain shipments, xxi, 71, 74, 84, 90–91, 126–28, 141, 145
Canadian Line, 9, 39
Canadian longshoremen: as seasonal labor, 89–90
Canadian National Railroad (CNR), xxi, 149–50
Canadian port development, 149–51
Canadian Steam Navigation Company, 32
Carlista, Frank, 199
Casale, Joseph (Portland mayor), 176
Casale, Samuel, 199
Casco Bay: naming of, 7
Caselden, John, 87, 97, 99, 100, 102, 125, 128, 133
The Cat (ferry from Ocean Gateway to Nova Scotia), xxiii, 188
Cathedral of the Immaculate Conception, xx, 80
Catholic church: denunciation of socialism, 122; influence on labor unions, 113–40; rulings on parochial schools, 116, 119; "ultramontane" (conservative) wing, 114, 119
Chamberlain, Gen. Joshua L., 34
Chamber of Commerce, 128. *See also* its precursor Portland Board of Trade
Chaplin, Carroll S. (Portland mayor-elect), 127, 128
Child, Mr. (Falmouth customs officer), 11–12
Child, Sir Josiah, 8
China clay shipping/steamers, 91, 99, 102, 148
Chlopek, Anthony J.: ILA presidency, 124, 125, 133–35, 141, 155
Chronology of Portland, Maine maritime history: xix–xxxiii
Churchill, Winston, 16
CIO. *See* Congress of Industrial Organizations (CIO)
Civil War period: Irish American role in, 69; labor union organization, 60–62; loss of ships during, 67

Clapp, Asa (Capt.), 23
Clapp, Charles Q., 38
Clarke, Charles B. (Portland mayor), 128
Cleeve, George, xix, 6
CNR. *See* Canadian National Railroad (CNR)
Coal handling/shovelers: union men and, 108; wage scales and, 99; work gang size and, 87
Coal shipping, 84, 91, 135, 146–47
Cobb, Matthew "King," 23
Cole, Peter, 50
Columbia Coastal Transport, xxiii, 187, 188, 190
Commercial Street (Portland): Grand Trunk cars and piers (c. 1875), *73*; shipbuilding trade, 10; Workingmen's Club, xxi, 121
Communism: anticommunism activities, 167–69; in labor unions prohibited, 134, 169. *See also* McCarthyism/Red Scare
Concannon, Marcus, 81
Concannon, Stephen "Steve," 81, 95, *144*, 161, 201
Congress of Industrial Organizations (CIO), xxi, 158–59, 160
Conley, Bartley, 164–65
Connolly, Bartley, 133, 199
Connolly, Jack, 111
Connolly, James, 93, 230n35
Connolly, John F., 199
Connolly, Larry, 194
Containerization: American standard measurement for containers, 172; McLean as container ship developer, 170–72; revolution in shipping, xxiii, 3, 169–74, 240n72
Corkery, Joseph L., 199
Corrigan, Michael (archbishop of New York), 119
Costello, Séamus, 201
Cottrill family, 66
Coughlin, Philip, 199
Counderakis, Nicholas, 158
Coyne, Joe, 111
Croly, D.G., 52
Cruise ship industry, 191
Cumberland and Oxford (C&O) Canal, xx, 34
Cumberland Steam Navigation Company, 26
Cunard-Anchor Line, 153
Cunard Line, 39, 133, 154
Cunningham, John J., 128
Curran, Philip A., 199

Curtis, Oakley C. (Portland mayor), 123
Cushing, Caleb, 67

Dana, Richard Henry, Jr., 54, 56
Davis, John, 111
Davis, Richard L., 95
Davitt, Michael, 62
Day of the Clipper (song by Steve Romanoff), 197–98
Dempsey, William, 10, 126, 127, 132
Derrig, John, 199
Devils on the Deep Blue Sea (Garin), 191
Dillingham Act (1921), xxi, 152, 153
Dingley, Nelson, Jr., 68
DiPietrantonio, Fiore, 199
Dirigio Insurance Company, 37
Dodge, Beverly, 138
Dolan, Hugh, 59
Dominic, Randolph, 223n12
Dominion Line, 99
Douglass, Frederick, 52
Dow, Neal (Portland mayor), 43, 49, 55
Downes, Capt. John, 23
Dwight, Dr. Timothy, 15
Dyro, Felix P., 199

Eastern Argus (daily newspaper), 51, 70, 98, 99, 227n5
Eastern Steamboat House: photo of, *34*
Eastman, Joel, 136
Eimskip (Icelandic container firm), xxiii, 186–87, 190
Elliott, Richard, 199
Elwell, Edward H., 7, 9, 17, 49, 55
Embargo Act (1807), xix, 16–18
Enterprise (USS): defeats the British *Boxer* (HMS), xix, 19–20
Essex decision (1805), 17
Export-import trade: Boston (1860), 25; commodities shipped (1895 and 1900), 70, 70 table; commodities shipped from Portland, 145–46; import trade volumes, 73–74; molasses trade imports, 41–43, 55; Portland (1860), 25; pulp, wood and paper shipping, 87, 91, 108, 145, 148; shellfish trade from Maine, 27; sulfur imports, 148; wooden boxes, barrels, and casks exports, 41. *See also* Shipping industry, Portland

Falmouth in Casco Bay, Maine: British destruction of town, 12–13; colonial commodities taxes, 10–13; early settlements, xix, 7–14, 219n4; mast trade, 10; population, 7, 9; shipbuilding trade, 9–10. *See also under its later name* Portland, Maine
Farnsworth, F. Eugene (KKK leader), 139
Federal Maritime Commission (FMC), xiv
Feeney, Patrick H., 199
Fenian Brotherhood, xx, 60, 62
Fernández-Armesto, Felipe, 7
Ferrante, Joseph, 199
Flagg, Charles F., 97
Flanagan, John J., 199
"Fly boat" or *fluit* (bulk cargo boat), 171–72
Foley, Albert S., 117
Foley, Mark, Jr., 199
Foley, Nan Conley, 201
Foley, Philip, 201
Foreign-born population, Portland: 57–58, 78 table
Fort Loyall, Maine: engraving of, 8
Foulke, Robert D., 7
Free Trade Union Committee for Human Rights, 169
Friendship (ship), 23
Furbish, Dependence H., 42

Garin, Kristoffer A., 191
Gault, M. H., 133
Geary, Patrick E., 199
General Dynamics Corporation, 174, 177
George Washington (steamship), 153
Gibbons, James (cardinal of Baltimore), 113, 119
Gignoux, Fred C., 133
Glasgow Line, 39
Gleason, Thomas W. "Teddy": ILA presidency, xxii, 125
Gompers, Samuel, 110, 123
Goold, William, 43, 45
Gorges, Sir Ferdinando, 6
Gorham, John P., 199
Gorham, Michael, 133
Gorham, Patrick, 88
Gorham's Corner: longshoremen culture, 142–43
Goth, Frederic R.: *Arrival of the SS Oregon, Portland ME, January 21, 1884*, pencil sketch by, 32, *33*

Grain exports. *See* Canadian grain shipments
Grand Army of the Republic, 115
Grand Trunk Railway (GTR): Canadian grain exports and, 71, 126–27, 135, 182; Depot (1854), *30*; leased A&StLRR, xx, 31; narrow gauge line, 29–31, 39, 65, 72–73, 182; ownership under Canadian National Railroad (CNR), xxi, 149–50; Portland terminus development, 73; railroad cars and piers (c. 1875), *73*; railroad yard photo, *71*; Station photo (c. 1904), *72*. *See also* Atlantic and St. Lawrence Railroad (A&StLRR)
Graves, Samuel, 12
Gray, William, Jr., 14
Great Depression (1930s), 142, 162–63
Great Northern paper mill (Millinocket), 148
Great Portland Fire (July 4, 1866), xx, 19, 38, 65
Great Western (steamship), 29
Greely, Michael, 199
"Greenhorns" (newly arrived immigrants), 81, 130
Green Memorial AME Zion Church, 138
Groves, Jack, 18, 49
GTR. *See* Grand Trunk Railway (GTR)
Gulf of Maine Ocean Research facility, xxii, 186

Haines, W. T. (Maine governor), 123
Halifax, Nova Scotia: port development, 4, 126, 135, 149–51, 185
Hapag-Lloyd, xxii, 178
Harding, Warren G., 136
Healy, Eliza Clark, 114
Healy, James Augustine (bishop of Portland): first African American Catholic bishop in America, xx, 114, *118*; meeting with Terence Powderly, xx, 115, 116, 233n7; opposition to Knights of Labor (KOL), 113, 114–19; opposition to "secret societies," 114–15, 116; profile of, 114; ruling on parochial schools, 116
Healy, Michael Morris, 114
Henshaw, John, 189
Hibernia (British steamer), 59
Hibernia (schooner), 12
Higham, John, 69
Hiring practices: nepotism, 50; racial preferences in hiring, 94–95; union preferences, 108
History of the English Speaking Peoples (Churchill), 16

Howard and Isles, 133
Hughes, Richard P., Jr.: ILA presidency, xxii, 125
Humeniuk, Jack, *144*, 174, 189, 192–93, 201

Ideal X (container ship), xxii, 171
Ignatiev, Noel, 51, 53
ILA. *See* International Longshoremen's Association (ILA)
ILWU. *See* International Longshoremen's and Warehousemen's Union (ILWU)
Immigration laws: Dillingham Act (1921), xxi, 152, 153; Johnson-Reed Act (1924), xxi, 152, 154; quota restrictions, 153–54; U.S. policy restrictions for "new" immigrants, 72, 136–37, 152–54
Immigration to U.S.: AFL position on, 154; American labor movement opposition to, 117, 141; "Americanization" or assimilation policy, 113; and "the American Dream," 2; family life in Portland, xiii–xiv; "greenhorns" (newly arrived immigrants), 81, 130; nationalism or nativism and, 69, 151; origin of first- and second-generation Portland immigrants, 78 table; Portland as port of entry (Maine State Pier), xxi, 146, 153. *See also* Irish immigrants
Imports. *See* Export-import trade
IMT. *See* International Marine Terminal (IMT)
India Street (*formerly* King Street): Clay Cove (engraving, 1840), *24*; shipbuilding trade, 9–10
Industrial Workers of the World (IWW, or Wobblies), 53, 109, 120
International Association of Lumber Handlers, 110
International Ferry Terminal: future freight operations, 187
International Longshoremen's and Warehousemen's Union (ILWU): Bridges' leadership of, xxi, 134; conflicts with other unions, 134; documentation of history of, 1–2; nepotism in hiring practices, 50
International Longshoremen's Association (ILA): affiliation with PLSBS, xxi, 85, 100, 103, 104–7, 112, 183; affiliations with North Atlantic ports, 100; black membership and leadership, 48–49; founding of, xx
—Local 861 (Irish longshoremen): archives, 2, 229n6; charter, *106*; closed shop or "Union all over," 110, 156; limited sling load issue, 111, 125, 156; state control of Portland waterfront supported by, 189; support for Pacific Coast strikers, 158–59
—Local 912 (Italian freight handlers), 2, 96, 145, 229n6; Local 1130 (checkers), 145; local unions in Portland, 145; origins of, 109–10; presidents of, 125
International Marine Terminal (IMT), 4; bond to rebuild, xxii, 175–76, 178; container facility proposal, 188; Maine Port Authority control of, xxiii, 193
International Seamen's Union, 110
International Steamship Company, xx, 26, 37
International Terminal Operating (ITO) Company, xxii, 190
Intolerable Acts (1774), 11
Ireland, John (archbishop of Saint Paul), 119
Irish immigrants: arrivals in Falmouth/Portland, 9, 57; Democratic Party and, 52; ethnic tensions with African American dockworkers, 36–64; "greenhorns" (newly arrived), 81, 130; infant mortality, 82; literacy of first- and second generation, 82; "narrow backs" (second- and later-generation), 130; nepotism in the workplace, 50–51; New England/Yankee xenophobia toward, 54; New York strike to dismiss black dockworker (1850), 53; population of Portland, 59, 65, 78, 78 table, 152; replaced African American longshore labor, 55–57, 64; steamship travel to Portland brings, 32–33, *33*
Irish Land League, 62
Irish nationalism, 62, 226n79, 236n68
Irish-speaking longshoremen, 80–81
The Iron Horse (movie), 31
The Issue (Socialist Party publication), 122
Isthmian Line (domestic brown-water shipper), 77
Italian Freight Handler's Union, 2, 96, 145, 229n6
Italian immigrants: ethnic tensions, 93–97, 117–18; impact on Portland longshoremen, 85, 117–18; strikebreaking and, 93–97, 117
IWW. *See* Industrial Workers of the World (IWW)

Jackson, Andrew, 23–24
Jacobson, Matthew, 54
Janzen, Olaf, 7, 181
Jarka Corporation (stevedore), xxii, 164, 167, 190
Jeanie Johnston ("famine ship"), 58
Jefferson, Thomas, 17
Jeremiah O'Brien (Liberty ship), 163
Jewett, Joseph, 14
Job security, 3, 107–8
Johnson-Reed Act (1924), xxi, 152, 154
John W. Brown (Liberty ship), 163
Joyce, Pat, 111
Joyce family, 199
Jusserand, Jules, 153

Kane, Charles R., 200
Kane, Daniel, 89
Kane, Mike, 175
Kavanagh family, 66
Keating, John B., 101
Keefe, Daniel J.: first ILA president, xxi, 125, 127, 155
Kellogg, Rev. Elijah, 45, 56
Kennebec (steamship), 25
Kennebec Steam Navigation Company, xix, 22, 25–26
Kenny, Kevin, 80, 94
Knights of Labor (KOL): cooperation with ILA, 104; Healy and Catholic episcopal church opposition to, 114–19; president Powderly's meeting with Bishop Healy, xx; race relations and, 53; relations with PLSBS, 118
Knobel, Dale T., 54
Ku Klux Klan (KKK): blacks, Irish Catholics and others as targets of, 137; headquarters in Portland, Maine, xxi, 139, *139*; parade on Cumberland Avenue, Portland (c. 1923), *138*; rebirth of the Klan, 137–40

Labor Disputes Act (1946), 167
Labor in Maine (Scontras), 168
Labor-Management Relations Act (1947), xxii, 142, 167
Labor union movement: Catholic hierarchical influence on, 113–40; Civil War period, 60–62; ethnic divisiveness, 117–18; post–World War I period, 123–24

Labor unions: antilabor legislation, 167–69; collective bargaining, 123; membership exclusions for black Americans, 47; membership levels (1917–20), 123; membership levels (1920s), 124; nonunion labor issue, 155; socialism in, 120; solidarity with other unions, 135; strikes and labor militancy alongshore, 84–112. *See also* names of specific unions or societies
La Follette, Robert M., Sr., 153
Landrum-Griffin Act (1959), 169
Larkin, James, 230n35
Larrowe, Charles P., 165
Leaving Queens (Ryan), 83
Leavitt, William, 99
Leavitt (Levett), Capt. Christopher, xix, 6, 153
Lee, Coleman, 107
Lee, Martin E., 200
Lee, Maureen Elgersman, 47
Legislator (steamship), 25
Lehman, John F., 174
Leo XIII (pope), 113–14, 119
Leonard, D. J., 48
Lion Ferry Pier. *See* International Marine Terminal (IMT)
Lloyd Line, 153
Lodge, Henry Cabot, 72
Longfellow, Henry Wadsworth: "My Lost Youth" (poem), vii, 20; on Great Fire of 1866, 38; Portland birthplace of, 33; remembering his hometown, 181
Longshore industry. *See* Shipping industry, Portland
Longshoremen: numbers of (1969), 170; numbers of (1999), 170
Longshoremen nicknames, 203–14
Longshoremen's Benevolent Association/Society. *See* Portland Longshoremen's Benevolent Society (PLSBS)
Longshoremen's Hall, 62
Longshoremen's Union Protective Association (LUPA), 104, 108
Lucey, William Leo, 120
Lydon, Joseph A., 200
Lynch, John, 68

Maersk Sealand (container line), xxii, 171
Mahalia, Michael, 111

Index

Maine: antilabor legislation, 168; foreign-born population (1860), 57–58, 78 table; prohibition laws, 43, 49, 55–56; social programs legislation, 122; state capital, xix, 22; statehood status, xix, 20–21
Maine Central Railroad, 31, 91, 147
Maine Historical Society (MHS), 2
Maine Port Authority, xxiii, 188–89, 193
Maine Protective League, 168
Maine State Federation of Labor (MSFL), 135
Maine State Pier (MSP): 100th anniversary of PLSBS, 175; as port of entry for immigrants, xxi, 146, 153; building project, 129, 133, 185; completion and opening of, xxi, 112, 140, 141, 149–50; Ocean Properties rebuilding contract, 185–86; photo of, *150*; waterfront development plans, xxii, xxiii, 185–86
Maine Steamship Company, 117
Maine Supreme Court: antilabor stance, 162
Malia, William H., 200
Malone, Patrick "Pat," *144*, *179*, 201
Manchester, Vincent, 200
Manning, Edward, 200
Margaretta (HMS): American seized, xix, 12
Marine Evangeline (cruise ship), 187
Mariner's House, Portland: photo of (1931), *15*
Maritime-related businesses, 15, 23, 36–38, 66–67
Maritime strikes: (1850), New York Irish dockworkers, 53; (1864), Portland Longshoremen's Benevolent Association, xx, 60–61; (1874), New York dockworkers, 84; (1900), dockworkers, 96; (1907), New York waterfront workers, 86, 93, 96; (1909), Boston longshoremen for handling bulk cargo, 86; (1911), Portland longshoremen, xxi, 84, 85, 86–93; (1912), Baltimore dockworkers, 96; (1913), Portland longshoremen, xxi, 84–85, 86, 97–103; (1921), Portland longshoremen, xxi, 121–33; (1931) Boston longshoremen, 156–57; (1934, May 9–July 31), Pacific Coast "Big Strike," xxi, 158–59, 161–62; (1934, July 5), San Francisco "Bloody Thursday," xxi
Maritime trade: British impressing of American seamen, 17, 221n42; "broken voyage" tactic, 17; federal role in development of, 68; first American naval battle in the Pacific, 23–24; fish and shellfish trade, 26–27; mast trade, 10; "Neutral Profits Era," 16; ocean schooners of 19th century, 66; pre–Civil War period, 15–17; steamship travel, 22, 25–26, 37, 67–68, 70–73; tourism replacing other development, 74; transatlantic commerce, 77. *See also* Export-import trade
Maritime transport: "blue water" or "deep sea" cargo (transatlantic), 70, 76, 77; "brown water" cargo (domestic), 70, 76, 77, 149, 170; "coastwise shipping" (via Panama Canal), 77
Marsh, George Perkins, 54
Mary F. Barnett (schooner), 137
Mayflower (ship), 7
McCallum (ship): arrival of, xix, 9
McCarthy, Sen. Joseph, 169
McCarthyism/Red Scare, xxii, 121, 142, 168
McClure, F. J., 73
McDonough, Bartley, 200
McDonough, Michael, 98, 101, 107
McDougall, J. M., 133
McGlinchy family, 60, 226n70
McGrath, James, 110, 129, 133, 165
McLaughlin, Francis, 103
McLean, Malcolm, xxii, 170–72, 240n75
McLean Trucking Company, 170–71
McLellan, Capt. Arthur, 18
McLellan, Bryce, 15
McLellan, Hugh, 15
McLellan, Joseph, Sr., 15
McLellan, Samuel, 18
McLellan, Stephen, 15
Mealy, Peter J., 200
Megantic (steamship), 126
Merchant Magazine, 23
Merriam, Frank (California governor), 158
Merrill, Henry F., 128, 129, 153
Merrill, P. D., 175
Merrill, P. E., 175
Merrill Marine: bulk cargo shipping, xxii, 4
Merrill Transportation Company, 175
Milliken, Carl (Maine governor), 124
Miscegenation, 51, 52
Monroe, Jeffrey, 187
Montgomery, David, 50, 91, 94
Montreal Ocean Steamship Company, 32
Montreal Steamship Company, 59
Moody, Capt. Lemuel, xix, 18, 19
Mooney, Thomas, 24–25, 181

Moran, John "Red," 169
Morrill, Charles, 27
Mowatt (Mowat), Henry, xix, 12–13
MSP. *See* Maine State Pier (MSP)
Mulkern, Thomas "Tom": officer in ILA, Local 861, 107; on accidents on the Portland docks, 111, 142–243; on Bridges' union leadership, 161; on china clay handling work, 148; on Irish-speaking longshoremen, 81; on KKK in Portland, 139; on labor unions, 145; on maritime transport, 77; on waterfront development, 174; oral history of, 201; photo of, *143*; retirement from PLSBS, 200
Mulkerrin, Catherine. *See* Brennan, Catherine (*nee* Mulkerrin)
Mulkerrin, Stephen, 102, 133
Munjoy Hill: black community at base of, 19, 40–41; life of immigrant family from, xiii–xiv; Observatory and Casco Bay Islands (engraving, 1845), *26*; Portland Observatory, xix, 18–19, *19*, 26
Mussey, John, 28, 38
Myatt, James, 200
"My Lost Youth" (Longfellow), vii, 20

Naples, Frank J., 200
Nash, Gary B., 40, 45
National Association for the Advancement of Colored People (NAACP), 137
National Association of Manufacturers (NAM), 151
National Labor Relations Act (1935), 167
National Labor Relations Board (NLRB), 169
National Maritime Union (NMU), 165
National War Labor Board, 123–24
Native Americans: ill treatment of, 7, 219nn8, 11; wars with European settlers, 6–7
Neal, John, 7, 28, 38, 44, 63
Neck (or peninsula), Maine, 7, 8, 9, 13
Neill, Mr. (stevedore for Allan Line), 48
Nelson, Bruce, 95
Nepotism, 50
New England Screwship Company, 37
New England Shipbuilding Corporation, 75
New England Society, 54
New Orleans: casual or seasonal labor, 91; "half-and-half" (racial allocations of work), 48; maritime labor, 231n47; population (1900), 47; race relations and dockworkers, 47–49

New York City: black dock laborers (1910 and 1920), 109; dockworkers strike to dismiss black worker (1850), 53; longshore workers, number of, 173; maritime strike (1850), 53; maritime strike (1874), 84; maritime strike (1907), 86, 93, 96; port development, 4; shipping from Falmouth, Maine, 9
Nilsen, Kenneth, 80
North Atlantic Line, 133
Norton, Fred, 103
Norton, James A., 111

O'Brien, Edward (American millionaire), 66
O'Brien, James, 200
O'Brien, Jeremiah, 12, 13
O'Brien, John, 12
O'Brien, Michael, 200
O'Brien, Patrick, 200
Ocean disasters: *Annie C. Maguire* (bark), wreck of, xx, 67; *Bohemian* (Royal Mail Steamer), sinking of, xx, 59, 67; Montreal Steamship Company and, 59; *Portland* (steamship), sinking of, xxi, 67; vessels lost in Portland Gale (1898), 68
Ocean Gateway facility, 33, 185, 188
Ocean Insurance Company, 37
Ocean Properties: Maine State Pier development project, xxiii, 185–86
O'Connell, William Henry (bishop of Portland), xxi, 113, 118; Baxter's views on, 120; concern for workingmen, 121; later cardinal of Boston, 119; meeting with Theodore Roosevelt, 120; pastoral letter on industrial relations, 121; ruling on parochial schools, 119; views on labor strife and strikes in Lawrence (Mass.), 120
O'Connor, Terrence V.: ILA presidency, xxi, 104–5, 124, 125, 134, 232n89
O'Donnell, Patrick, 107
O'Donnell, Philip J., 200
O'Donnell, Philip "Phil," 81, 94, 111, 132, 142, 148, 161, 174; oral history of, 201; photo of, *143*
O'Donnell, Philip T., 200
Old Town Fuel and Fiber, xxiii, 193
Oliver, Jim, 194
Olympia Company: MSP development project and, xxiii
O'Malley, John M., Jr., 200
O'Malley, Patrick "Pat," *144*, 200, 201

O'Neal, Michael and Ann, 60
O'Toole, James M., 118, 140
O'Toole, Patrick, 201

Pacific Coast longshoremen: "Big Strike" (1934), xxi, 158–59, 161–62; documentation of history of, 1–2, 238nn31, 32
Palmacci, Joseph, 200
Patent (steamer), 25
Payson, Rev. Edward, 17–18
Perkins, Frances, 159
Petroleum pipeline (Portland to Montreal). *See* Portland Pipeline
Philadelphia: biracial workforce, 108–9; longshoremen ethnic and racial cohesiveness, 50–51, 53, 94–95, 223n98; racial preferences in hiring, 94–95; shipping tonnage (1855), 16
Phillipo, Joe, 200
Pittsburgh: steel strike (1919), 124
PLSBS. *See* Portland Longshoremen's Benevolent Society (PLSBS)
Pocahontas Coal Company, 147
Polish immigrants: ethnic tensions, 96
Poor, John Alfred: birth of, xx, 27; death of, xx, 31; legacy of Portland development visionary, 4, 27–31, 38, 65, 182; portrait of, 26
Population of Portland. *See* Portland population
Portland, Maine: as state capital, xix, 22; chronology of, xix–xxiii; European colonial settlement, 6–13, 219n1; form of government, 23, 139–40; "Golden Years" (1832–1866), xx, 24–27, 37–38; Great Fire (1866), xx, 19, 38, 65, 224n32; incorporation as city (1832), xx, 22; map of harbour (1823), *21*; maritime economic growth (1865–1880), 63; motto *Resurgam*, 13; naming of, 13; pre–Civil War history, 3, 6–35; street name changes, 23; Town Hall or City Halls, 47, 224n32
Portland, Rutland, Oswego, and Chicago Railway Company, 31
Portland (sloop): launching of, xix, 14
Portland (steamship): sinking off Cape Cod, xxi, 67; steamship travel (1835 to 1850), 26
Portland Board of Trade, 31, 70, 72, 90, 101–2, 185. *See also* Chamber of Commerce
Portland Board of Trade Journal, 70, 71
Portland Central Labor Union (CLU), 135
Portland Company (steam engine manufacturer), 37, 39, *71*

Portland Daily Press, 60
Portland Dry Dock Company, 39
Portland Express (newspaper), 98
Portland Glass Company, 37
Portland Head Light, *14*
Portland Longshoremen's Benevolent Association, xx, 53, 60
Portland Longshoremen's Benevolent Society (PLSBS): affiliated with ILA, xxi, 85, 100, 103, 104–7, 112, 183; archives, 2; banner on parade (1894), *79*; *formerly* Portland Longshoremen's Benevolent Association, xx, 53, 60; incorporation and charter (1880), xx, 36, 60, 62–64, 118, 182; Irish nationalism and, 62, 226n79; membership exclusion for African Americans, 48; membership levels (1882–1978), 214–15 charts; membership levels (1899), 86; membership levels (1899–1900), 79; membership levels (1899–1910), 84; membership levels (1900), 64, 78–79, 228n38; membership levels (1914), 112; membership levels (1919), xxi, 141; membership levels (1919–23), 79; membership levels (1920), 123; membership levels (1941), 173; membership levels (1941–49), 164; membership levels (1945–47), 79; relations with Knights of Labor, 118; retirement roster, 199–200; support for Southern Ireland, 154; veterans membership opposed, 164
Portland Longshoremen's Union (phantom union), 92
Portland Mutual Fire Insurance Company, 37
Portland Observatory, xix, 18–19, *19*, 26, 221n49
Portland Packing Company, 27
Portland Pipeline, xxii, 4, 163–64
Portland Pleasure Boat, 37
Portland population: blacks (1840 to 1860), 44–45, 44 table; blacks (1860 to 1900), 50; foreign-born (1860 to 1900), 57–58; foreign-born (1900), 78 table; Irish (1860 to 1900), 57–58; Irish (1900), 65; total (1800–1900), 66 table; total (1860 to 1900), 57–58; total (1900), 65
Portland Press (newspaper), 98
Portland Shipping Ceiling Company, 133
Portland Shovel Manufacturing Company, 37
Portland Steam Packet/Steamship Company, xx, 37, 69

Portland Sugar Company/House, xx, 38, 39, 42–43; photo of (c. 1850), 42
Portland Town (song by Steve Romanoff), 195–96
Portland Transcript, 49
Ports America (stevedore firm), xxii, 190
Potomac (U.S. frigate), 23
Powderly, Terence, xx, 115, 116, 233n7
Preble, Ebenezer, 14
Preble, Edward, 14
Preble, William (Judge), 28
President Polk (steamship), 153
Prince of Fundy (cruise ship), 178, 186, 187
Prohibition laws, in Maine, 43, 49, 55–56
Pullen, Warren, 190
Pulp, wood and paper shipping, 87, 91, 108, 145, 148
Pyrrhus Venture (Dominic and Barry), 223n12

Race and labor relations: competition for longshore labor and, 52–53; interracial cooperation, 137; Irish and African American dockworkers, 3, 36–64, 225n61; Irish immigrants replaced African American longshoremen, 55–57; miscegenation, 52; New York dockworkers strike to dismiss black worker (1850), 53; preferential hiring systems, 94–95; resources on, 231n47; segregated education, 40; WASP Americanism, 54–55; "whiteness" theory and studies of whiteness, 51, 54–55
Railroad Brotherhood of Trainmen, 101
Railroad development: federal role, 68; Portland to Montreal narrow gauge rail link, 27–31; rate structures, 39; transcontinental railroad, xx, 31. *See also* Grand Trunk Railway (GTR)
Randall, Charles H. (Portland mayor), 72
Randall & McAllister, 147
Read, Lt. Charles W., 67
Reagan, Ronald, 174
Red Scare. *See* McCarthyism/Red Scare
Red Shield environmental plant (Old Town), xxiii, 188, 189, 190, 193
Reed, Thomas Brackett, 120
Reed-Johnson Act (1924), xxi, 152, 154
Religion and Catholic influences, 3, 55, 113–40
Rerum novarum (Of New Things), 116–17, 119

Resurgam ("I will rise again"), 13
Reuben James (USS): sunk by German U-Boat, xxi
Rich, Maurice G., 101
Richmond, John, 6
Robert Reford Company, 73, 133
Roediger, David, 51–53
Rogers and Webb Line, 154
Roosevelt, Franklin Delano, 162
Roosevelt, Theodore, 120
Rosenberg, Daniel, 47
Rowe, William Hutchison, 10, 42, 56, 67
Royall, Anne, 22
Rumery, Samuel, 27
Rum trade, 43, 86
Ryan, Joseph P.: allegations of corruption, 141, 160, 165; ILA presidency, xxi, 124, 125, 155–58, 164; McCarthyism supporter, 168; on nonunion labor issue, 155; personality struggle with Bridges, 159–61; photo of, 156
Ryan, Kate Moira, 83

Safety issues: hatch-to-hatch restrictions, 133; limited sling loads, 3, 87–88, 110–11, 132–33, 154–55; marine-related accidents, 111; work gang size, 3, 50, 86–87, 166, 167
Sailors' Union of the Pacific (SUP), 162
Saint Dominic's Church, xix, 34, 80, 116, 142
Saint John, New Brunswick: port development, 4, 126, 135, 149–51, 182, 185; wage scale, 100; winter steamship terminal, 59
Saint Patrick's Catholic Church, xix
Sarah Sands (steamship), xx, 57, 73, 228n23
Scontras, Charles A., 47, 61, 168
Scotia Prince (cruise ship), 187
S. D. Warren Paper Mill (Westbrook), 87, 147–48
Sea-Land Container Company: founding of, xxii; merger with Maersk container line, xxii
Seasonal migrations of laborers, 89
Security. *See* job security
Sewall, Arthur, 68
Seydlitz (steamship), 153
Shamrock (container ship), xxii, 186
Shape-Up and Hiring Hall (Larrowe), 165
Shepard, Steadman, 49
Shipbuilding: Falmouth mast trade, 10; in

Falmouth, 9–10; in the 19th century, 66; Liberty ships launched from Portland, xxii, 75, 163; sailing ship to steamship conversion, 75–76

Shipping Board (U.S.): strike intervention, 124, 131

Shipping industry, Portland: Canadian legislative restrictions, 136; companies operating, 4, 39, 71; destinations of, 71; feeder ports and, 170; reasons for decline and losses, 136, 141–42. *See also* export-import trade; maritime transport

Shipping tonnage: commodity tonnages study (1935), 70; Baltimore (1855), 16; Boston (1855), 16; Boston (1860), 25; Philadelphia (1855), 16; Portland (1798), 17; Portland (1812), 18; Portland (1860), 25; Portland (1866), 16; Portland (1871 to 1874), 63; Portland (1898 and 1899), 74; Portland (1915–19), 135

Ship repair facility, 174

Shipwrecks. *See* ocean disasters

Siggs, John, 49

Silke, John, 164–65

Sling load, limited, 87–88, 110–11, 125, 128, 132–33, 141, 154–56, 164–76; definition of, 3

Smith, Robert M., 99, 133

Smith, Sen. Margaret Chase, 168, 169

Smith, Thomas (Parson), 9, 10, 40, 220n13

Snow and Burgess (sailing ship), 76

Socialism: Catholic church denunciation of, 122; in labor unions, 120

South African Paper and Pulp Industries (SAPPI), 175, 176, 188, 189

South Portland Shipbuilding Corporation, xxii, 163

Spanish-American War, 69

Sperry, Howard, 158

Sprague Energy Marine Terminal, 188, 189

Stakeman, Randolph, 40

Steamship travel: eclipsed sailing ships, 75–76; transatlantic sailings to and from Portland, 22, 25–26, 37, 67–68, 70–73. *See also names of specific steamship lines*

Stevedore agents (hiring bosses): definition of, 87; longshoremen relations with, 87, 129

Strikebreakers (scabs): ethnic tensions and, 93–97; in Boston strike (1911), 85, 92; in longshore strike (1921), 124; Italian immigrant laborers, 93–97, 117; rerouting as tactic for strikebreaking, 97; violence against, 61

Strikes: by black workers (1866), 46; journeymen mechanics (1849), 37; Pittsburgh steel strike (1919), 124. *See also* maritime strikes

A Strong Arm and a Mother's Blessing (Kellogg), 45, 56

Sweat, Clinton T., 133

Taft-Hartley Act (1947), xxii, 142, 167

Tall Ships (Wilson), 221n42

Tate, Capt. George, Sr., 10

Thomas Laughlin Company, 33

Thompson, Gen. Samuel, 12

Thompson and Donaldson Lines, 73

Thompson Line, 133, 154

Thornton, John, 107

Todd Shipyard of Philadelphia, 163

Torrance, John, 97, 99

Tourism, 74

Trefethen and Dugan (stevedore firm), 87–89

Truman, Harry S, 167

Tucker, Richard, xix, 6

Tuscania (steamship), 153

Two Years Before the Mast (Dana), 54–55

Underwood, William, 27

United Mine Workers, 95, 168

United States Line, 153

Valleau, Tom, 176

Viking (schooner), 75

Wage scales/schedule, 84, 90, 92, 98–99, 102

Wages for dockworkers: for bulk cargo (1909), 86; for general cargo (1921), 125–26; for grain handling (1921), 126, 127; freight handlers' hourly wages, 94; ILA wage agreement (1922–23), 134; longshoremen's daily wage (1864), 60; longshoremen's hourly wages, 94; stowing cargo hourly wages (1864), 60; wharf workers hourly wages (1864), 61

The Wages of Whiteness (Roediger), 52

Wagner Act (1935), 167

Wainwright, W. W., 73–74

Wakeman, George, 52

Waldo, Francis (first tax collector), 11
Waldo, Samuel (Brig.), 10
Walker, James: beating death of, xxi, 137, 225n61
Walsh, Louis Sebastian (bishop of Portland), xxi, 113, 118; and Longshore strike (1921), 124, 128–32; Catholic hierarchy and the unions, 121–23, 130; Ku Klux Klan opposition to, 138–40
Walsh, Patrick J., 200
Walsh, Thomas, 200
War of 1812: impact on Portland, 19–20
Warren, William E., 165
Warren and Thomaston, 66
Washington, George: on Falmouth affair, 13
WASP (White, Anglo-Saxon, and Protestant), 53
Waterfront development: in Portland, 174–79; in Portland, future of, 191–94; Marine Trade Center, 186; Ocean Gateway facility, 33, 185; referendum and moratorium passed (1987), xxii, 177; working waterfront development needs, 192–93. See also Maine State Pier (MSP)
Welch, Lawrence "Larry": on Canadian Scotch whiskey shipment incident, 132; on china clay handling work, 148; on export commodities shipments, 145–46; on Irish longshoremen, 80; on local blacks' exclusion from unions, 137; on loss of work, 136; on maritime transport, 77; on racketeering/Mafia, 160, 161; on working conditions, 80, 155–56; opposition to Ryan, 165; oral history of, 201; photos of, *143*, *146*; positive view of Bridges, 161–62; videotape for Maine Television of, 201; waterfront as "rich man's playground," 194

Westbrook, Col. Thomas, 10
Western Steamship Company, 133
West Indian molasses trade, 41–43, 55, 86, 223n17
W. H. Dugan and Sons, 133
White Star-Dominion Line, 97, 99, 100, 126, 127, 133, 154
Willis, William, 11, 15, 40, 63, 69
Wilson, Hazel, 221n42
Winslow, Calvin, 93
Winslow, J. M., 60
Winter, John, 7
Wobblies. See Industrial Workers of the World (IWW, or Wobblies)
Woodard, Colin, 191
Work gang size, 3, 50, 86–87, 166, 167
Workingmen's Club, Portland, xxi, 121
Work rules and conditions: Boston local work rules, 156–57; eight-hour day, 123; for limited sling loads, 3, 87–88, 110–11, 125, 128, 132–33, 141, 154–56, 164–67; for quick steam hoisting, 110; length of contract, 127–28; nonunion labor issue, 155; ten-hour day (journeymen mechanics strike, 1849), 37; union losses after maritime strike (1921), 132; union negotiations maritime strike (1921), 128
Works Progress Administration (WPA), 163
World War II: Liberty shipbuilding in Portland, xxii, 75, 163; "Rosie the Riveter" campaign, 163
Wright, Allan Jeffrey, 151

Yankee Clipper (container ship), xxii, 178

CPSIA information can be obtained
at www.ICGtesting.com
Printed in the USA
LVOW11s0307160118
563058LV00001B/109/P

9 780813 037226